brian ENO

Please return on or
before the last date
stamped below.
Contact:
01603 773 114 or
01603 773 224

1 1 FEB 2013

1 4 OCT 2014

2 7 NOV 2015

0 4 SEP 2017

brian ENO

His Music and the Vertical Color of Sound

Updated Edition

Eric Tamm

DA CAPO PRESS

Library of Congress Cataloging in Publication Data
Tamm, Eric, 1955–
   Brian Eno: his music and the vertical color of sound / Eric
Tamm.—Updated ed., 1st Da Capo Press ed.
     p.   cm.
   Discography: p.
   Includes bibliographical references (p.   )
   ISBN 0-306-80649-5 (alk. paper)
   1. Eno, Brian, 1948– . 2. Composers—England—Biography. 3. Eno, Brian,
1948- —Criticism and interpretation. I. Title.
ML410.E58T3 1995
780′.92—dc20
[B]
                                                                    95-21602
                                                                    CIP

First Da Capo Press edition 1995

This Da Capo Press paperback edition of *Brian Eno* is an unabridged
republication of the edition originally published in Boston in 1989,
here supplemented with a new epilog, a section on Eno on the Internet,
and updates to the bibliography and discography. It is reprinted by
arrangement with Faber and Faber, Inc.

Published by Da Capo Press, Inc.

A Member of the Perseus
Books Group

Manufactured in the United States of America

DEDICATION

This book is dedicated to my parents, Igor Tamm and Olive Pitkin Tamm. In my childhood, my father sang bass and strummed guitar; my mother played piano and violin and sang in choirs. Together they gave me a love and respect for music that will be with me always.

TABLE OF CONTENTS

PART I. ENO IN THE WORLD OF MUSIC

PART II. ENO'S MUSIC

ACKNOWLEDGMENTS

I want to take this opportunity to thank Professor George Skapski of California State University, Northridge, for his enthusiasm for musicological studies, which did much to whet my appetite for further work in the field.

This book grew out of my doctoral dissertation research in the Music Department at the University of California, Berkeley. I am grateful to a number of faculty members there: John Swackhamer, whose broad view of contemporary music and sense of humor helped me see the light at the end of the tunnel; Bonnie Wade, whose interest in a wide range of world music has always been refreshing, and who supervised the independent study that led ultimately to this book; Anthony Newcomb, who gamely steered my research through its early stages; Christopher Brown, who with good cheer and open-mindedness took on a fruitful advisory role; Olly Wilson, whose course in Afro-American music was one of the highlights of my studies at Berkeley, and whose continuing scholarly and personal involvement with that tradition set a valuable example for me; and Philip Brett, my dissertation adviser, who was a delight to work with, offering many valuable suggestions, and whose firm editorial guidance taught me much about writing itself.

Professor Charles Hamm of Dartmouth College served as an active yet unofficial reader and adviser from the earliest stages of the dissertation, and for his penetrating comments, informed by a lifetime's study of popular music, I am grateful.

I do not know exactly how to express the depth of my admiration for and obligation to Robert Fripp, the most effective teacher with whom I have ever had the privilege of studying music, whose Guitar Craft XII seminar in 1986 opened up many doors for me, and who inspired my interest in undertaking a study of the work of his colleague, Brian Eno.

I would also like to thank Professor Howard DeWitt of Ohlone College, whose encyclopedic knowledge of rock and roll and massive record collection lightened my research load considerably; Charles Amirkhanian, Joshua Kosman, and Joe Paulino, who supported the project from early on and were kind enough to loan me a number of obscure records and tapes; Lin Barkass and Anthea Norman-Taylor at Eno's management firm, Opal Ltd., London, who answered my queries about Eno in a timely fashion and supplied several pertinent articles and brochures; David Snow at Opal Ltd., Los Angeles; and Betsy Uhrig of Faber and Faber for her warmth and editorial assistance in the preparation of the final manuscript.

This book could not have been written without the constant support of my wife, Kristina Holland, who agreeably proofread typescripts and put up with long stretches of antisocial behavior on my part. Finally, I must thank my daughter Lilia, now seven years old and no great Eno fan, for helping me keep everything in perspective. After repeatedly playing Eno records on the home stereo and running on about how wonderfully "mysterious" his music is, I asked her one day if she liked it. "Turn it off!" she said. "It makes me feel like *I* am a mystery."

part I Eno in the World of Music

chapter 1

Eno's Work in Perspective

Brian Eno (b. 1948) is a contemporary British musician and artist whose public creative career began in 1972 with his synthesizer playing for the rock group Roxy Music. Through securing a niche in the music industry and building up an audience for his progressive rock music, Eno has been able to diversify his creative efforts considerably. He is a prime example of a new type of composer who draws freely on the resources of many types of music and ideas about music. These include popular genres, such as rhythm and blues and rock and roll, progressive rock, punk, and new wave, as well as African, Middle Eastern, and Asian styles. Also notable among his influences are minimalism, experimental new music, post-Cage avant-garde theory, and electronic music. Eno has combined music with visual art (in the forms of video and sculptural installations), has lectured on musical subjects extensively, and is the author or coauthor of a number of written materials. Although he has performed live, his primary arena of operation is the recording studio, which he has called his "real instrument." In addition to the knobs and switches of the mixing board and multi-track tape recorder, Eno plays keyboards (primarily synthesizer), guitar (primarily electric), electric bass, and a variety of percussion instruments; he is also a singer.

The scope of Eno's musical activity is impressive.[1] Between 1972 and 1988 he released eleven solo albums ranging stylistically from progressive rock to what he has called "ambient" music—a gentle music of low dynamics, blurred edges, and washes of sound color, produced primarily through electronic means. As a songwriter he developed a technique of lyric writing based in part on the procedures of phonetic poetry. It is on his solo albums that we may observe the unfolding of Eno's musical personality in its purest form; in the role of composer he has been keenly interested in working with the traditionally neglected or at least downplayed realms of timbre (tone color) and texture, and in the process of pursuing that interest he has been of seminal importance in the development of the "new age" or "space music" genre. "Timbre" is a term that refers to the color of sound: it is what makes the same note, played on a violin, a trumpet, or a xylophone, sound different. This aspect of musical sound can be thought of as "vertical," since it depends to a large extent on the harmonics, or barely audible frequencies, that are stacked "vertically" on the primary heard note itself. The vertical harmonic spectrum determines the color of the sound, and how our ears and minds interpret the harmonic spectrum determines whether we hear the characteristic sound of a guitar or a flute, or whether, for example, we hear the vocal syllable "ooh" or "aah."

Collaboration with other rock and non-rock musicians has been a very important aspect of Eno's activity. Two albums of tape-looped synthesizer/guitar duets with King Crimson guitarist Robert Fripp were among Eno's first publicly available experiments in the ambient sound. Eno has worked with conceptual rock group 801 (a live band, formed around ex-Roxy Music players Phil Manzanera on guitar and Eno on synthesizer), with Kevin Ayers and John Cale (producing a live album), and with the German synthesizer group Cluster (producing several albums of ambient-inflected music). Eno's collaboration on three albums with glitter/art rocker David Bowie mixed hard rock, disco/funk, and electronic excursions in a unique combination of styles. With David Byrne, leader of Talking Heads, Eno made the controversial album *My Life in the Bush of Ghosts,* which used African and American radio "found sounds" in a number of musical collages in which complex rhythms and textures set up a kind of sonic frieze. Entirely apart from the rock realm, Eno has collaborated on albums with composers Harold Budd, Jon Hassell, Daniel Lanois, Michael Brook, and Roger Eno, creating a marvelous variety of soundscapes and musical concepts. Eno's role in all of these collaborations has varied, but in each he has been credited as a co-composer, and in some as the producer.

Eno's expertise in the recording studio has been much sought-after since about 1975, and he has produced at least twenty-three albums on which he is not listed as one of the composers. As a producer of these albums his role has varied from that of a simple recording engineer to that of a *de facto* co-composer of the total sound. Again the represented types of music are diverse. Eno produced two albums for the Portsmouth Sinfonia, the "world's worst symphony"—an ensemble committed to high-camp satire and consisting of non-musicians and musicians playing instruments they didn't know how to play, stumbling through deliberately butchered versions of the classical repertoire.

Eno independently created a record label, Obscure Records, which released eight albums during the 1970s. In several statements, Eno described the Obscure intention as essentially to aid in the dissemination of experimental music. The Obscure records included pieces by contemporary composers Gavin Bryars, Christopher Hobbs, John Adams, Max Eastley, John Cage, Jan Steele, Michael Nyman, the Penguin Café Orchestra, Tom Phillips, Fred Orton, and Harold Budd.

The rock acts whose work Eno has produced include John Cale, Robert Calvert, Talking Heads, Ultravox, Devo, and U2. Eno also produced the compilation *No New York* (documenting the New York punk scene of the late 1970s, with music by the Contortions, Teenage Jesus and the Jerks, Mars, and DNA), an album featuring the ethereal music of hammer dulcimer player Laraaji, and a record by the Ghanaian pop group Edikanfo.

Eno has appeared as an instrumentalist (playing synthesizer, percussion, bass, and guitar) and vocalist on at least twenty-three albums, ranging from the fabled Scratch Orchestra's recording of Cornelius Cardew's experimental vocal composition, *The Great Learning*, to David Byrne's music for Twyla Tharp's Broadway production, *The Catherine Wheel*.

During the 1980s Eno's approach to music has found favor among filmmakers, television executives, and playwrights. Among other things, Eno produced the "Prophecy Theme" for David Lynch's film *Dune*, and the music for the PBS series *Creation of the Universe*. Eno compositions were used as background music for the acclaimed *Nova* film *The Miracle of Life*, which featured stunning color footage of human internal physiology and reproductive processes. In 1978 Eno released an album of original compositions entitled *Music for Films; Music for Films, Vol. II* followed in 1983. The pieces on these albums have been used in film, TV, advertising, dance company, and planetarium applications in the United Kingdom, the United States, Australia, Japan, and the Netherlands.

Since 1979 Eno has been working in the area of audiovisual installations— shows in galleries and other public places in which taped music, video monitors or video "sculptures," and the spatial features of a given site are encouraged to complement each other, to create an aesthetic whole. He has set up such installations in over fifty locations in the United States, Canada, France, Australia, the Netherlands, England, Italy, Austria, and Germany. Sometimes the required technology has been elaborate, as at La Forêt Museum in Akasaka, Tokyo, where he used thirty-six video monitors.

Owing to the expansive, multifaceted nature of his ideas and, doubtless, to his highly publicized collaborations with rock stars like David Bowie, Robert Fripp, and Talking Heads (whose work has been much more popular with the record-buying public), Eno's music has received sustained critical attention out of all proportion to the (rather meager) number of records he has sold. In his early work with Roxy Music and subsequent solo progressive rock albums, Eno styled himself a rock musician, capturing the attention of the rock press and public with his imaginative approach to the synthesizer, his constant textural experimentation, the dry, witty irony of his lyrics—and with his public image as a sort of cerebral hermaphrodite (with Roxy Music he wore women's clothing and makeup). His credentials as as an outré rock innovator thus established, he continued to pique the imagination of his public when, with the release of a number of albums of quiet, gentle compositions, often entirely without pulse or melody, his music turned away from rock forms, rhythms, harmonies, and styles. It is doubtful whether Eno's ambient music would have found its way to the forefront of popular music discourse had he not begun his public career working more or less within the rock mainstream. Eno has thus become, for many critics, a symbol of the potential of "art rock": he has not only applied philosophy, experimentation, and self-conscious "artistry" to the creation of what might be called rock music for the thinking person or aesthete (as have musicians like Frank Zappa and Robert Fripp), but has worked within new, non-rock genres essentially of his own creation.

Fascination with Eno extends beyond the world of the music press; his life and music have been treated in general-interest magazines like *Esquire, Omni, People Weekly,* and *Time,* as well as art periodicals like *Artforum, Art in America,* and *Flash Art.* Critical response to specific solo albums by Eno range from effusions of enthusiasm to pronouncements of boredom or indignation; both extremes are often found in different reviews of the same work.

If Eno's approach to music can be summed up here, it is in terms of inventing systems and setting them in motion; sustaining an open mind and childlike curiosity about the infinite range of musical possibility; taking command of technology's array of music-making equipment, from tape recorders to synthesizers to mixing consoles; generally working within a relatively narrow range of expressive possibilities for any given piece; and accepting happy accidents at any stage of the creative process. "Honor thy mistake as a hidden intention," says one of the *Oblique Strategies,* a set of oracle cards Eno produced and marketed in 1975 with painter Peter Schmidt, and subsequently used extensively as a compositional aid.[2]

Let's take a step back and try to view Eno's broad output and accomplishments in some kind of perspective. The challenge to the observer of today's multifaceted musical scene is to avoid easy identification with attitudes and assumptions promoted by the many "interest groups" involved and to cultivate an open view. Contemporary music should be viewed as a pluralistic whole. In the age of the global village, the mass media, and worldwide record distribution networks, music ranges freely across geographical and cultural boundaries. It may range more freely across some borders and in some directions than across others, and certainly the day has not yet come when each culture knows about the music of every other, or wants to know. But in a growing number of cities worldwide, the living history and present character of the world's music are concentrated on discs in libraries and record stores, available to whoever has the means and curiosity to listen; and radio makes available a similarly wide array of musical traditions and treasures.

In this pluralistic situation, some musical genres remain traditional, self-consciously insulated from the explosion of musical information; others mix and mingle, whether through the directed efforts of musicians, composers, and ethnomusicologists or through the inexorable processes of acculturation. In his recent book, *The Western Impact on World Music,* Bruno Nettl traces the ways in which such Western musical norms as functional harmony, such Western instruments and ensembles as violins and orchestras, and such Western institutions as the classical concert have affected musical life and concepts of music in diverse cultures throughout the world. Although Nettl's ethnomusicological study concentrates on the influence of music from the West on the music of other parts of the world, intercultural musical exchange works both ways.

Nettl's short chapter on "pop" is notable for its opinion, all too common in musicological circles, that "if there is any trend in world music that might justify the fear of musical homogenization, it would have to be in [the] realm of popular music."[3] Such an opinion must be heard in the context of a long history of musicologists' refusing even to recognize the existence, let alone the diversity and vitality, of popular music. Yet even a cursory survey will show that some of the most interesting intercultural developments have taken and are taking place in popular music. History has become an all-embracing present, and today is an exciting time to be alive in the world of music, in the music of the world.

Despite today's unprecedented opening up of musical possibilities, many of the institutional frameworks of Western music exert pressure on the individual musician to conform. Many orchestras, opera companies, vocal groups, chamber music ensembles, and their audiences, are reluctant to take chances with the new, no doubt because since Schoenberg "emancipated dissonance" few composers have made many efforts to make their music accessible to a wide audience. Many academic institutions still assess musical training largely in terms of the attainment of competence in the performance of a repertory which has not changed much during the past half-century or more. And although a few composers have undertaken experiments in tone color—notably through extended instrumental and vocal techniques, inventions of new instruments, and electronic music—the timbral norms of academic new music have remained substantially those associated with the instruments of the traditional orchestra, which has grown in size but which structurally and organizationally has not changed much for over two centuries.

Popular music is considerably less insular than modern art music. In the Western world, a decisive musical development of the twentieth century has been the rise to prominence of a spectacular variety of Afro-American musical genres and associated styles: ragtime, big-band jazz, be-bop, and rhythm and blues; the development leads from rhythm and blues directly into the rock and roll of the 1950s and the subsequent stylistic explosion. Rock music exists in an abundance of varieties, many of them drawing their vitality from fresh infusions of non-Western sources. On the face of it, there might appear to be considerably less pressure to conform within the area of popular music than in the area of modern art music, more incentive to innovate, to create hybrid musics, to experiment along the borderlines between genres; and indeed a great deal of such experimentation has been done. But as any popular musician can testify, the pressure to conform in the world of popular music comes not from the academic imperative of upholding a tradition of supposed structural sophistication and intellectual validity, but from the need to make music that is "commercial." Group after group has died from a creative standpoint after making one or two albums that have attained commercial success: having come up with an original sound, the musicians—and especially the musicians' management and record company—are reluctant in subsequent efforts to significantly alter the original formula, for fear of lost audience and income. Few have the courage to avoid this trap and follow their artistic destiny.

The situation is thus simultaneously exhilarating and perilous for the contemporary musician who has something important to say. Finding or creating an audience is only part of the problem. The musician must also find the strength to resist both intellectual and commercial pressures. What a paradox: the global musical/informational network allows access to fantastic riches in terms of sources, ideas, and styles; but, simultaneously, old and new institutions—existing performance groups, genre-oriented audiences, the academy, the music industry—may inhibit the musician from forging anything truly new from these precious materials.

Eno's music, in its sweeping eclecticism, represents—one might even say epitomizes—the new freedom felt by many younger composers during the second half of the twentieth century—composers for whom the traditional forms, forums, and aesthetic and intellectual ideas of Western art music have never seemed especially preferable to those of other kinds of music. The difference between classical and popular music presents itself to Eno as a matter of differing forms of social organization and performance practice, not as a matter of degrees of craft and aesthetic worth. In Eno's music we find qualities that are commonly, if somewhat superficially, associated with art and popular music respectively: on the one hand, a genuine concern for values of thoughtfulness, reflection, craft, creativity, and originality; on the other hand, an acknowledgment of the needs of the audience, a sense of music as a functional, social phenomenon, and a lively interest in the full global spectrum of contemporary musical styles and tendencies.

Throughout his creative life, Eno has been fascinated by different kinds of processes and systems. In a statement whose implications have been vigorously debated, he summed up his attitude in 1975: "Since I have always preferred making plans to executing them, I have gravitated towards situations and systems that, once set into operation, could create music with little or no intervention on my part."[4] Though this might seem to imply a relatively passive role for the artist, Eno has been tirelessly active in the creation and investigation of the properties of different systems of composition and music making, and in his choice of specific limitations he has typically determined the outcome to a fairly high degree. His craft is widely acknowledged and admired, and the product or residue left by his "self-regulating or self-generating systems" includes a body of music of compelling beauty and originality.

It seems to me that it is not really the point to ask whether Eno's music is "art music" or "popular music," yet a discussion of what is meant by such terms can help to situate his music in the contemporary scene. In recent years considerable scholarly and polemic energy has been directed toward determining the difference between, and the relative social and aesthetic positions of "art music" and "popular music." (For the truly interested, the Bibliography at the back of this book includes a variety of writings on this topic.)

In his recent book, *Analysis and Value Judgement*, the German music historian Carl Dahlhaus, expressing a viewpoint that is widely shared among musicologists and classical music critics, writes that "A listener capable of doing justice to a Beethoven symphony is generally equipped to cope with the musical issues of a pop tune, but the reverse is not true." This seems to me patently false: the musical issues raised by the Beethoven symphony and the pop tune are simply not comparable, and there is no point in pretending that they are. Dahlhaus's explicit generic prejudice is made outrageous by the sting in the tail of the disclaimer that follows: "Arrogance of the initiated must not be defended, but that nobody has the right to blame musical illiterates for being illiterate does not change the fact that illiteracy provides a weak foundation for aesthetic judgements."[5] For Dahlhaus, and for those who share his extreme view, apparently the eye is more important than the ear when it comes to appreciating music: if you can't read it, you can't really understand it. And woe to the music that is not even written down to begin with! The substantive problem with this line of reasoning is that reliance on notation as a criterion for aesthetic judgment inevitably leads to the ignoring, by traditional analysts, of aspects of musical style which are extremely important in popular music, but which are difficult or impossible to notate, such as overall "sound" (or what are known as "production values"), timbre, vocal quality and nuance, and ornamentation.

A broader view of the art/popular dichotomy is prevalent in the discipline of ethnomusicology—whose history, however, can be read as a tale of predominantly Western scholars slowly coming to terms with their own ethnocentricity and genre preferences. Over the past century, ethnomusicologists have suggested various ways of classifying the musics of the world. Bruno Nettl summarizes:

> At one time [in the late nineteenth century] there was a tendency to recognize only two classes, Western art music in the one and everything else in the other. Soon, recognition of the fact that Asian cultures had a stratification of music not unlike that of Europe led to a tripartite model, primitive, art, and folk music. . . . A third stage is implied in [Mantle] Hood's statement [in 1963] to the effect that art, folk, popular, and primitive music are the norm. . . . Eventually, further, there also came the realization that each culture has its own way of classifying music. . . . I suggest that while most cultures do indeed have their own way of classifying music, so that the terms "folk," "art," and "popular" are at best culture-specific to the West, each culture tends to have some kind of hierarchy in its

musical system, a continuum from some kind of elite to popular. Where the lines
should be drawn is a subject of discussion.[6]

This struggle over where to draw the lines can yield some insights into the
position of Eno's music in the schema of musical types. The British-born popular
music scholar Philip Tagg has published an "axiomatic triangle" that represents
a recent attempt to classify musical types into folk, art, and popular.[7] Folk
music is produced and transmitted primarily by amateurs, writes Tagg; art and
popular music are largely the work of professionals. Popular music usually is
mass-produced; folk and art music usually are not. The three types of music
have different primary modes of storage and distribution: folk music by oral
tradition, art music by musical notation, and popular music by recorded sound.
Types of music vary with types of culture: folk music emerges mostly in nomadic
or agrarian societies, art music develops in agrarian or industrial societies, and
popular music is largely a phenomenon of the industrialized world. The production and distribution of folk music occur independently of a monetary economy; art music relies on public funding; and popular music's economic domain
is free enterprise. An organized, written body of music theory and aesthetics
is uncommon to folk and popular music, but it is the norm with art music.
Finally, folk music is usually composed anonymously, while art and popular
music are not.

What Tagg has done is to systematize the standard musicological wisdom
with regard to the three types of music. Unfortunately—and a growing number
of scholars and critics are beginning to recognize this—there is a lot of music
out there that refuses to be classified so neatly. Eno's music, for example. Eno
is certainly a professional, in the sense that he gets paid for what he does; yet
he has largely given up live performance and, as we shall see, he positively
revels in the "amateurish" nature of his instrumental abilities, going so far as
to characterize himself as a "non-musician." Is his music "mass-distributed"?
In the sense that multiple pressings are made of his records, yes; but he has
certainly set no records for numbers of copies sold, sales figures of each of his
solo albums hovering between 50,000 and 100,000. The "main mode of storage
and distribution" of Eno's music is certainly "recorded sound"; and while the
genesis of some of his compositions includes a written sketching stage (though
not in musical notation), the only existing scores of his music have been produced by others for copyright purposes, and in Eno's opinion bear little resemblance to the music itself. A point to be made about modes of storage and
distribution as criteria for distinguishing art from popular music, however, is
that surely in 1989 musical notation can no longer be considered the main
storage mode of art music: although the written score may still enjoy a certain
ontological supremacy, in reality most people experience classical music more
through recordings than through scores. Sound recording is the great equalizer
of musical genres: regardless of the original social context of a piece of music,

a record is a record, whether it sits on the shelves of a research library or is played on the home stereo system.

According to Tagg's criterion, Eno's music would seem to be art music, if only because Eno himself has surrounded his music with a glittering halo of theory and aesthetics in dozens of statements ranging from interviews and album liner notes to published articles. But the issue is more complex: Tagg's distinction between popular and art music, on the basis of the absence or presence of a body of theory and aesthetics, is increasingly dubious. Paul Taylor's fine, extensively annotated bibliography, *Popular Music Since 1955: A Critical Guide to the Literature*,[8] devotes a chapter to "Artistic aspects of popular music" which cites works concerned specifically with aesthetics, musical criticism and analysis, and songs as poetry. Finally, Eno's music is not anonymously composed; but the double or multiple authorship of many of the pieces Eno has worked on introduces a complicating detail, if one argues that collective authorship is more characteristic of folk and popular music than of art music. In short, it would be impossible, on the basis of Tagg's axiomatic triangle, to decide whether Eno's music should be classified as "art" or "popular."

So much for this level of abstraction. Everyone knows that at least since the 1920s musicians have been deliberately blurring the distinctions between popular, art, and folk music. Charles Ives and Aaron Copland wrote symphonic works incorporating American folk themes. Igor Stravinsky composed pieces like the jazz-inflected *Ebony Concerto*. Many critics consider the music of Duke Ellington, Charlie Parker, and John Coltrane to be art of the highest order. And with the rock music of the 1960s and beyond, the experimentation has become increasingly intense. There are, of course, many examples of superficial blendings of pop and classical styles, such as Walter Murphy's "A Fifth of Beethoven" or the Swingle Singers' jazzy renditions of Bach. There is everything from Joshua Rifkin's *Baroque Beatles Book* (actually not so superficial as all that) to Muzak versions of "Yesterday."

Attempts at deeper syntheses of art and pop are sometimes categorized as art rock or classical rock. Such music includes not only the rock operas of the Who, the Kinks, and others, and the massive, virtuosic, grandiose compositions of 1970s groups like Yes and Emerson, Lake & Palmer, but also more restrained, subtle examples of "baroque or classical sound/structure" in rock, such as the Beach Boys' "Surf's Up" or the Beatles' "Eleanor Rigby."[9] Other groups often associated with the classical rock concept are the Moody Blues, the Electric Light Orchestra, the New York Rock Ensemble, Procol Harum, and Renaissance.

"Progressive rock" is one of the most useful yet exasperating terms within the rock orbit. It gained currency in the late 1960s and early 1970s among rock critics and audiences; it meant, essentially, rock music with substance, rock music that was more than just entertainment or Top-40 pop, rock music that was serious, with something serious to say, whether that "something" involved a political or artistic message. Progressive rock music was heard on "underground," progressive FM radio stations in the United States—stations whose disc jockeys did not have to follow some corporate line or the weekly dictates of the charts but could play what conscience and sensibility demanded—typically not singles, but cuts from albums featuring musicians who creatively or politically seemed to be above the rough-and-tumble of the music industry and its merely commercial demands. Progressive rock was the brutal, straightforward rock and the sexual/political posturing of the Rolling Stones; the majestic, finely produced sound-tapestries of the Beatles; or the hip honesty and moralizing verbal pyrotechnics of Bob Dylan. It was the uncompromising musicality and innovation of Gentle Giant, Jethro Tull, King Crimson, Queen, Traffic, Blind Faith, Steely Dan, or Frank Zappa.

With the history of progressive rock—a term not much used since the late 1970s—came the rather startled realization, on the part of many critics as well as of some of the genre's leading musicians, that certain of its "progressive" musical tendencies were too closely allied for comfort with classical techniques. In other words, unbridled "progressivism" in rock had led to a strange development in which rock was risking its status as an innovative musical form and symbol of the youth culture through its increasing reliance on the harmonic, formal, and orchestrational trappings of the music whose cultural base it was supposed to be rebelling against. Thus progressive rock ultimately included, and for many listeners was epitomized by, the grandiose synthesizer gestures and elaborate formal layouts used by the groups that some commentators pigeonhole separately under classical rock—groups like Yes, Genesis, and Emerson, Lake & Palmer. One reference source defines progressive rock as "a form of rock music in which electric instruments and rock-band formats are integrated with European classical motifs and orchestrations, typically forming extended, intricate, multisectional suites."[10] The excesses of classicized progressive rock constituted one of the major reasons why many creative rock musicians, Brian Eno among them, felt so refreshed when the development of the new wave genre during the late 1970s seemed to offer a progressive musical alternative to the increasingly manneristic and self-stultified genre of progressive rock itself.

I shall refer to the music of Eno's early solo albums as "progressive rock" because in the historical matrix of rock genres—an imperfect but functional typology—that is where it belongs. During the late 1960s and early 1970s, before the allegedly counterproductive tendencies of the classicization of rock had run their course, numerous musicians, who at the time were unflinchingly referred to as "progressive," glimpsed great possibilities. Eno was among the few who, in retrospect, gave the impression of hopping gracefully from the progressive rock to the new wave genre without making any essential changes in his approach to music. All along, of course, Eno was coping, on both conceptual and practical levels, with entirely different musical genres, notably minimalism and post-Cage experimentalism; the overtly "classical" aspects of progressive rock never interested him much. The term "progressive rock" is not without its ambiguities, since for some its progressivism was a political or philosophical matter, and for others it was a purely musical tendency or ideal; furthermore, unlike many of rock's sub-genres, progressive rock does not denote a specific musical style so much as a complex of styles, united, if at all, only through a common interest in musical experimentation and diversification. Progressive rock musicians were interested in playing about on the borderlines between musical genres, notably on those between classical music, jazz, avant-garde music, non-Western music, and rock.

Thus, in spite of the problems associated with the term, progressive rock must be viewed as the generic background for Eno's first recorded musical efforts. The term "art rock" is less suitable, primarily because of the inevitable association of the word "art" with the Western European classical music tradition. The leading proponent of the term "art rock" is John Rockwell, who in his fine article of that title in *The Rolling Stone Illustrated History of Rock & Roll* found the distinguishing feature of the genre in the self-consciously artistic attitude of its diverse practitioners.[11] Self-consciousness is what makes Stravinsky's *Rite of Spring* not a primitive, but a primitivist piece; a similar act of removal or distancing is what made the mid-1970s performances of art-rockers like Patti Smith, or of Talking Heads who followed, not simply primitive rock shows, but statements about primitive rock shows. This sort of detachment, according to Rockwell, is one of the things that makes art rock "art." Eno's primacy of place in Rockwell's scheme of things is clear in his placement of Eno, along with Frank Zappa, the Velvet Underground, and Pink Floyd, in their own separate, unqualified discographical categories; all other art-rockers are grouped by subject headings, some of them slyly derogatory—"Chart-Topping Classical Bombast" (Moody Blues, Emerson, Lake & Palmer, Yes), "Arty Primitivism" (John Cale, Terry Riley, Patti Smith). The catholicity of Rockwell's point of view, which deserves close attention from anyone interested in the shifting and blending of popular, art, and folk genres in the world of twentieth-century music, is also evident in his book *All American Music*, which finds Neil Young's "rock populism and transcendental primitivism" alongside Milton Babbit's serial structuralism, and Keith Jarrett's "mystical fusion romanticism" rubbing shoulders with Laurie Anderson's performance art.[12]

Brian Eno began his public career during the early 1970s, working primarily within the genre of progressive rock, toying with the expectations that are part of the listener's experience of any genre. In ways that I shall examine fully in Part II, he pushed back the boundaries of progressive rock until much of his music could not be called rock at all by any stylistic criterion, lacking, as it did, drums, a steady pulse, and vocals.

Most of Eno's music is characterized by a certain simplicity of conception, a sense of confidence in making a simple thing work. This, along with a preoccupation with the formal elements of music, is reminiscent of Mozartean classicism; certainly romantic breast-beating of the nineteenth-century variety finds few parallels in his work. Some of his ambient music is of such apparent surface simplicity that one critic, Jon Pareles, has questioned whether the allegedly bland results of his conceptual approach do not "hedge against questions of content or intrinsic interest."[13] Ed Naha has accused Eno of walking "the fine line between the musically artistic and autistic,"[14] while Lester Bangs has written of "still waters that don't necessarily run deep."[15]

Such criticism illuminates a paradox that must be faced when confronting Eno's music, a paradox that can be expressed in a number of ways. Is Eno's music divinely simple or merely simplistic? Is it primal and elemental, or primitive and elementary? If it proceeds from a wondrous, enchanting "What if?" attitude, do the results sometimes call for a cynical "So what?" response?[16] Eno himself combines a sophisticated, well-read intellectual sensibility with a vulnerable, childlike curiosity, in an alchemical mixture as rare in the rock world as outside it. Faced with the paradox, the listener must ultimately make his or her own decision.

Background and Influences

In interviews, Eno has discussed his musical influences and ideas on a sizeable array of intellectual topics repeatedly and in considerable detail, while he has been guarded, if not positively secretive, about his personal life—relationships, day-to-day movements, personal habits. In the published interviews, the journalists do not even *ask* personal questions, so it is likely that among Eno's ground rules for the interview is a prohibition against delving into purely biographical matters. While such guardedness is certainly refreshing when seen against the backdrop of scandal and confessional that typifies the press's treatment of popular musicians, it leaves us a bit at a loss in terms of knowing Eno as a human being.

Nevertheless, the basic outlines of Eno's life, or at least of his public life, are well known. Born May 15, 1948, at Woodbridge in Suffolk, England, he was christened Brian Peter George St. John le Baptiste de la Salle Eno. His early education (1953–64) was under the nuns and brothers of the de la Salle order at Ipswich. Although he was brought up Catholic, he does not practice the religion; in fact, his main references to this part of his background have to do with the sense of guilt which the church instilled in him at a young age— a sense which even as an adult he has not fully exorcised. From 1964 to 1966 he pursued foundation studies at Ipswich Art School, and in 1969 he received his Diploma in Fine Art from Winchester Art School. That is the extent of his formal education; we shall return to his art school experiences later, in the context of how they decisively shaped his musical outlook. Throughout most of the early and middle 1970s, Eno lived in London, working in recording studios, though he traveled and was frequently on tour. In 1978 he moved to a loft in New York City's Greenwich Village and made himself very much a part of the vital new downtown music scene. Subsequent travels took him to San Francisco, among other places, where he lived for six months around 1980. During this period he spoke of the psychological wear and tear of frequent travel and moving. Eventually he moved back to England, where he lives still, although since 1979 he has continued to pursue a rigorous regimen of almost bi-monthly trips to countries all over the world, setting up his audiovisual installations.

Eno's personality is complex. While he is capable of expounding at length and in a seemingly authoritative fashion on musical and philosophical subjects, many interviewers have noted a certain self-effacing quality that comes across when one talks to the man: he needs to be sure that his interlocutors are following him, that his ideas are not sounding too pompous or outrageous; he blushes easily. Although his ambient music is quiet and contemplative, he has been described as an extrovert, a sociable person who is able to make friends easily and take on new situations confidently. Eno speaks in long yet clearly structured sentences, and his easy sense of humor comes through by means of varied inflections of his voice.[1] As an artist, and perhaps also as a person, one of his primary assets is a profound capacity for wonder: he never seems to stray far from a sense of the inherent mystery of the world, and that sense of mystery excites and motivates him. Eno's favorite adjective is "interested." The word denotes to him more than a merely intellectual flirtation with a passing idea; when he is interested in something, it has awakened that sense of wonder, and he is palpably engaged in it, fully, existentially, and personally.

Composers today have available to them the entire world of music: it is no farther away than the local library or record store. One consequence of this state of affairs is that to an ever-increasing degree, the whole matter of "influences" is becoming less and less clear-cut. Things were simpler in earlier periods, and the historian's task in dealing with earlier music is rather different. It is one thing to note that Bach copied out Vivaldi scores by hand, or to trace the history of the parody Mass during the sixteenth century: in those instances, the musical tradition in question was more or less insular; the music available to the composers was limited in quantity, style, and genre; and the biographical facts available to the researcher were minimal. When "influences" can be positively identified, their identification usually represents a triumph of intrepid musicological sleuthing as well as a confirmation of the traditional, linear interpretation of music history.

It is quite another thing to take note of the music that Eno has counted among his influences. He exemplifies a new type of composer whose musical background is astonishingly diverse: he has exposed himself to a variety of traditions ranging from rock to classical, from avant-garde to experimental, as well as to a variety of non-Western musics such as Arabic, African, and Bulgarian. Today, the "chain of influence" is more likely to be a complex network or web, with many points of intersection that can become difficult or impossible to sort out. When the vast array of influences is processed and reprocessed in the mental melting pot of a modern composer like Eno, the resulting work sometimes suggests specific ties with specific traditions; but just as frequently, an individual piece will manifest no certain origins, its influences having been so completely assimilated into the composer's personal voice that no outstanding traces of them are left. Perhaps something similar may be true of the work of some earlier composers, but this does not alter the radical difference between the contemporary and historical musical situations.

Eno grew up in the English countryside. His decisive musical influences came not from indigenous English folk or popular traditions, however, but from two large U.S. air bases located within five miles of Woodbridge, which eventually housed about 15,000 G.I.'s. The many local cafés had juke-boxes well stocked with contemporary American popular music, and Eno had a sister who used to go to the PX stores and "come back with all these really very interesting records that you never heard in England otherwise. They never were on the radio."[2] It was a musical environment strikingly similar to that of the young Beatles' Liverpool, where sailors brought in the latest American records, which attracted young listeners with their contemporaneity and their exotic quality. Eno has described the curious mix of music he heard:

> Feeble, weedy English pop music and then the American stuff, full of what I still find to be menace and strangeness. I listened to Chuck Berry, Little Richard, Bo Diddley, I was a listener for a long, long time—I used to sing, too, I was always singing a lot, Buddy Holly, Elvis. This was American music, African music, in the middle of the English countryside. . . . I think the echo on Elvis's "Heartbreak Hotel" is better than the song itself, by far. Nobody could tell me what that was, in my family. They didn't know what to make of that sound. It turns the studio into a cave. . . . When I was young, the most overpowering sense of wonder was inspired in me by music.[3]

Eno, like many English rock musicians of his generation, has been harshly critical of his own country's popular music of the '50s. "English music at that time was *really* boring. Cliff Richard and Tommy Steele and . . . just a lot of very poor imitations of the larger American stars."[4] On another occasion, Eno used the phrase "Martian music" to describe the alien, *other* quality of the 1950s doo-wop which he heard emanating from the G.I. culture of the air bases.[5] In 1981, he waxed philosophic on the question of why such music seemed so full of mystery to him, and on its lessons for his own creative work:

> I suppose people here [in the U.S.A.] might think it's strange to regard doo-wop as magical music, but I did, because in England we had no tradition of it whatsoever. . . . It could have been from another galaxy for all I knew. I was absolutely entranced by it, from the age of seven or eight, when I first heard those early songs like "Get A Job" [The Silhouettes, 1958]. I thought, "This is just *beautiful*." I had never heard music like this, and one of the reasons it was beautiful was because it came without a context. It plopped from outer space, in a sense. Now, in later life I realized that this removal of context was an important point in the magic of music.[6]

Eno's imagination was galvanized by early rhythm and blues and rock and roll, and he would play certain records incessantly on his parents' auto-repeat record player: "I used to leave it on all day, every day."[7] He was also exposed to big-band jazz:

> And then another [group] I heard was, funnily enough, the Ray Conniff Singers. Because I had an uncle who had to leave the place he was living, and he parked

his record collection with my parents for a while. And his taste was '40s big-band jazz. The sound of those voices on the Ray Conniff records I thought was superb. . . . I remember these winter mornings, hearing these amazingly lush, soft, silky voices, and I thought it was a beautiful sound.[8]

Again, Eno was fascinated by the sound itself, having at this point no historical or cultural context in which to place such music: "I was just interested in it, for some reason. I didn't know where it came from or what jazz was."[9] The Enos also had a player piano, which Eno "absolutely loved" and "played all the time. All we had were . . . old hymns, like 'Jerusalem' and so on, which I thought were beautiful. And I think that the kind of melancholy quality of those is something that's actually persisted in anything I've done since."[10]

Traces of all of these early musical influences show up in Eno's own published musical output, which begins about a decade later. The sense of strangeness resulting from contextlessness is something he has explicitly endeavored to capture in most of his music. Echoes of early rhythm and blues and rock and roll turn up in the "idiot energy" (the phrase is Eno's) of some of the songs on his solo albums of the early 1970s—songs which occasionally borrow specific instrumental textures from music of the 1950s, whose generally economical and transparent arrangements Eno attempted to emulate. His fascination with Afro-American rhythms is most clear in his 1981 collaboration with David Byrne, *My Life in the Bush of Ghosts,* though it is also evident elsewhere. What Eno calls the "lush, soft, silky" quality that he admired in the Ray Conniff Singers is a nearly constant feature in his ambient music, finding its most literal expression in the electronically treated vocals of *Music for Airports.* And finally, the "melancholy" strains of the player-piano hymns resonate particularly strongly in several of Eno's ambient synthesizer pieces, which resemble grand, textless, diatonic organ hymns.

Among his influences from the popular music world of the 1960s, Eno has singled out for special mention the unique New York band, the Velvet Underground, and the prototypical British rock band, the Who. By the 1960s, Eno's conceptual world had expanded to the point of having more of a context in which to place the music. In the case of the Velvet Underground, context is all-important, since they were directly associated with the pop art movement of Andy Warhol—who in 1965 used them to provide the music for his moveable multimedia show, the Exploding Plastic Inevitable. Context was also important to the Who, who began as heroes of the Mod scene in England and were among the first to create concept albums—a development that culminated in their rock opera of 1969, *Tommy.* Both bands were known for their self-conscious primitivism, and they showed Eno "that it was possible to occupy an area between fine art sensibility and popular art, and have the ambiguity work."[11] More specifically, Eno dreamed of a blend of music that would utilize the Who's and Velvets' approach with the more soulful sound of Afro-American music—a musical marriage of the "stiff, totalitarian" aspect of rock with the "fluid, sensual quality of black music":

I think it would make a saleable combination if Kraftwerk employed Parliament, or the other way around. It would be interesting if you had the Parliament group playing bass, and Kraftwerk playing the drums. There would be a cross-cultural hybrid, especially if everybody stuck to their guns.[12]

Although Eno played clarinet with the Portsmouth Sinfonia, and although he has systematically attacked the "pyramidical" social structure of the classical orchestra (in a crucial article treated in Chapter 5), in interviews he seldom discusses Western European art music. If he owes a debt to that tradition, it is to its avant-garde, experimental factions, which rallied to John Cage's proclamation during the 1950s and 1960s that "everything we do is music," and to the group of composers, now called "minimalists," who have followed paths set out by La Monte Young and Terry Riley.

Eno read Cage's epochal book, *Silence*,[13] during the 1960s. Glancing through its contents today, one is struck by the frequency of passages that presage Eno's own approach to music and the philosophy of music. Cage quotes from an article by Christian Wolff:

> Notable qualities of this music, whether electronic or not, are monotony and the irritation that accompanies it. The monotony may lie in simplicity or delicacy, strength or complexity. Complexity tends to reach a point of neutralization: continuous change results in a certain sameness. It goes in no particular direction. There is no necessary concern with time as a measure of distance from a point in the past to a point in the future, with linear continuity alone. It is not a question of getting anywhere, of making progress, or having come from anywhere in particular, of tradition or futurism. There is neither nostalgia nor anticipation. Often the structure of a piece is circular. . . .[14]

Though the sounding surfaces of Wolff's examples—Pousseur's *Exercises de Piano* and Stockhausen's *Klavierstück XI*—are about as diametrically opposed to Eno's ambient music as they could be, Wolff could be describing any number of Eno pieces written since 1975, and it is easy to imagine Eno during the 1960s reading such a passage and turning it over in his mind. Cage's essay on Erik Satie likewise contains quotations that could almost have appeared in the liner notes to an album like *Music for Airports*, an album that is in a sense a response to Satie's challenge. Cage quotes Satie:

> Nevertheless, we must bring about a music which is like furniture—a music, that is, which will be part of the noises of the environment, will take them into consideration. I think of it as melodious, softening the noises of the knives and forks, not dominating them, not imposing itself. It would fill up those heavy silences that sometimes fall between friends dining together. It would spare them the trouble of paying attention to their own banal remarks. And at the same time it would neutralize the street noises which so indiscretely enter into the play of conversation. To make such music would be to respond to a need.[15]

Eno's own philosophy of ambient music is not so peevish as Satie's, and Eno has been more interested in enhancing and incorporating the environment's extraneous noises than in neutralizing them. Nonetheless, the parallels are obvious. Cage's description of Satie's proto-minimalist work, *Vexations*—a piece lasting, in Cage's estimation, "twenty-four hours; 840 repetitions of a fifty-two beat piece itself involving a repetitive structure: A, A₁, A, A₂, each A thirteen measures long"[16]—immediately brings to mind Eno's piece, "Discreet Music" (in which a couple of short synthesizer melodies meander, repeat, and randomly overlap during a period of thirty minutes) and Eno's recent audiovisual installations (in which repeating, overlapping cycles can go on for as long as six weeks). In discussing Satie's music as accompaniment to the sounds of knives and forks, Cage says that "It is evidently a question of bringing one's intended actions into relation with the ambient unintended ones."[17] Although Eno has never publicly said so, Cage's concept of "ambient" sounds very likely informs Eno's own concept of ambient music, or at least Cage's use of the word is likely the source of his own use of it. Later on the same page, Cage characteristically defines silence as "ambient noise."

Cage quotes Satie again:

> They will tell you I am not a musician. That's right. . . . Take the *Fils des Etoiles* or the *Morceaux en forme de poire*, *En habit de cheval* or the *Sarabandes*, it is clear no musical idea presided at the creation of these works.[18]

Again, although one may not be exactly sure how to interpret Satie's blend of irony, bitterness, and wit, the statement "I am not a musician" was taken up eagerly by Eno in the 1970s, and became almost his motto or credo, however numerous the misunderstandings to which it has given rise may be. (I shall return to this issue in Chapter 4.) Eno specified that it was the "systematic" Satie with whom he strongly identified: "He was a systems composer, you know, planning chord changes by numerical techniques. In the midst of extraordinary chromatic experimentalism, with everyone doing bizarre things, he just wrote these lovely little pieces of music."[19]

Apart from such specific references, there is much in *Silence* that clearly influenced Eno: the fascination with chance operations, which Eno was to incorporate in his deck of oracle cards, the *Oblique Strategies*, in the mid-1970s (see Chapter 5); the Zen anecdotes and the excursions into Eastern philosophy; the mildly, jocosely irreverent attitude toward canonical principles of Western art music, with regard to both musical structure and social setting; the unconventional typography and free mix of musical and written media (as in Cage's "45' for a Speaker"); the idea of "Composition as Process" (another chapter title); and the ever-repeated axiom that all sounds have the potential for being experienced as music. *Silence* served Eno, like countless young artists and musicians of the last few decades, as a somewhat ad-hoc, yet more or less comprehensive survey of major developments in experimental music during the early and mid-twentieth century.

Eno has acknowledged Cage's influence on several occasions. His first published reference to Cage is in a 1972 interview. Eno was discussing the tape-delay technique he had recently been exploring with Robert Fripp, the results of which can be heard on their 1973 album, *No Pussyfooting*. Eno was aware that Terry Riley had just gone public with a similar delay system. Then the interview quotes him as having said: "Actually, soon afterwards I found out that John Cage had discovered the same things years ago. But he was a creep, and anyway he didn't know how to use it!"[20] By 1977, Eno no longer had to adopt the aggressive attitude of the *enfant terrible* feeling his oats: " 'Art is a net,' Cage said. Years later I read Morse Peckham. He said, 'Art is safe.' I realized that's what Cage meant. You're creating a false world where you can afford to make mistakes."[21]

In 1980, after again acknowledging Cage's influence on the development of his ideas, Eno revealed that he had sent Cage a score of his own around 1966, and that he had received in return "a circular, I guess, [that] he sends out to the thousands of people a week who send him scores, and it said, 'thank you very much for the score. It has been duly filed and appreciated,' or something of that type." Eno added, with a self-deprecatory laugh, "I was very pleased to get this accolade from John Cage."[22]

More revealing still are comments Eno made in a 1981 interview. Calling Cage "the most influential theorist" he had encountered at a certain point in his life, "a completely liberating factor," Eno goes on to say that Cage "reintroduced the notion of spirituality into the making of music." Much musical composition during the first half of the twentieth century struck Eno as sterile: "The history of music was seen as the breakdown of the old tonal system and the move into chromaticism and the tone row, and everything was being discussed in these terms." The formal and technical agenda had replaced or submerged aesthetic concerns, and

> to be a good composer, what you had to do was understand what had happened on a formal level and then break certain of those rules. Now clearly, this has never been what good music was about. In fact, the quality that one seeks is the spiritual quality, which incidentally sometimes breaks the rules. . . . So what Cage did that was so important was to say, "Look, when you make music you are acting as a philosopher. You can either do that consciously or you can do it unconsciously, but you're doing it."[23]

One of the points of Cage's program was to make musical compositions "the continuity of which [is] free of individual taste and memory (psychology) and also of the literature and 'traditions' of the art."[24] As we shall see, Eno is emphatically not interested in making music that is "free of individual taste and memory (psychology)": looming large in his artistic intentions is a desire to make music that has a frankly seductive surface and arouses the emotion of wonder; and, at least in recent years, he has consciously tried to create a unique sense of physical space for each piece.

In 1985, Rob Tannenbaum scored a remarkable journalistic coup by bringing together John Cage and Brian Eno for the first time. During the 1980s, Eno has been somewhat reluctant to give interviews, apparently bored with repeating himself, and often wondering "why people just don't research the extant material."[25] Tannenbaum coaxed him out with the prospect of meeting Cage —who was in London for performances of the Cunningham Dance Company which featured his music—and doing a joint interview. Among other topics, the two amicably discussed their methods of composition, their knowledge of each other's work, their status as legends, their views on modern music, and the role of the composer. Tannenbaum reports that Eno was deferential, seeming "reluctant to quiz Cage on anything other than gardening,"[26] a shared interest. At one point, Tannenbaum posed the dilemma: "Both of you have defended the idea that you can be a good composer whether you're trained or untrained. . . . So what is it that separates untrained composers who aren't worth listening to from untrained composers who are?" Cage responded with a characteristic conceptual twist:

> I think the term "worth listening to" depends on who's listening. I think it would be right to say that no matter what, if it is sounds, one could listen to it. I haven't yet heard sounds that I didn't enjoy, except when they became too musical. I have trouble, I think, when music attempts to control me. I have trouble, for instance, with the "Hallelujah Chorus." But if the sound is unintentional, then I have no problem.[27]

Eno picked up the train of thought and said:

> That's right. Some sound comes so heavily laden with intention that you can't hear it for the intentions. . . . But the question you asked about trained and untrained musicians. . . . In fact, I must say that [to Cage] you're the reason, or you're the excuse for why I became a composer. The alibi, I should say. Because I never learned to play an instrument, and still haven't.[28]

Eno paid homage to Cage in 1976 by producing an album that included performances of five Cage pieces.[29] If there is a gulf that separates the two men, fundamentally it has to do with age and background. Cage is the elder statesman of the avant-garde; he studied with Schoenberg, and his views on music, summarized in *Silence*, revolve around developments in the Western art music tradition—indeed represent developments more or less specific to that tradition; some of his chance music bears an aesthetic surface strikingly similar to that of serially composed music, to which it is so adamantly opposed at the philosophical level. Eno's *musical* roots are in popular music traditions, and this is reflected not only in his somewhat superficial knowledge of the classical tradition and his disdain for its institutional infrastructure, but in his music itself, which, even when it is not outright rock, is by far more consonant and accessible than much of Cage's music.

Cage's influence on Eno has thus been significant, but as is true of Cage's impact on many composers, it has been more conceptual than specifically musical in nature. A more concrete musical influence has been that of minimalist composers such as La Monte Young, Terry Riley, and Steve Reich, whose music has influenced Eno more than any others', with the possible exception of the popular music of the 1950s. To Eno, minimalism represents the most significant and potentially fruitful aesthetic point of departure during the twentieth century—a new musical meta-idea, so to speak, which promises untold riches not simply in the development of compositional techniques, but in the development of new ways of listening.

The prehistory of minimalism goes back at least to Satie's *Vexations*. But one of the earliest examples of minimalism proper is by Terry Riley (b. 1935), who, shortly after graduating from the University of California, Berkeley, with a degree in composition, wrote the seminal work, *In C* (1964). The score consists of fifty-three notated melodic fragments, which the performers, who may vary in number, are to play one after the other, in synchronization with a steadily repeated "pulse" on the top two C's of the piano keyboard, repeating any given fragment an indeterminate number of times and pausing between fragments as they see fit. The piece ends after everyone reaches the fifty-third fragment. Typical performances last between forty-five and ninety minutes, though one *In C* marathon in Mexico City in 1982 lasted for three hours. The effect of the music depends to a large extent upon the quality of the interaction among the musicians in the ensemble. Thus a large amount of repetition and a requirement of active listening by both performers and audience are built into the structure of the piece.

Although Eno has spoken with admiration of Riley's music, a more decisive minimalist influence on his work were the phase tape pieces of Steve Reich (b. 1936). In a 1985 interview he singled out Reich's *It's Gonna Rain* as "probably the most important piece that I heard, in that it gave me an idea I've never ceased being fascinated with—how variety can be generated by very, very simple systems." Reich made short tape loops of a black preacher saying "It's gonna rain," so that what we hear is this one phrase repeated over and over again. The tape machines are running at slightly different speeds, however, so that as the piece progresses, the loops gradually shift out of phase with each other. Eno comments:

> . . . Any information which is common, after several repetitions, you cease to hear. You reject the common information, rather like if you gaze at something for a long time, you'll cease to really see it. You'll see any aspect of it that's changing, but the static elements you won't see.[30]

Reich's *It's Gonna Rain* was a remarkable experiment in the psychology of musical perception: for although one could hear each individual voice if one tried, far more fascinating was the composite, subtly changing rhythmic texture that arose from the phase shifts. New, unforeseen musical events were formed, as it were, out of the chinks between the words; the listener's attention could be riveted by any one of a multitude of possible composite patterns, and could flip back and forth between patterns of interpretation. A visual equivalent to such flipping might be the diagrams used in experiments on perception that are open to different interpretations: a vase in silhouette appears also as two heads facing each other, or a rabbit also as a duck. The graphic artist M. C. Escher made such perceptual shifts major components of his style, for instance, in his mind-bending, multiple-perspective stairway drawings.[31] In music, Reich's phase shifts constituted a use of repetition inviting or requiring a new mode of listening; if one listened in the old way, all one heard was hundreds of boring repetitions of the same phrase. Eno was aware of this, and even found an analogy in the biological world:

> There's an essay called "What the Frog's Eye Tells the Frog's Brain," by Warren McCulloch, who discovered that a frog's eyes don't work like ours. Ours are always moving: we blink; we scan. We move our heads. But a frog fixes its eyes on a scene and leaves them there. It stops seeing all the static parts of the environment, which become invisible, but as soon as one element moves, which could be what it wants to eat—the fly—it is seen in very high contrast to the rest of the environment. It's the only thing the frog sees and the tongue comes out and takes it. Well, I realized that what happens with the Reich piece is that our ears behave like a frog's eyes. Since the material is common to both tapes, what you begin to notice are not the repeating parts but the sort of ephemeral interference patterns between them. Your ear telescopes into more and more fine detail until you're hearing what to me seems like atoms of sound. That piece absolutely thrilled me, because I realized then that I understood what minimalism was about. The creative operation is listening. It isn't just a question of a presentation feeding into a passive audience. People will sometimes say about Reich's piece, "Oh yes, that one with that voice which keeps hammering into your head," and indeed, if you're not especially listening to it that's exactly what it is.[32]

Reich went on to develop this technique in such works as *Violin Phase* (1967); later works, such as *Music for a Large Ensemble* (1978) and *Tehillim* (1982), abandon strict phase technique but continue to explore the possibilities of long-term repetitions of one sort or another. As Eno said, "Reich sort of abandoned that system as a way of working, which is rather fortunate because that meant I could carry on with it. [Laughs.] And *Music for Airports* is one of the products of that."[33] In the liner notes to his 1970 composition *Four Organs*, Reich stressed his belief in the expressive power of gradual processes in music, and in the importance of not burying structure in mathematical formulae. His statement could almost have been made by Eno himself: "The use of hidden structural devices in music never appealed to me. Even when all the cards are on the table and everyone hears what is gradually happening in a musical process, there are still enough mysteries to satisfy all."[34]

Eno's experience of hearing what he has called the "aural *moiré* patterns"[35] of *It's Gonna Rain* was additionally refreshing because it seemed to run against the trend toward the unnecessarily complex and grandiose in rock music:

> I heard this in the early 1970s, which was just at the time that most of the people that I was involved with were doing exactly the opposite thing. Twenty-four track recorders had just become current, and the idea was to make more and more grotesque, Gothic pieces of music, filling up every space and every corner of the canvas. And to hear something that was as alive as this Reich piece, and so simple, was a real shock to me. . . . I thought, "I can do this. It's not hard." [Laughs.][36]

La Monte Young (b. 1935) is a composer whose conceptual works fitted perfectly into the anything-goes, avant-garde, anarchic artistic atmosphere of the 1960s. In his *Composition 1960 #3* the duration of the piece is announced and the audience is told they may do whatever they wish until it is over. In *Composition 1960 #6* the performers stare at the audience as if they were the performers. Another 1960 composition contains only two notes, B and F♯, "to be held for a long time." John Lennon and Yoko Ono later indulged in this genre of composition: in one Lennon/Ono piece, fans blow open the pages of a Beethoven symphony, and the players are directed to play whatever is before them.[37] But it is Young's works in the specifically repetitive realm that inspired Eno's imagination. In Young's 1960 piece *X for Henry Flynt*, the performer is instructed to produce a single unspecified sound over and over for an unspecified interval of time. Eno performed this piece on piano around 1967—it was "the first piece of music I ever performed publicly,"[38] he said—by playing large clusters of notes with both forearms once a second for a period of an hour. He later philosophized on what the piece had taught him:

> Now, until one became accustomed to this fifty-odd note cluster, the resultant sound was fairly boring. But after that first ten minutes, it became progressively more absorbing. This was reflected in the rate at which people left the room— those who didn't leave within ten minutes stayed for the whole performance. One began to notice the most minute variations from one crash to the next. The subtraction of one note by the right elbow missing its top key was immediately and dramatically obvious. The slight variations of timing became major compositional changes, and the constant changes within the odd beat frequencies being formed by all the discords began to develop into melodic lines. This was, for me, a new use of the error principle and led me to codify a little law that has since informed much of my work—"Repetition is a form of change."[39]

3

On Other Music:
Eno as Critic

Eno's impressions of the world of music were gathered primarily during the 1950s, 1960s, and 1970s. During those years, he was exposed to a great deal of rock and other popular music, to a good deal of experimental and avant-garde music, to a fair quantity of non-Western music, and to some traditional Western art music. Since 1980, however, Eno has evinced less interest in keeping up with contemporary trends and with listening to other people's music in general. The club scene began to pall for him, as he explained in 1986:

> I used to go to clubs now and again, but I gradually stopped going because I couldn't find one that did the kind of thing that I wanted. The accent of a club is towards somehow speeding you up, presumably with the idea of obliterating what is assumed to be an otherwise average existence. Well, I wanted the opposite of that. I wanted to find places that would actually be slower, bigger, more open and would make me think in some interesting way. Clubs, in fact, prevent me from thinking.[1]

It is a fairly common phenomenon among composers that, after a certain point in their creative lives, they lose the desire or will to listen to a great deal of other music. In 1985, Eno said, "I don't listen to records much." The interviewer asked, "Is that a deliberate thing, or do you find you just don't want to?" Eno answered:

> I don't think about it. I don't have a record player, funnily enough. I think life's too short to listen to records, at the moment. Well, I do listen to *some* things, but I usually like to listen to the same thing over and over for months.
> I'm quite happy to accept that I don't know most of what's going on in the world of music. I never have done. You have a choice when you get interested in culture. You have a choice of trying to absorb it all, the American style of "doing the sights" in two days, or else you can just decide: "I'll stay in this one place, because I like it here anyway, and I'll really understand this. I'll really find out about it." That's what I do.[2]

In 1982, Eno was pessimistic about the public value of airing his opinions on music (after having done precisely that for a decade, it should be added).

He felt that he had run out of interesting things to say about pop music, and that whenever he started talking about it, people stopped listening. More than that, he wanted to distance himself philosophically from pop: "Pop music isn't by any means the central issue of my life; it's hardly a peripheral one."[3]

Eno has always had paradoxical views on the subject of rock music, and even with his solo progressive rock albums of the early 1970s, in a sense he was not so much making rock music as he was making music about rock music. As I noted in Chapter 1, critic John Rockwell has singled out such a self-conscious attitude as the unifying factor behind the genre of art rock; and if Stravinsky was right in saying that the real criticism of a piece of music lies in other pieces that are "about" that piece, then we should expect to find Eno's real critical voice in his music itself. However committed to his art he has been and continues to be, Eno is simultaneously curiously aloof, removed from everyday pop realities. In 1974, early in his career, he was interested in somehow uniting the two kinds of music that interested him most: the "fiercely intellectual, fiercely anti-physical" quality of avant-garde music and the "fiercely physical, fiercely anti-intellectual" quality of rock. "I wanted to try to find a meeting of the two which would actually not be frightened of either force. Rock musicians are frightened of any kind of discussion of what they do. . . . I do think that rock music is the most important art form right now."[4]

The key detail here is Eno's reference to rock as an art form. This was a concept idealistically shared by many musicians, critics, and fans during the late 1960s and early 1970s. For Eno, rock held out this possibility—that music could be mentally stimulating as well as sensuously accessible, intellectual as well as physical, conceptual as well as popular. That this was more often an ideal than a reality was one of the main lessons of Eno's experiences with Roxy Music. In 1975 he discussed their early and subsequent music:

> If I listen to the first album now, I still find it a bold statement. But what happened is what happens to most bands: they become successful. . . .
>   Unfortunately, if you want to make a lot of money in rock music you have one good idea and then you do it again and again. You don't even have to have a good, original idea if you conform to the existing pattern.[5]

Clearly, if Eno had once proclaimed rock the most important contemporary art form, he stopped far short of embracing all rock music as equally valuable, and he was only too aware of the homogenizing pressures of the music industry. In a 1980 interview he argued strongly for risk-taking and experimentation, criticizing rock musicians for being too narrowly goal-oriented, unwilling to "dabble and play." "Any music worth anything is born in clumsiness and chaos. . . . Rock isn't dangerous any more." Eno thought that rock was losing one of its greatest strengths: its ability to incorporate ideas from a variety of musical traditions. Rock was becoming "a progressively more insular form."[6]

Part of Eno's criticism of rock doubtless stemmed from the fact that after his collaborations with David Bowie and Talking Heads during the late 1970s, he found himself personally less drawn to rock as a medium. With those collaborations he thought, at least temporarily, that he had taken rock as far as he wanted to go with it. He began to draw less sustenance from the types of sound that rock had to offer. In 1982, he said:

> Effectively, what I've done is abandoned rock music, because, for me, rock isn't capable of producing that spiritual quality anymore. And, in fact, I don't really hear anything at the moment that disputes my feeling. Despite all the criticism that's been made of psychedelic music, it certainly was committed to the production of an expanded awareness.[7]

And a year later:

> I don't get the feeling of discovering new worlds from pop music that I used to get, just of being shown old ones over and over. One automatically thinks that's because I'm getting old, which is true but that doesn't mean one is getting jaded. I still get feeling and experience from other areas, but not rock.[8]

More recently, Eno made the following personal observation:

> One of the nice things about the kind of music I'm doing now is that it makes me feel quite unimportant. I like that feeling. Rock music, on the other hand, tends to make you feel *very* important.[9]

How much of Eno's loss of interest in rock music is due to personal factors—his own musical background and development—and how much may be attributed to a real stagnation in the field of rock music itself? The question is a complex one, and there is no simple answer. Some rock critics have tended to extol the music of the 1950s and 1960s, and to denigrate the 1970s and 1980s as decades of homogenization, commercialization, and creative stagnation. Compared with those years of bland corporate rock, the late 1960s are frequently portrayed as a kind of golden age of experimentation, variety, and intense musical ferment. The critics who make such statements are of course themselves children of the 1950s and 1960s, inevitably tending to see the music of their youth as belonging to a kind of golden age. Many who during the 1930s and 1940s grew up on the music of the big bands, Broadway, and Tin Pan Alley lost all interest in the development of popular music beyond those particular halcyon days.

Critics with a sociological bent, like Simon Frith, go so far as to define rock as the music of youth, and make no further bones about it.[10] There is plenty of statistical data on age-linked patterns of music consumption to back him up. After reaching the age of thirty or so, people in Britain and the United States buy few rock records, and are inclined to tune in to radio stations that offer "adult contemporary" music as well as a significant proportion of oldies.[11]

To some extent, Eno may be said to have followed the pattern of his generation in rejecting or at least abandoning rock music upon growing into adulthood. For most people over the age of thirty the social context for rock music diminishes; and for musicians, particularly creative ones of Eno's talents, the sounds of ordinary rock are almost bound to start sounding repetitive and worn. Yet it ought also to be acknowledged that during the late 1960s, when Eno was absorbing rock music at a great rate, a peculiar conjunction of the popular and avant-garde musical worlds was taking place—a conjunction not exactly without historical precedent (think of the fascination of traditional composers with jazz during the 1930s, cool jazz and third-stream music during the 1950s, and new wave music and performance art during the late 1970s and early 1980s), but a conjunction that provided an ideal cultural backdrop for Eno's own developing ideas. The late 1960s were the era of happenings, of pop art, of the Beatles' most progressive work, of rock music appearing to *matter* in musical, political, and intellectual spheres. They were also the era of psychedelic music, which Eno singled out as a phenomenon whose ideal value and purpose—the production of an expanded awareness—he has found lacking in the run of more recent rock.

If the pop/art cultural interaction of the late 1960s provided the twenty-year-old Eno with broad-ranging stimulation and plenty of raw material for his own theories, and if the Eno of the 1980s has abandoned rock after having repeatedly criticized it broadly and incisively, during the 1970s he still leapt to its defense when he thought it was being treated pompously by the wrong people for the wrong reasons. In 1978 he reportedly let loose the following diatribe:

> One of the things I'm finding quite infuriating at the moment is the continuous attempt by middle-class critics to validate rock music. They're saying to people, "You can't fucking hear anything because you're dumb, but this or that is terribly important." That's no basis for liking something. If you approach something on that basis, "God, this is important," then it doesn't give you any real information.
>
> Rock music is such a liberated form, and will remain that way as long as the middle-class critics stay off it. It doesn't have any snobbishness about its development. People aren't afraid of just playing old Chuck Berry riffs still, twenty years later. There aren't all those petty restrictions about how you've got to innovate, it's got to be new.[12]

The apparent contradiction between this statement and Eno's own criticisms of the trap of repetitiveness that befalls rock musicians may be partially resolved if we recognize his position as a straddler of a fence between two worlds: "I have different circles of friends, and some of the people I know come from so-called serious music backgrounds and others are from popular music backgrounds. And whenever I'm with one group, I'm always defending the other."[13]

Out of the vast array of rock musicians active in the 1960s, Eno has found only a handful interesting enough to mention in interviews. In 1980 he wished to set himself apart from what he called the "cultural myth" represented by groups like the Rolling Stones—a myth that

> has to do with the view of the musician or artist as an impulsive, drug-taking romantic. I don't reject that view, I know some artists like that and they do good work as well. But there's another kind of artist who thinks about what they're doing and talks about what they're doing and wants to articulate it and who doesn't believe as some do that talking about it reduces its mystique or deflates the work. . . . I think you can make a work richer by seeding it with a number of connotations, which you can do by talking about it. I suppose my difference from [groups like the Rolling Stones] is that one has the sense they improvise at almost every level. I don't—except at certain levels.[14]

Onstage, especially during the 1970s when they increasingly played to audiences numbering in the tens of thousands, the Rolling Stones' musical act was notoriously unpolished—but this was part of the whole myth: the Stones were cultural symbols who just happened to sing and play instruments, and they played out of tune, played sloppily and lost the beat, almost with a vengeance. They were allowed to, because part of the whole idea of rock music at that level was that it was music that anybody could play. When Eno would say he was not a musician, however, he meant something quite different, as we shall see in the next chapter; he resented the kind of musical thoughtlessness epitomized by the Rolling Stones. He indeed used improvisatory techniques himself, but always in the context of a larger plan: in the context of the process of shaping an immaculately polished musical product. His interest in improvisation was reflected in his appraisal of Bob Dylan albums like *Blonde on Blonde* (1966). He suspected that Dylan had used a technique of writing lyrics rather like his own: "When I've got a set of sounds that I think works musically in an interesting way, then I listen to those sounds and try to make them into words. It's a bit like automatic writing, the way you scribble until words start to appear."[15]

Eno has singled out a number of musicians who, he believes, consciously tried to realize the potential of that grand new musical instrument, the recording studio: Glenn Gould (whose technique of recording many performances and editing them together Eno greatly admired); Jimi Hendrix (who would fill as many as twenty-six separate tracks on a thirty-two-track tape recorder with guitar solos, then begin the real creative process of blending, mixing, and deleting); Phil Spector (who "understood better than anybody that a recording could do things that could never actually happen"); the Beach Boys, the Jefferson Airplane, and the Byrds (whose experimental and psychedelic approach Eno appreciated); the Beatles (whose 1966 album *Revolver*, recorded on four-track with George Martin at the controls, Eno described as "my favourite Beatles album"); and Simon and Garfunkel ("The song 'Bridge Over Troubled Water' [1970] is perfection in its way. I'm told it took 370 hours of studio time to record—that's longer than most albums, but it is such an incredible *tour de force*. It's the World Trade Center of production in a way; you might not think that the building is necessarily beautiful, but you cannot help but be impressed by it.").[16]

Although I have argued that Eno's early solo albums belong in the genre of progressive rock, he has been constantly at pains to disassociate himself from some of the most popular manifestations of that genre. In 1978 he took the following broad view of recent rock history and his place in it:

> At the end of the 1960s, there were two mainstreams, one that came from the Beatles, with big sales, and one from the Velvet Underground and the early Who and Bo Diddley—much rougher, more urban and less Gothic. I always felt I was part of that second thing. Technology is a separate issue. It just happened that the fantasy bands got involved in technology because they could afford it, rather than because it was a particular predilection of theirs or particularly belonged with that kind of music.[17]

By the "Gothic fantasy bands" Eno doubtless means groups like Yes and Emerson, Lake & Palmer, who managed to turn an unlikely blend of elements—an instrumental virtuosity previously unheard of in rock, a grandeur of conception rivaling that of Mahler and Strauss, a widely expanded harmonic and rhythmic technique (with roots in both nineteenth-century art music and jazz), and an infatuation with the possibilities of synthesizers and twenty-four-track recording technology—into one of the most commercially successful musical blends of the era. Eno has attacked this kind of music on a number of occasions, calling it "grotesque" in one instance,[18] making a snide remark about "the well-known and gladly departed orchestral rock tradition" in another,[19] decrying "really dumb bands who've tried to make a kind of academic form out of rock music" in yet another.[20] What apparently has bothered Eno most about progressive rock of this type is not its seeming to want to claim a vicarious and inappropriate respectability for itself by borrowing so blatantly from late-Romantic ideals (the aspect that has troubled most critics); rather, Eno, ever the Apollonian technophile, seems genuinely offended by its sheer technological excess, its lack of restraint. In 1983 he recalled

> the early 70s, when recording had just gone from four to 24 tracks in a very few years. Rock became grandiose and muddy, like a bad cook who puts every spice and herb on the shelf in the soup. . . . I started thinking in reductive terms.[21]

Infatuation with technological means is something Eno has no use for; he thinks it tends to get in the way of the functioning of the most important link in the musical chain—the human ear. In the early 1980s, a visit to Stanford University, home of one of the world's most sophisticated computer music studios, proved disillusioning: "Techies don't listen to what they're doing. . . . I'm no techie."[22]

The last movement within rock to capture Eno's sustained interest was the new wave music of the late 1970s. He moved to New York in 1978 in order to be in the thick of the latest developments. The rawness of the British punk sound may have intrigued him for a while, but he was never attracted to its overtly political, anarchistic message; the New York new wavers, on the other hand, seemed to be experimenting with music and with ideas:

> The New York bands proceed from a "what would happen if" orientation. The English punk thing is a "feel" situation: "This is our identity, and the music emanates from that." I've always been of the former persuasion. . . .
> But there's a difference between me and the New York bands. They carry the experiment to the extreme; I carry it to the point where it stops sounding interesting, and then pull back a little bit. What they do is a rarefied kind of research; it generates a vocabulary that people like me can use. These New York bands are like fence-posts, the real edges of a territory, and one can maneuver within it.[23]

The New York scene of the late 1970s impressed Eno as a kind of paradigm of the developmental process in rock:

> What's going on in New York now is one of those seminal situations where there are really a lot of ideas around, and somebody is going to synthesize some of them soon. . . . That's always been the way of rock music as far as I can see, this forming of eclectic little groups of disciplines.[24]

Eno felt he had indirectly contributed to this ferment by having steadily maintained, over the previous several years,

> that it was possible to go in there [the recording studio] with a childlike enthusiasm and dabble about and come out with something that was interesting, and my own work, as far as I was concerned, was a proof of that. . . . And I think that this was one of the many currents that flowed into what became new wave, because as you know, many of the new wave groups are in much the same musical position as me. They have enthusiasm and good ideas, but no or little technical skill, and they don't worry about that. You design your music to accomodate the level of skill you have available to you, rather than sitting at home and thinking, "Boy, I wish I could play like Eric Clapton," which is what people were doing when I started making records.[25]

Finally, to Eno new wave music symbolized a healthy turning away from the overblown, grandiose, crowded synthetic perfection of twenty-four-track rock; as many writers have pointed out, the means of making music were once more in the hands of the people, rather than limited to those few who could afford the ever-increasing costs of studio time, professional producers, and the latest electronic equipment:

> One of the great liberating things about new wave was the idea that people could once again release demos and things done in garages and very crude acoustic

situations, and one didn't regard these things as "Oh, it's a great song . . . what a pity it's so badly recorded"; one said, "Isn't that an interesting recording quality."[26]

It is possible to consider black music and white music as having separate histories since the mid-1950s; and indeed the surgical categorization of the charts in *Billboard* and similar trade magazines encourages one to do so. But in fact, at least since the middle of the nineteenth century, interaction between white and black popular music styles has been a chief feature of both of their developments. And particularly since the rise of the phonograph and the radio, the audiences for music made by blacks and whites have overlapped to a considerable degree. Since the rise of rock and roll, many if not most of the greatest white stars have paid homage to the black musicians whose records showed them new musical possibilities. John Lennon, Bob Dylan, Mick Jagger, Eric Clapton, and Paul Simon are just a few of the white rock musicians who have cited black musicians at least as frequently as they have cited whites when called upon to discuss those who have influenced their work. Although much of Eno's music appears on the surface to owe little directly to black sources, he has frequently expressed admiration for a variety of black popular music. Part of the attraction of Afro-American music for him is due to what he has called its sensual properties; but characteristically, he also admires the production values that have informed specific records by specific musicians—the way they have approached the recording studio. For instance, in a 1980 interview he pointed to developments in studio technique during the mid-1960s:

> The rhythm instruments started becoming very important. Instead of being simply rhythm, that is to say simply things that gave you a comforting thud in the lower part of the sound spectrum, they started having real vocal lines and singing parts, and a kind of compression started taking place where the voice wasn't the dominant, melodic instrument, necessarily. [In the Supremes' "Reflections"], you hear a number of interesting things going on: first of all the electronics are being used in an interesting way; secondly, the acoustic space is quite fictional; thirdly, the bass guitar has quite as much to say as Diana Ross's voice, I think.[27]

In addition to Tamla/Motown musicians, Eno cited Sly Stone as "one of the formative influences of the '70s, in how he reshuffled all the instrument roles. . . . He started using rhythm instruments in a vocal fashion and conversely often using the voices in a rhythmic fashion."[28] As an example, Eno offered the song "Everyday People" (1969). In Sly's "Thank You" (1970) Eno pointed out that the bass is active to the point of being "the most interesting melody on the track."[29] Such examples may be historically naive to the extent that they underestimate the importance, in much Afro-American music since the nineteenth century, of an active bass line, a heterogeneous sound-ideal, and a spreading of rhythmic duties over the whole ensemble. But in the present context, the point is Eno's fascination with a different approach to texture and studio technique making itself felt in the world of mainstream popular music.

In black music, as in white music, Eno finds overindulgence in electronics irritating. "Stevie Wonder's synthesizers are interesting, but in general the machines have been very badly used for decorative effects or as gravy to glue a track together. It's very disappointing."[30]

One of the musicians, black or white, for whom Eno has shown the highest degree of respect, is a man whose music has always been difficult to pigeonhole into this or that tradition: Jimi Hendrix. During a radio interview in 1975 Eno called Hendrix "probably still the greatest guitar player of all time," but not on the basis of instrumental virtuosity: "He was the first guitar player to realize that the guitar was more than a piece of wood that hung around his neck, and he really understood that there was a relationship between the room acoustics and the amplifier he was using, the whole situation."[31]

Eno proceeded to play a recording of Hendrix's solo electric guitar version of "The Star-Spangled Banner" from the soundtrack to *Woodstock*. When the recording was over, Eno was temporarily stunned into speechlessness by the music. When he had sufficiently recovered, he said, "I think that's one of the most extraordinary historical documents, that piece. The first time I heard it, it just made me cry."[32]

Eno admired Hendrix's choosing to limit himself to a restricted range of timbral possibilities. Unlike the many rock musicians, particularly in the age of synthesizers, who waste time and energy chasing after novel sounds, Hendrix "always worked with a Stratocaster and a particular type of amp,"[33] searching for a deep understanding of this setup.

> Frequently in the studios, you see synthesizer players fiddling for six hours getting this sound and then that sound and so on, in a kind of almost random search. What's clear, if you're watching this process, is that what they're in search of is not a new sound but a new idea. The synthesizer gives them the illusion that they'll find it somewhere in there. Really, it would make more sense to sit down and say, "Hey, look, what am I doing? Why don't I just think for a minute, and then go and do it?" Rather than this scramble through the electrons.[34]

In this context, Eno cited Glenn Gould once again: "He has been working with the same piano for years and years. Clearly he understands that piano in a way that no synthesizer player alive understands his instrument."[35] In addition to Hendrix's guitar playing and approach to the electronic situation, Eno found his lyrics exemplary: citing the "strange and mysterious lyrics" of "Little Wing" from *Axis: Bold As Love* (1968), he said:

> All the best lyrics I can think of, if you question me about them, I don't know what they're saying, I really don't, but somehow they're very evocative. . . . [Hendrix] has given you the impression that he's saying something, and it's being said with an intensity of some kind, and that's the important thing.[36]

In 1978 Eno discussed his changing views on black "funk" music in these terms:

> . . . In 1974 or '75, I absolutely despised funky music. I just thought it was everything I didn't want in music. And suddenly, I found myself taking quite the contrary position. . . . I suddenly found that, partly because of what [David Bowie] was doing and one or two other things—mostly Parliament and Bootsy and those people—I suddenly realized that if you took this a little bit further it became something very extreme and interesting.[37]

In another interview from the same year, Eno extended this view of funk:

> . . . A lot of the most interesting things in electronic music have come from that area—they haven't come from people who are dealing with electronics exclusively. They've come from people searching for gimmicks, something as banal as "What kind of sound can we get now that nobody's got before?" What I like about the Parliament/Funkadelic people is that they really go to extremes. There's nothing moderate about what they do.[38]

And here Eno reiterates his dream of bringing together the "strange, rigid" electronic music of Kraftwerk with the "weird physical feeling" of Parliament: "Put those two together and say, 'Make a record.' "[39] In addition to Eno's own *My Life in the Bush of Ghosts*, which was then in the planning stages with David Byrne, a large quantity of popular music during the 1980s has turned out to parallel Eno's dream rather closely: with Prince and Michael Jackson leading the way on the black side and Phil Collins and Peter Gabriel on the white, synthesizers have begun to dominate the sound of popular music, and many musicians have learned how to take the hard, metallic edge off of electronic sounds, or to use them creatively at cross-purposes with their mechanical nature.

Although Eno was momentarily enthusiastic about funk and disco, at least with regard to their possibilities when taken to creative extremes, by 1983 he had had enough of "the formula disco style where it has to have this or that and it has to have the girls doing a refrain. You hear so much of this junk coming out all the time."[40]

Like many other white musicians of the late 1970s (notably the Police, who forged a distinctive popular style based on the angular vocal melodies and off-beat bass lines of reggae), Eno was fascinated with the sounds of Jamaican reggae music. Again, it was how the music was put together, as much as the sound itself, that interested Eno:

> The contemporary studio composer is like a painter who puts things on, puts things together, tries things out, and erases them. The condition of the reggae composer is like that of the sculptor, I think. Five or six musicians play; they're well isolated from one another. Then the thing they played, which you can regard

as a kind of cube of music, is hacked away at—things are taken out, for long
periods.

A guitar will appear for two strums, then never appear again; the bass will
suddenly drop out, and an interesting space is created. Reggae composers have
created a sense of dimension in the music, by very clever, unconventional use
of echo, by leaving out instruments, and by the very open rhythmic structure of
the music.[41]

Clearly the "sculptural" approach has influenced Eno's own way of composing.
It is characteristic that he has shown no interest in reggae's political implications, either in terms of the indigenous philosophy or life-style of Rastafarianism
or in terms of Western white musicians and audiences wanting to express
solidarity with the Third World through the reggae beat (Bob Dylan's use of
a Jamaican rhythm section on his 1983 album, *Infidels*, being a typical case).
Eno's interest is in the sound of the music, in its engineering, in what the
music can teach him as a composer; if a "political" meaning of music is important
to Eno at all, it is restricted to the local level of interaction between musicians
and between musicians and audience.

In addition to reggae, other non-mainstream black music has consistently
commanded Eno's attention. In 1977 he remarked that the highlife music of
Fela Ransome-Kuti and Africa 70 was "the only music that makes me want to
dance."[42] The experience of working with the Ghanaian group Edikanfo was
simultaneously inspiring and depressing: "All the interactions between players
and all the kind of funny things going on with the rhythm . . . When I started
listening to the stuff that we did with the Talking Heads, it was just so wooden
by comparison. I couldn't get very excited by it anymore. I could still get
excited about it in other terms, but not in rhythmic terms any more. It seemed
to be really naive."[43]

Eno is familiar with Western art music at least enough to criticize the academic
serialist tradition of the twentieth century and the pyramidical organization of
the classical orchestra (as we shall see in Chapter 5). Such sweeping judgments
aside, he has rarely talked about actual pieces from the classical repertoire.
Curious exceptions to this rule are various slow movements from Haydn string
quartets and Mozart concertos. Eno explained in 1986 what he found attractive
about such music: it "didn't produce emotional surprises, [but rather] presented
an emotional situation that held steady for quite a long time. In other words,
a 'steady-state' kind of music."[44]

An interviewer recently asked Eno to define his relationship to the English
classical tradition of composers like Elgar, Delius, and Vaughn Williams. He
expressed guarded admiration for it, but quickly moved on to his own agenda:

They didn't interest me for a long time, but recently I found that I actually like
them. . . . As I grew up I saw a lot of people taking very extreme positions, like

"Let's make a piece of music eighteen hours long," or "Let's make a piece of music that has only one note and lasts for six years,"—that kind of thing. It's all interesting, and it's nice to know that these possibilities exist, but I don't want to listen to them or at least not more than once. I found that the artists I liked were aware of these possibilities, but had taken up less extreme stances—usually ones which, given the tastes of the contemporary art world, made them look as if they were playing it safe.[45]

Whether in recent English classical music or Haydn slow movements, it is evidently the sensuous quality that appeals to Eno, as well as the sense of restraint and balance, the drawing back from an extreme position, whether intellectual or emotional. It is with somewhat similar criteria that Eno has criticized recent experimental music. Reporting in the *Village Voice* on Eno's lecture at the "New Music, New York" festival hosted by the Kitchen in 1979, Tom Johnson wrote: "He told us that experimental music involves too much intellect and not enough sensuality, that creating charisma is a useful and even necessary thing, and that experimental composers should think more about marketing their work."[46]

For all his own use of technology's array of music-making and recording equipment, Eno consistently has been critical of electronic music without a heart. This brings us back to rock, which Eno was still touting in 1980 for its conceptual attractiveness:

Rock music has always been teetering on two borderlines. One is the borderline of a very advanced technology, and the other is a borderline of people using it who don't have a clue of what to do with it. . . . The big problem with computer music is that everyone knows how to use it too well. It just doesn't have the idiosyncratic, human element. You can't imagine anything in computer music like [Elvis Presley's "Heartbreak Hotel"]. No one would dare do it.[47]

Likewise, Eno has professed to be "totally bored" with electronic realizations of classical scores, such as Walter Carlos' ground-breaking album of 1968, *Switched-on Bach.*[48]

If, as Eno has said, the entire world of music is available to the modern composer, what, besides the Western popular, classical, and avant-garde traditions are some of the other types of music Eno has heard from? In 1986, he recounted how hearing a gospel record on the radio in the Bahamas during a Talking Heads recording session "changed my life." His subsequent search for the record led him

into gospel shops and I found about 200 other great gospel albums, and finally the one I was looking for, but in my search I had discovered what an incredible musical form gospel is. You have this very simple formula that's been ornamented in such original and moving ways. It's so alive, and keeps changing—new styles come up, while the traditional style still goes on.[49]

Eno has also expressed admiration for unspecified "folk music." Perhaps predictably, one of the things he likes about folk singing is its sense of casual harmonic randomness. Created by untrained musicians, the music often contains

> strange and lovely harmonies that are actually inadvertent. They result from the fact that somebody can't sing in the register that the main voices are in, so they just find a pitch at some peculiar interval above or below and stay in parallel harmony from there onwards. So in folk music you often have this sense of a limitation being turned into a strength.[50]

It is easy to understand Eno's attraction to certain kinds of Japanese music. As he explains,

> When I sit at home listening to things on a quiet evening I find I really am capable of listening to uneventful things with great pleasure. In fact almost the degree to which they are uneventful is interesting to me. For instance I'm very keen on shakuhachi music and koto music, partly because it has those very long spaces and very restrictive pitch palate . . .[51]

Since the late 1970s, Eno has listened to and drawn lessons from Arabic popular music. During a trip to Ibiza, an island off the coast of eastern Spain, he tuned into North African radio stations and was inspired by the vocal styles he heard:

> I was prepared to give up completely because I think they have the edge on us in singing. Not only the Arabs, but the Thai, Japanese, Africans, and so on. . . . What's really interesting about these pieces is the way they quite effortlessly accomodate electric organs and instruments we tend to associate with rock music, just build them in with no problem whatsoever.[52]

During the radio interview from which this quotation is taken, Eno played a tape he had made in Ibiza, and confessed that he had no idea what the singer was singing about. In the interview with John Cage, he said that he usually listens to gospel and Arabic music while he is "cleaning the house."[53]

As is the case in so many realms of experience that Eno has dwelt in, one detects a mixture of childlike enthusiasm and naiveté, of deep reflection and a certain contextlessness. Like any other thoughtful person of the late twentieth century, he confronts an explosion of information, and he faces the dilemma of how to forge meaning out of it all. The contemporary musicologist Joseph Kerman has succinctly posed the dilemma as it affects the direction and goals of his own discipline: "[We have] more and more facts, and less and less confidence in interpreting them."[54] In his creative work, Eno has drawn on a very broad range of musical "facts," and he has come up with some extremely provocative and beautiful results.

In this survey of music that has attracted, repulsed, and influenced Eno, doubtless much has been left out. An alert journalist, during a visit to Eno's New York loft in 1981, noted "a tidy stack of records: *Les Liturgies de l'Orient, Music of Bulgaria, Actual Voices of Ex-Slaves,* Parliament's *The Clones of Dr. Funkenstein.* . . ."[55] Like any other modern person, Eno inevitably if inadvertently has heard countless pieces of music on the radio, on television, in movies, and through other invisible loudspeakers in public places—pieces whose titles, authorship, and strains have faded from his memory (if indeed they ever lodged there to begin with). Given the modern ubiquity of music of so many types, the task of tracing "influences" is not so simple as it once seemed.

4 The Ear of the Non-Musician

ART SCHOOL AND EXPERIMENTAL WORKS: PROCESS AND PRODUCT

As many have observed, there was something about the atmosphere of British art schools during the late 1950s and 1960s that seemed to breed rock musicians. Among the leading rockers to emerge from art school backgrounds were John Lennon of the Beatles, Pete Townshend of the Who, Bryan Ferry of Roxy Music, and Ray Davies of the Kinks. Eno's experiences at Ipswich Art School between 1964 and 1966 decisively altered his views of art and the nature of creativity. As he has described it,

> I guess that we were all united by one idea—that art school was the place where you would be able to express yourself, where the passionate and intuitive nature that you felt raged inside you would be set free and turned into art. As it happened, we couldn't have been more wrong. The first term at Ipswich was devoted entirely to getting rid of these silly ideas about the nobility of the artist by a process of complete and relentless disorientation. We were set projects that we could not understand, criticized on bases that we did not even recognize as relevant.[1]

The emphasis of Eno's art school education was on "process over product"; a major element of the 1960s avant-garde philosophy was that the residue left by an artistic gesture was less important than the conceptual nature of the gesture itself. Under this set of ideological conditions Eno thrived, producing a variety of student works completely consonant with the artistic climate of the times. With Ipswich's taping facilities, he made his first musical piece by recording the sounds of striking a large metal lampshade and then altering the speed of the tape—a process which resulted in pronounced acoustical beats. He made "sound sculptures," such as a vertical cylinder with a big loudspeaker mounted on top, with various objects placed on the speaker which moved themselves into different arrangements according to the nature of the vibrations shaking the membrane. Eno hung loudspeakers from trees in a park and piped different music into each one. He made a painting and placed it at the bottom of a river. Rarely did he work on making pictures for their own sake; he found himself too impatient to finish a canvas, and more interested in designing "scores" "to tell myself how to construct a painting. I looked for designs that would contravene ordinary decisions about whether something looked nice or didn't look nice."[2] Paintings became performance pieces. In one experiment,

> I did a whole series . . . that involved more than one person doing the painting. In one, I gave four people identical instructions of the type, "Make the canvas such-and-such square, make a mark 14 inches from the top right-hand corner, and then measure a line down at 83 degrees and find a point here . . . ," and so on. Each instruction built on the one before. If there was any error, it would be compounded throughout the picture. I ended up with four canvases that were clearly related but different from each other, and they were stuck together to make one picture.[3]

The line between music and other forms of art was obscured in many such experiments, yet Eno became more and more attracted to music itself, since here was an art form that had always been a "performance art" involving real-time processes. He found it increasingly difficult to finish his paintings, which tended to look "as if I'd got bored half-way through, which in fact is what had happened." Music, on the other hand, offered an activity that was more immediate, that involved instantaneous feedback between process and product; Eno also thought that music was "an activity that has a more direct emotional appeal" than painting.[4] What ultimately intrigued him most about music, however, was not its performance aspect, but the possibilities of the tape recorder, which seemed to make composing directly analogous to painting: "I realized you could mess with time—storing it and then distorting it any way you wanted—and this made music into a plastic art. It instantly struck me as more interesting than painting."[5]

Thus the processes involved in making artworks had a peculiar fascination for Eno: he saw them as valuable not only in terms of their ability to stimulate composition and to lend insight into craft, but as interesting ideas in themselves. His enthusiasm for talking about process has impressed most of the writers who have interviewed him, and indeed it is his acute awareness of the varieties of the creative process, and his ability and willingness to articulate his experiences with them, that have set him apart from a host of progressive rock musicians of the early 1970s. (An occasional writer found Eno's preoccupation with process irritating: Lester Bangs declared Eno's much-discussed methods "boring as shit to talk about at much length and probably unnecessarily complicated, but they've given us some of the most amazing albums of the decade.")[6]

However, by 1981, if not earlier, disillusioned by the proliferation of self-indulgent conceptual debris being passed off as art, and with a much clearer —and perhaps more traditional—conception of what is involved in making a piece of music, Eno had come to the position that there were definite limits to the interest that could be sustained by an artist's dwelling on process as a sort of artistic product in its own right:

> I was taught in art school that process is everything, which is another way of saying that having an idea is enough. Since I'm basically lazy, I liked that idea, but I no longer think it's true. The structure or process that I used in *Discreet Music* is almost identical to the structure of Reich's *It's Gonna Rain*, for example, but the *sound* of the two pieces is very different.[7]

> The process is supposed to be interesting in itself. I don't go for that. I think if something doesn't jolt your senses, forget it. It's got to be seductive.[8]

Eno has criticized such things as Nam June Paik's multi-screen video installations and imitations of William Burroughs's "cut-up" technique, in which random bits of text are selected and pasted together: "Sure, 'cut-ups' can be fascinating, but it *does* matter what the input is." The idea "that as long as the process was interesting it didn't really matter what went into it" was

> part of the John Cage legacy. The failure of that inheritance is evident when you hear some pieces of systems music that you like, and others that don't hold your attention at all. You come to the inevitable conclusion that the difference doesn't lie in the differing degrees of elegance in the systems, but in their content.[9]

ON LISTENING

Although Eno has never had any formal ear-training, he is evidently listening all the time—and not just to the sounds of what we normally call "music." Taking a cue from Cage, Eno uses his ears to scan the environment, putting himself into a music-listening mode even in the absence of music. He has frequently criticized musicians, particularly those seduced by the glamor of high-tech electronic instruments, for being unable or unwilling to *listen* to what they are doing. In his 1979 lecture "The Studio As Compositional Tool" he remarked that "almost any arbitrary collision of events listened to enough times comes to seem very meaningful," adding, "There's an interesting and useful bit of information for a composer, I can tell you."[10] The context of these remarks was his discussion of improvised jazz, but their implications lead far beyond the conventionally "musical" into the realm of environmental sounds. For Eno, music is not necessarily restricted to relationships between pitches and rhythms:

> Classical music works around a body of "refined" sounds—sounds that are separate from the sounds of the world, pure and musical. There is a sharp distinction between "music" and "noise," just as there is a distinction between the musician and the audience. I like blurring those distinctions—I like to work with all the complex sounds on the way out to the horizon, to pure noise, like the hum of London. If you sit in Hyde Park just far enough away from the traffic so that you

don't perceive any of its specific details, you just hear the average of the whole thing. And it's such a beautiful sound. For me that's as good as going to a concert hall at night. [11]

Eno's ideas about listening to the environment as music are shared by modern composer Pauline Oliveros, who has used such concepts as the basis of actual pieces. The instructions for the fifth of her *Sonic Meditations* (1974) read as follows: "Take a walk at night. Walk so silently that the bottoms of your feet become ears." *Sonic Meditations XVII* is somewhat similar: "1. Enhance or paraphrase the auditory environment so perfectly that a listener cannot distinguish between the real sounds of the environment and the performed sounds. 2. Become performers by not performing."[12]

The concept of "the environment as art" reached its height in the 1960s and early 1970s. Andy Warhol's putting Brillo boxes in a museum was perhaps the most celebrated example of an artist encouraging his audience to take a closer look at the sensuous qualities of everyday objects, though the painter Robert Rauschenberg had done something similar much earlier with his "white paintings"—monochromatic canvases that invited the viewer to become involved in the play of light and shadow on the "empty" surface. The most direct musical analog to these experiments is John Cage's "silent" piece, *4'33"*, in which a performer takes the stage and does nothing for the duration: the audience is given the opportunity to experience the ambient sounds of the hall as music. Eno clearly took the lessons of such experiments to heart: he is a person who has spent a great deal of time simply listening, and it shows in much of his ambient music, which is a music of understated inner strength and few outwardly vigorous events.

Much of Eno's music is constructed on a *vertical* basis: to a great extent, it is music concerned with the sheer color of sound, rather than with the linear (horizontal) growth of melodies. Each moment in Eno's music presents certain tone colors or timbres, and the interest lies in the relationships between these colors rather than in the evolution of thematic material (which has been the norm in most Western art music for centuries). What Eno hears sitting in Hyde Park is a composite, geographical, ambient music, with no need of horizontal teleology or the logic of linear development. Such vertically-oriented musical experiences can be had using conventional instruments as well. In 1985 Eno cited the grand piano, the tambura (the four-stringed Indian drone instrument), and the electric bass guitar as his favorite instruments. It is the piano which he most enjoys:

I like it because of the complexity of its sound. If you hold the sustain pedal down, strike a note and just *listen* . . . that's one of my favourite musical experiences. I often sit at the piano for an hour or two, and just go "bung!" and listen to the note dying. Each piano does it in a different way. You find all these exotic harmonies drifting in and drifting out again, and one that will appear and disappear many times. There'll be fast-moving ones and slow-moving ones. That's spell-binding, for me. [13]

Eno discussed what he hears in piano harmonics in terms of equal temperament ("There are a lot of books about this. It's an interesting subject."), [14] explaining that the slight out-of-tuneness of piano fifths, thirds, and so on, make for extraordinary vertical richness. He went on to say: "I used to think: Piano? Compromise? Pathetic instrument, can't be tuned. But now I think what makes a piano so interesting is that it's generating so much complex information." [15]

What we are dealing with here are different modes of perception and receptivity. Expectations—often unconscious—have a great deal to do with how we listen. Beethoven's Fifth Symphony is, aside from all of its programmatic "fate" connotations, a piece of music about the unfolding of a brief melodic fragment in time: the first four notes, G-G-G-E♭, with their characteristic rhythm, appear in all four movements of the Symphony in different guises. On the other hand, the sound of a single piano tone struck with the sustain pedal down, or the sounds of the hum of London in Hyde Park, are, or have the potential to become, purely timbral, though unexpectedly complex musical experiences. One cannot approach Beethoven's Fifth in the Hyde Park mode of perception, or vice versa. One cannot approach a Bach fugue from the "frog's eye" perspective, nor can one approach Reich's *It's Gonna Rain* from the Western, linear-ear perspective. There is an analogy in the visual arts, in the growing field of video artworks. If in his music Eno is interested in cultivating a radically different approach to the listening process, in his video works a similar concern comes into play with regard to the video screen itself. In 1986 he criticized in precisely these terms some of the videos shown at "The Luminous Image" exhibition at the Stedelijk in Amsterdam: "Most of the pieces had a narrative structure, so you ended up looking at the screen, and looking at a screen is a different experience from looking at an object. You look *into* a screen, and by doing so you accept all its visual conventions." [16]

One of the things Eno is after, then, is using the senses—vision and hearing—in new ways, ways that have little to do with traditional artistic conventions. When he speaks as a critic, he is especially preoccupied with innovative uses of conventions, with the vertical color of sound, and with engineering aspects of the work of art.

CRAFT AND THE NON-MUSICIAN

If Eno rejects much in the way of traditional artistic conventions, he also rejects many conventional ideas about musicianship. A full understanding of his often quoted assertion that he is "not a musician" is crucial to a grasp of his music. Before discussing what this assertion really means, we must allow that Eno is

in fact a talented and versatile, if intuitive and marginally skilled, multi-in-
strumentalist: he has played synthesizers, piano, organ, other electronic keyboards, electric guitar, electric bass guitar (which he called in 1985 "the only
instrument I have the remotest hope of learning to play before the end of my
life—though I don't know what I'll do with it once I've learned"),[17] and assorted
traditional and "found" percussion instruments such as ashtrays and flexible
plastic pipes. His technical capabilities on all of these instruments are limited:
on keyboards, he stays within a small range of keys around C major; in his
guitar playing, he sticks with a limited number of bar chords and simple, slow
melodic lines; his bass work tends to consist of single long sustained notes. In
his singing, he typically uses only the middle and lower registers of his chest
voice, without much dynamic flexibility; he does, however, consistently sing
nearly perfectly in tune with no vibrato. Thus, although Eno's manual and
vocal skills may be limited in depth, they are broad in scope; furthermore, his
sense of rhythm and timing, a primary constituent of good musicianship by any
definition, though it is not exceptional, is completely adequate for the type of
music he has been interested in playing.

Eno's knowledge of traditional music theory is at least as limited as his manual
skills. Lester Bangs asked him in 1979, "Have you ever had any formal music
or theory training at all?"

"No."

"Have you ever felt the pressure that you should get some?"

"No, I haven't, really. I can't think of a time that I ever thought that, though
I must have at one time. The only thing I wanted to find out, which I did find
out, was what 'modal' meant; that was, I thought, a very interesting concept."[18]

On another occasion, when an interviewer said, "You don't know music
theory and things of that sort," Eno responded, "No, I don't. Well, let's say I
know many theories about music, but I don't know that particular one that has
to do with notation."[19] By this "notation theory," we can probably assume that
Eno is referring to music theory as it is taught in school: the fundamentals of
notation and the principles of harmony, counterpoint, and voice-leading which
developed during the so-called "common practice" period of music history
(essentially the eighteenth and nineteenth centuries). When we look at Eno's
music, particularly his progressive rock albums, we shall see that like many,
if not most, popular musicians, he uses standard major, minor, and seventh
chords in traditional, but also in unpredictable, "empirical" ways—ways that
ignore the statistical tables of "common," "less common," "strong," and "weak"
chord progressions of some standard harmony textbooks.[20] Particularly striking
in this regard is his almost complete avoidance of the tonic-dominant relationship, which almost inevitably brings with it the gravitational pull of functional
tonality. (For instance, in a piece in C major, the dominant chord G7 feels like
it is "pulling" the music toward the tonic chord of C; when G7 leads to C the
listener feels a sense of tension followed by a resolution. Eno tends to avoid
such "classical" tension/resolution chord pairs.)

One aspect of the rock tradition—indeed, part of the significance of the rock tradition—has been its refusal to let arbitrary technical standards of musicianship interfere with the music-making process. Much of the joy of early rock and roll, and of the skiffle music in England that preceded it, sprang from their implication that anybody could grab a guitar and yank a few sounds out of it: here was music by and for non-specialists in music, and a certain anti-elitism concerning instrumental and vocal technique was part of its whole ideology.

The Beatles provided the most stunning early examples of how far one could go with a limited, unexceptional technique. Like Eno, John Lennon and Paul McCartney were versatile but technically rather ordinary multi-instrumentalists who knew exactly what kinds of sounds they wanted to get out of the instruments they played—guitars, piano, other keyboards, assorted percussion, and bass. And when, like Eno, they moved into the modern recording studio to produce such epochal albums as *Revolver, Sergeant Pepper's Lonely Hearts Club Band,* and *Abbey Road,* the studio itself became their instrument, and their ears became much more important than their hands. Lennon once said that if one were to compare his guitar-playing with that of blues great B. B. King, "I would feel silly. [But] I'm an artist and if you give me a tuba I'll bring you something out of it."[21] In the late 1960s and early 1970s, of course, instrumental virtuosity found a place in rock, with audiences responding to the pyrotechnics of guitarists like Eric Clapton and Jimi Hendrix and keyboard players like Rick Wakeman and Keith Emerson much as nineteenth-century European audiences were ignited by the Paganinis of the day. And, in their turn, the unschooled sounds of the punk and new wave movements of the late 1970s represented another swing of the same pendulum: again, the point seemed to be that anybody with something to get off his or her chest could make music.

The contrast between "Inspiration and Gymnastics" is the subject of a chapter in Bruno Nettl's recent book, *The Study of Ethnomusicology;* here he shows how these two approaches to music-making have shaped concepts about music in many different societies at many different times. Nettl contrasts "the concept of 'divine inspiration' (according to which music-making should be easy)" with "the 'athletic view' of music (according to which music-making—composing, improvising, performing—must be difficult to be truly great)."[22] Eno, the Beatles, and the new wavers fall into the "inspired" camp; Eric Clapton, Keith Emerson, and many progressive rockers are of the "gymnastic" musical type.

Eno has talked about his ideas on craft (or the lack of it) and musicianship since the beginning of his public career. Just prior to the release of his first solo album, *Here Come the Warm Jets,* he said:

> I'll make a prediction here. I think, in fact, I shall be seen as a rock revivalist in a funny way, because the thing that people miss when they do their rock revival rubbish is the fact that early rock music was, in a lot of cases, the product of incompetence, not competence. There's a misconception that these people were

brilliant musicians and they weren't. They were brilliant musicians in the spiritual sense. They had terrific ideas and a lot of balls or whatever. They knew what the physical function of music was, but they weren't virtuosi.[23]

Two years later he told an interviewer, "I'm an anti-musician. I don't think the craft of music is relevant to the art of music."[24] "Anti-music" has a specific meaning for some critics, including David Cope, who in his book *New Directions in Music* discusses the following categories in his chapter on "Antimusic": danger music (involving physical or mental hazard to the performer and/or audience), minimal and concept music (Cage's famous *4'33"* representing these genres' archetypal qualities), biomusic ("music created by natural life functions rather than by necessarily conscious attempts at composition"), and soundscapes (typically involving the focusing of attention on manipulated or natural environmental sounds).[25] Much of Eno's music, particularly since about 1975, can certainly be seen in terms of these categories, with the exception of the "danger music" category.

But I doubt that Eno, in referring to himself as an anti-musician, was intent on allying himself with any of these movements. Rather, he was making a specific statement about the way he deals with his own creativity. In 1981 he said, "I don't consider myself a professional musician, though I do consider myself a professional composer."[26] In one sense, Eno's saying he is not a musician, or his saying he is an anti-musician, is nothing radical: he is merely casting himself in the role of the traditional composer whose function is to conceive the music and communicate it to the audience in some way—without necessarily being competent to perform it himself. But there is a difference between Eno and the traditional composer. The composer's final product is a musical score—a more or less conventional system of written signs that tell the performers what to do with more or less accuracy and completeness. Eno's final product, on the other hand, is a sound recording that has only to be cued up on playback equipment to be heard—and up to the point of playback, Eno has had total control over the composition. Eno, like many if not most popular musicians, does not read music. The exact ways in which he conceives and works with sound, and the ways in which he communicates his intentions to his performers, are the subjects of the next chapter. Here it will suffice to quote Eno's answer to an interviewer who asked him whether his not reading music was a deliberate choice:

> It wouldn't be very useful for me. There have been one or two occasions where I was stuck somewhere without my tape recorder and had an idea, tried to memorize it, and since a good idea nearly always relies on some unfamiliar nuance it is therefore automatically hard to remember. So on those very rare occasions I've thought, "God, if only I could write this down." But in fact, quite a lot of what I do has to do with sound texture, and you can't notate that anyway. . . . That's because musical notation arose at a time when sound textures were limited.

If you said violins and woodwind that defined the sound texture; if I say synthesizer and guitar it means nothing—you're talking about 28,000 variables.[27]

Eno goes on to reflect on the "transmission losses" that inevitably occur when a traditional composer or pop arranger takes a sounding idea and fixes it in written form, musicians read the written form, and then they play it: the potential for distortion of the original information is present at each stage of the process. Any composer who uses notation can attest to the painfulness of this dilemma.

Eno sees himself as having precisely the right amount of manual instrumental skill to do what he needs to do in order to make his music. He apparently does not feel that a higher level of instrumental technique might open the door for him to other kinds of musical expression. An interviewer asked him in 1981, "Do you ever practice things on a keyboard or a guitar in order to be able to execute them to your satisfaction?" He answered: "Not very often. . . . If I have a phrase that has a fast series of notes, I might break the phrase down into three simpler ones, and do them as overdubs."[28]

This resolute lack of technique has become an integral part of Eno's whole philosophical approach to music-making. Whether from inner or outer defensiveness, or from honest self-examination, he has come up with a variety of justifications for remaining a "non-musician." One is that lack of technique almost forces one to be creative: it makes one confront one's vulnerability. Eno explains:

I've seen musicians stuck for an idea, and what they'll do between takes is just diddle around, playing the blues or whatever, just to reassure themselves that, "Hey, I'm not useless. Look, I can do this." But I believe that to have that [technique] to fall back on is an illusion. It's better to say, "I'm useless," and start from that position. I think the way technique gets in the way is by fooling you into thinking that you are doing something when you actually are not.[29]

Robert Fripp—who is, however, one of the most technically proficient and polished guitarists in rock—has built his approach to music-making around a similar idea. Fripp has said:

You have to be *there*—with attention. And if you are, your state is changed from the normal and dozy condition we wander around within. And in the condition of heightened sensitivity and awareness, music is possible. You see, for a good player to just play licks, running on automatic, there's no music there. It only *seems* to be music. There is what we would call musical sound and forms of organization, but there's no quality. It's only mechanical.[30]

Eno and Fripp arrive at the same point from opposite directions. As Eno has said, "The reason Fripp and I have always had a good rapport is because we stand at two ends of that spectrum. He's the virtuoso and I'm the idiot *savant*, if you like. The middle territory of pointless displays of skill and obvious next moves doesn't interest either of us."[31]

For Eno, another positive aspect of his lack of instrumental and theoretical proficiency is that it can lead to results that a trained musician would have ruled out or might not even have considered. He illustrates this point by recalling a recording session in which Fripp had called him in to work on one of his albums. Fripp asked Eno what could be added to a particular song, and Eno said he had in mind a melodic part and some harmonic backing. Fripp asked what kind of harmonies, and Eno said, "I won't know until I play them." From that point, Eno proceeded empirically, building up the song track by track. Fripp listened to the final result and said, "That's very interesting, because nobody would have arrived at that harmony by writing it out. There's a wrong chord in it." Eno concludes: "Had I known that [there was a 'wrong' chord], I probably would have dismissed it as a possibility, even though it sounded good. Retaining my lack of proficiency to a certain extent allows me to make interesting mistakes."[32]

One of the *Oblique Strategies* cards says, "Honor thy mistake as a hidden intention." And indeed one of the most delightful aspects of Eno's creative personality is his inclination to take the idea of this oracle seriously, whether in searching empirically for the right harmonies by laying track after track on top of each other, in accepting the piano's equal temperament as its most beautiful characteristic, or in sometimes finding charm and wonder in an out-of-tune live recording. In speaking of the live album he did with Kevin Ayers, John Cale, and Nico, *June 1, 1974*, he describes their encore performance of his song, "Baby's on Fire," in glowing terms:

> The instruments were incredibly out of tune, so out of tune you wouldn't believe it. But it sounds fantastic. There's one little bit in it where there's a riff between the guitar and one of the bassists, and they're so out of tune it sounds like cellos. Amazing! I mean if you tried to make that sound in the studio it would have taken you ages. You wouldn't have thought of making it, in fact, it's such a bizarre sound. And the piano and guitar are quite well out of tune as well. Ha![33]

This quality or discipline, which might be called "retroactive creativity"— consisting in affirmations that mistakes can work out for the best—forms an important part of Eno's work. Still other benefits that Eno has derived from his lack of manual technique are an abiding love of the simple and an ear for realizing the potential for the marvelous in the most rudimentary of musical materials. This has created problems in studio situations where, in their efforts to be creative, the skillful musicians he works with sometimes can't help but produce complex musical ideas. Paradoxically, if an idea is musically complex to begin with—containing a lot of fast notes or difficult harmonies, for instance—Eno feels he can do less with it: his creative options are limited. "So the problem with musicians is always telling them to have confidence in a simple and beautiful thing, to know that there's a whole world that can be extracted from a simple sound. . . . It's not that because it's simple, any idiot can do it. There's sensitivity in the way you can strike just one note."[34]

Eno's primary asset, as for any composer, is his ear. Particularly since he works with sounds on tape rather than notes on paper, listening is his primary compositional activity. He has stressed again and again that the problem of many musicians, whether studio instrumentalists, instrumental virtuosi, synthesizer wizards, or computer-music composers, is that they do not listen to what they are doing. For his part, he is content to work with sound materials that he can understand, however minimal they may seem. As he has said, "The greater you understand the structure of something, the more you'll be amazed at the tiniest movement within it. In that sense the possibilities are limitless."[35]

As we have already seen, some of the musicians Eno admires most are those who have realized that "there are really distinct advantages to working within a quite restricted range of possibilities."[36] Ultimately, this line of thought can become a transformational philosophy applicable to the whole of life, not just to musical composition. Eno has advised, "Regard your limitations as secret strengths. Or as constraints that you can make use of."[37]

By 1981, if not before, Eno had come to the conclusion that the recording studio and the empirical method of composing had created a new art form, a whole new kind of "music": "In some sense it's so different that it really should be called by a different name. The only similarity is that people listen to it, so it enters through the same sense, but in the way it's made it's really a different thing."[38]

Since Eno came to these conclusions, the music world has been transformed by the application of computer technology to musical instruments and music data storage methods. MIDI (Musical Instrument Digital Interface) has been invented, and now different brands of synthesizers and computers happily talk to each other in a common language. A composer or rock band can create complex multi-track music on a MIDI sequencer, store it on a floppy disk, edit it by computer, and print it out in notated form or play it back in a flawless "performance" at the touch of a button. The new digitial music technology is a non-musician's dream; that is, one needs very little traditional musical skill to produce impressive masses of sound. As prices come down, more and more musicians and amateurs are getting their hands on electronic equipment, building little home studios, and experiencing firsthand the kind of empirical compositional process Eno has described in detail. Even if we still call it music, the methods by which sounding substances are made and thought about have been changed radically, perhaps forever.

chapter 5 Listeners and Aims

ENO'S AUDIENCE

Judging by sales figures of his recordings, Eno's audience is not very large by rock standards; compared with composers of avant-garde or contemporary fine art music of the academic variety, however, he has a substantial following. According to George Rush, each of Eno's progressive rock albums has sold between 100,000 and 150,000 copies, as has *Music for Airports;* his other ambient music albums have sold about 50,000 copies each.[1] Although Eno has said he receives "encouraging letters from listeners, whose ages range from twelve to sixty,"[2] the drop-off represented by the sales figures of his ambient music records indicates that there are many young listeners who found his brand of progressive rock exciting and worth buying, but who have not been willing to follow his career closely as it has gone into the ambient.

Eno has constantly searched for a kind of middle ground between the rarefied realms of high art and the everyday ephemera of popular culture. It stands to reason that he would view his audience as people interested in that same territory. He tries to make his music accordingly, making pieces that "seduce people to the point where they start searching." If a piece of music has a seductive sounding surface but no real content, or conversely, if the content of a piece is obscured by complicated and unattractive surface procedures, Eno believes the music has failed. What interests him is "sitting on that line" between seductive surface and meaningful content.[3]

Although Eno has made few concert appearances over the last decade, the sense of making music for an audience, however abstract, is important to him: "If I ever found I was doing work that nobody was interested in, I would seriously doubt it. I wouldn't want to be in the position of not feeling *connected* anymore."[4] Thus, unlike Milton Babbitt[5] and many other contemporary composers who see their work as a kind of research and development in the cause of music advancement, not needing the approval of or feedback from the public or any particular segment thereof, Eno is unable to be quite so detached about his work: his position is more traditional, more that of an artist doing work that his audience can appreciate and understand and is willing to pay for. He makes, as Wayne Robins has put it, "music you can live with."[6]

During the 1980s Eno's relationship to his primary chosen medium—the phonograph record—has been ambivalent. After a string of ambient solo albums and collaborations, he has recently been devoting much more time to his audio-visual installations. An interviewer asked him in 1983: "You mentioned that you've gotten very suspicious of records lately. Can you elaborate?" He replied:

> I don't like the form much anymore. I've become more and more interested in music that has a location of some kind, like gospel music—you go somewhere and you become part of something in order to experience the music. You enter a whole different social and acoustic setting. There's a whole context that goes with the music. Just sitting in your living room and sticking on some record is a whole other thing.[7]

As an analogy with the new music that is completely studio-produced, Eno recalls the birth of photography in the nineteenth century: initially, the new technology was used as a substitute for painting, to make inexpensive portraits; the desire to imitate painting went as far as the use of canvas-textured photographic paper. Similarly, the early history of filmmaking shows producers interested essentially in putting traditional dramatic ideas to work on celluloid. And with early sound recordings, the idea was to capture a live musical performance as faithfully as possible. With time, however,

> a point was reached where it became realized that this medium [film] had its own strengths and limitations, and therefore could become a different form through its own rules.
>
> I think that's true of records as well. They've got nothing to do now with performances. It's now possible to make records that have music that was never performed or never *could* be performed and in fact doesn't exist outside of that record. And if that's the area you work in, then I think you really have to consider that as part of your working philosophy. So for quite a while now I've been thinking that if I make records, I want to think not in terms of evoking a memory of a performance, which never existed in fact, but to think in terms of making a piece of sound which is going to be heard in a type of location, usually someone's house. . . . I assume [my listeners] are sitting very comfortably and not expecting to dance.[8]

Discussing film on another occasion, Eno doubted whether "naturalism" was really possible:

> The concept of naturalism in any of the recorded media is worthy of debate. Has a film got anything to do with real life? I don't think it does. . . .
>
> What do Fellini's films have to do with naturalism? He works with the inaccuracies of memory. In *Amarcord* there's the tobacconist with the very big tits. In real life they were probably not that big. But they were his *first* big tits, and he remembers them as being very big. It's the opposite direction from naturalism:

elevating things to mythical, archetypal status. Make them more dreamlike. That's a feeling *I* like a lot.[9]

The conscious recognition that in his studio-created music he is dealing with an inherently non-naturalistic medium analogous to that of the art film, abstract painting, or modern photography has given Eno's work a certain quality of depth consistent with its "mythical, archetypal" conception. Such ideas are not unique in modern music: electronic music composers since the 1950s have been confronted with the dilemmas of performerless and placeless music, though after the initial flirtations and experiments with synthesized sound and tape recorders had run their course, many composers gave up purely electronic music since something indeed seemed to be missing. Eno is unusual in how carefully he has thought through the whole matter, and in his courageous persistence in seeking an audience for this elusive music that is made, yet is not performed. In speaking of what he termed the "landscape music" of ambient-style ablums like *On Land,* he said, "I don't quite know what it is. There isn't any tradition for it. . . . The problem is always calling it music. I wish there were another word for it."[10] This dissatisfaction with the traditional word is reminiscent of Edgar Varèse, who preferred the term "organized sound," and of Igor Stravinsky, who, in searching for a formulation for the sound of Anton Webern's music, came up with the term "illuminated noise."

Thus Eno is fully aware of the transformation in the meaning of music that results from the revolution in listening habits and environments made possible through the availability of inexpensive, high-quality playback equipment. He is fond of referring to Marshall McLuhan's idea that all music is now all present: ". . . Not only is the whole history of our music with us now, in some sense, on record, but the whole global musical culture is also available."[11] In this transformed aural habitat, what sort of meaning does Eno see for his own music? To what sorts of purposes does he imagine people putting it to use? Facing these questions, Eno has been most forthright about his ambient music. In a statement from 1982 which is worth quoting at length, he discussed his ambient music and its uses:

> I like it ["ambient music"] as an ambiguous term. It gives me a certain latitude.
>
> It has two major meanings. One is the idea of music that allows you any listening position in relation to it. This has widely been misinterpreted by the press (in their infinite unsubtlety) as background music. I mean music that can be background or foreground or anywhere, which is a rather different idea.
>
> Most music chooses its own position in terms of your listening to it. Muzak wants to be back there. Punk wants to be up front. Classical wants to be another place. I wanted to make something you could slip in and out of. You could pay attention or you could choose not to be distracted by it if you wanted to do something while it was on. . . . Ambient music allows many different types of attention.
>
> The other meaning is more pronounced on *On Land:* creating an ambience, a

sense of place that complements and alters your environment. Both meanings are contained in the word "ambient." . . .

When *Music for Airports* came out and sold fairly well, I thought people assumed it was going to be another *Before and After Science*. It takes a long while to learn whether you're selling on the momentum of your successes. I don't think that's so anymore. I've almost shifted audiences. I meet people who never knew I made a record of songs.

Critics can't stand these records, by and large, because in their search for eternal adolescence they still want it all to be spunky and manic and witty. They come back to rock music again and again, expecting to feel like kids. That isn't what I want from music anymore—not in quite that way. I'm interested in the idea of feeling like a very young child, but I'm not interested in feeling like a teenager. [12]

The last paragraph in this quotation ties in with Eno's many reservations about rock in general. Clearly, his ambient music has been aimed at a different audience than his progressive rock music, or at least at a different mode of receptivity. With his ambient works, Eno has tried explicitly to make music that is not too self-assertive, that does not intrude too much, that neither dares its audience to listen nor threatens them if they choose not to—yet, at the same time, music that is complex and deep enough to sustain and reward close listening. His ambient music is designed to be played at low or medium volume; high-volume settings do violence to the sense and spirit of the music. Close listening reveals a constantly changing soundscape; yet, paradoxically, the same music can seem static, uneventful, and benign if one is not really paying attention. Critics of Eno's ambient works have often complained that nothing much happens in the music. He answers such criticism by comparing his musical works to paintings, in their quality of being "a sort of continuous part of the environment" that one can choose to notice or to ignore:

If a painting is hanging on a wall where we live, we don't feel that we're missing something by not paying attention to it. . . . Yet with music and video, we still have the expectation of some kind of drama. My music and videos do change, but they change slowly. And they change in such a way that it doesn't matter if you miss a bit. . . . The conventional commercial notion that people want a lot of stimulus and constant change simply isn't true. [13]

ENO'S ARTISTIC INTENT

The question of "artistic intent" is always a slippery one when dealt with verbally, for there is a significant sense in which the artist's intent is fully evident only in the artworks themselves; furthermore, it is not at all logically or philosophically necessary to posit the concept of a linear, clearly formulated intent. [14] Eno has spoken unsympathetically of music that "comes so heavily laden with intention that you can't hear it for the intentions."[15] Yet Eno has frequently addressed the issues of what it means to him to make music and what sorts of meaning he hopes his music will convey to his audience.

In his progressive rock music, Eno was attempting a synthesis of avant-garde artistic concepts with the stylistic forms of rock music; until about 1974 he was unflinching in his declaration that "rock is the most important art form right now."[16] The quality that was to bind everything together was what he called his "idiot energy"—a kind of gleeful abandon, a reveling in the possibilities of such a synthesis and in the improbable results that sometimes ensued. Shortly after he left Roxy Music, he explained his position:

> What it [Roxy's first album without Eno] lacks for me is one of the most important elements of my musical life, which is insanity. I'm interested in things being absurd and there was something really exciting in Roxy at one time. We were juxtaposing things that didn't naturally sit together.[17]

Roxy's early work held for Eno the attraction of "the element of clumsiness and grotesqueness. . . . There was terrific tension at one stage in the music, which I really enjoyed."[18] Exactly how Eno succeeded in working the qualities of insanity, absurdity, clumsiness, and grotesqueness into his progressive rock music is the subject of Chapter 9. Such qualities contrast sharply with the qualities of mystery, wonder, seductiveness, and transparent beauty that characterize the intent of his ambient music. But even in his early career Eno was interested in more than making a specific kind of rock music:

> My role in rock music isn't to come on with New Musical Ideas in any strict sense. It's to come on with new concepts about how you might generate music. It's always time to question what has become standard and established. I figure that in a way, my contribution . . . will be more on a theoretical basis, about suggesting greater freedom in the way people approach music.[19]

The complexity of this intent should always be borne in mind when considering Eno's music. If his belief that music is about other music cannot be applied to all music, it certainly does apply to much of his own. There has always been this element of distancing in Eno's relationship to his own music; it is as though he has never been quite willing to say of his music, "Here it is, this is it, this is my music and that's all there is to it." His intent encompasses a larger conceptual territory than that of simply making music for its own sake; his ambivalent, paradoxical statement about calling his ambient works "music" at all bears this out.

If Eno has been anxious that his listeners understand his work in a large historical and conceptual context, however, he is decidedly uninterested in being identified with any particular school of musical practice, including rock itself. As we have already seen, he has criticized progressive rock for its "Gothic" tendencies and technological excesses. On the other hand, he has not been anxious to identify completely with the avant-garde. Not even the ideas of Cage have met with his unconditional approval or endorsement. At the same time, Eno does not wish to get stuck in some extreme artistic fringe, but rather wants his music to be rooted in the real world of real listeners. Furthermore, he acknowledges, both explicitly (in verbal statements) and implicitly (in the character of his music), the active and ongoing relationship of his music with other musical traditions. The complexity of Eno's debt to other traditions, though, should be evident. In the interview with Eno and Cage, the latter said:

> When I was just beginning there were only two things you could do: one was to follow Schoenberg and the other was to follow Stravinsky. If you want to be a modern composer now, there are so many things to do, and people do them. . . . It's a changed world. It's not a world in which we are obliged to follow a mainstream, represented by X or Y.

Eno readily concurred: "That's right, you don't have to belong to a pantheon or even know about it."[20]

"I want to make things that put me in the position of innocence, that recreate the feeling of innocence in you."[21] Eno has said this in different ways on many different occasions. The emotional component of his work is extremely strong, even if in his ambient music its range is somewhat limited. Wonder, mystery, melancholy, subdued joy, and a sense of the strange-yet-familiar are what he has systematically been trying to achieve in his wordless ambient music. If the emotional component is strong, however, it is usually present as a kind of deep undercurrent: it does not burst from the surface of the music or confront the listener with unambiguous, expressionistic intent. This is, by and large, as true of his progressive rock as of his ambient music, and it may be construed as reflecting a "classical"—as opposed to a "romantic"—strain in Eno's temperament. In 1978 he criticized

> bands who want to give the illusion by their music that the music itself is the result of incredible, seething passions and turmoil from within, and all this music comes out as a direct result of that. It's a case of, "Boy, are we in a sort of emotional turmoil, here it all comes."
>
> The way I work, and the way a lot of other people work, is to create music that creates a feeling in you. You set out in a rather deliberate way to do this by carefully constructing a piece that will evoke in you the feeling that you want. It's not the other way round, where you have all these feelings that then suddenly force this piece to exist in whatever form it takes.[22]

Eno's "classicism" does not necessarily imply unambiguous, direct expression; part of the sense of mystery arises from the listener's uncertainty as to the precise nature of the music's emotional content. Eno is apt to throw up barriers to interpreting any given piece in any one single way; the veiled, multiple, obscure, or discreet intention is part of his whole aesthetic. Even in the lyrics to his progressive rock songs, Eno was at pains not to make his emotional statements too explicit, too prone to any one interpretation. To him, that would defeat the purpose of making a *musical* statement at all. For instance, although he has written songs that appear to be more or less about lust ("The Great Pretender") and about male/female companionship ("St. Elmo's Fire," "Julie With . . ."), Eno has not produced anything that could indisputably be called a "love song" in the popular music or rock traditions. In 1979 Lester Bangs asked him, "But isn't it difficult and mysterious enough to try to understand why you love a certain person? Isn't that feeling worth writing about?" Eno responded:

> No, not for me. I'm not interested in it. I mean, I'm not interested in writing about it. It's certainly not something that I would ever use music to discuss, at least not in clear terms like that. You see, the problem is that people, particularly people who write, assume that the meaning of a song is vested in the lyrics. To me, that has never been the case. There are very few songs that I can think of where I even remember the words, actually, let alone think that those are the center of the meaning. For me, music in itself carries a whole set of messages which are very, very rich and complex, and the words either serve to exclude certain ones of those, or point up certain others that aren't really in there, or aren't worth saying, or something.[23]

Another aspect of intent involves what making music means to Eno personally. What attracts him to being a composer, and what keeps him at it? Eno has often discussed the fact that his earliest musical experiences came without a context: one reason that do-wop and big-band jazz seemed so wonderful to him was that such music appeared completely "alien," totally other: he had as yet acquired no inner historical framework. Increased knowledge inevitably led to a certain disillusionment, diffusing some of the music's mystery, and it is precisely that sense of mystery that he wishes to put back into the music he makes, by deliberately dismantling or shifting the stylistic contexts of the materials he works with.[24]

Composing also takes on the aspect of an introspective search—a search for undiscovered territory within the self:

> I think the trait common to most artists is an attraction towards the thrill of uncertainty, and an impulse to again and again put themselves in a precarious position, even if it's in a very insulated way. Making records doesn't threaten your life. If you fuck it up you're not gonna die, but nonetheless, the thrill is to do something that takes you by surprise, that makes you wonder, god, what in me does this concept connect with? What part of me have I discovered now?[25]

The element of risk is important to Eno in creative as well as in day-to-day situations. In 1976 he told an interviewer, "My interest in danger is at a peak.

The real risks are the ones which threaten your mental stability—I mean which threaten your ability to have a ready answer."[20] Indeed, many if not most of Eno's compositions are begun without a clear idea of what they will ultimately end up sounding like—quite a different process from that in which Mozart is said to have "seen" entire symphonic movements, fully orchestrated, in moments of brilliant inspiration.

"Generating and Organizing Variety in the Arts"

Eno's primary written statement concerning compositional processes in the abstract and social aspects of music-making was an article published in 1976.[27] In its broad outlines, the essay consists of a polemic against traditional methods of composition and the educational and institutional structures that have evolved with and around the concept of the composer during the past two centuries, an examination of some alternative compositional options, and a bold attempt to integrate the point of view of cybernetics—"the science of organization"— with musical and compositional strategies. It is densely written, in a detached and formal style that refrains from excessive rhetorical posturing while still managing to express a definite point of view.

Eno opens with a provocative statement: "A musical score is a statement about organization; it is a set of devices for organizing behaviour towards producing sounds." While composers of the past two centuries have concentrated on the specific instructions given to the performers, the mode of social organization and interaction implied by the use of a score has remained essentially static. "A traditional orchestra is a ranked pyramidical hierarchy of the same kind as the armies that existed contemporary to it." The pyramid of power has the composer and his absolutely binding "intentions and aspirations" at its apex; in descending positions of power are the conductor, leader of the orchestra, soloists if they are called for, section principals, section subprincipals, and finally, rank-and-file members at the bottom. This ranking system has three characteristics that are in Eno's view problematic or symptomatic. First, it "reflects varying degrees of responsibility." Second, "like perspective in painting, it creates 'focus' and 'point of view.' " In the foreground is the intent of the composer, the conductor's interpretation, and the performance of the soloist(s); the playing of the rank-and-file members is liable to be perceived as a kind of background phenomenon. Third, the orchestra's ranking system

predicates the use of trained musicians. A trained musician is, at the minimum, one who will produce a predictable sound given a specific instruction. His training teaches him to be capable of operating precisely like all the other members of his rank. It trains him, in fact, to subdue some of his own natural variety and thus to increase his reliability (predictability).[28]

Eno never comes right out and says that he believes this variety-reducing effect of the institutions of classical music to be undesirable or entirely negative. Rather, he borrows from cybernetics, holding up as an ideal for musical composition and performance the concept of an organism or system whose behavior is determined not through predictable subservience to a centralized control structure, but through "a responsive network of subsystems capable of autonomous behaviour."[29] Musical scores composed with this ideal in mind would not be conceived as a means of controlling the behavior of the performers to the sole end of carrying out the composer's intent. Rather, musical scores would be heuristic, attempting to take advantage of, rather than to suppress, the natural variety occasioned by the performers and the performance situation. Eno quotes and endorses cybernetician Stafford Beer's definition of a "heuristic": "a set of instructions for searching out an unknown goal by exploration, which continuously or repeatedly evaluates progress according to some known criterion."[30] Eno cites Beer's example of a non-musical heuristic: "If you wish to tell someone how to reach the top of a mountain which is shrouded in mist, the heuristic 'keep going up' will get them there."[31]

Much of Eno's essay consists of a discussion of examples of contemporary experimental music whose scores can be considered heuristic. Cornelius Cardew's "Paragraph 7" (from *The Great Learning*) is the piece he treats at greatest length.[32] This is a vocal score in which considerable freedom is given to the performers in terms of which pitches to sing and how long to hold them. The overall effect is one of meditative calm and tranquility—a slowly shifting, complex yet not too dissonant chord with a sense of one central drone pitch. What fascinates Eno about "Paragraph 7" is how the score stipulates not a specific result, but a range of possible results; how it accomodates the instincts and respects the choices of performers of all levels of musical training; and how elements not inherent in the score become primary features of the sound (beat frequencies appear between different sustained sung notes, and the strongest pitch, which naturally evolves from the minimal instructions, becomes the resonating frequency of the room itself, which will vary from performance to performance: the singers pick it up intuitively). Eno sums up his discussion of "Paragraph 7":

> Something quite different from classical compositional technique is taking place: the composer, instead of ignoring or subduing the variety generated in performance, has constructed the piece so that this variety is really the substance of the music.
>
> Perhaps the most concise description of this kind of composition, which characterizes much experimental music, is offered in a statement made by the cybernetician Stafford Beer. He says: "Instead of trying to specify it in full detail, you specify it only somewhat. You then ride on the dynamics of the system in the direction you want to go." In the case of the Cardew piece, the "dynamics of the system" is its interaction with the environmental, physiological and cultural climate surrounding its performance.[33]

Another experimental piece that Eno praises for similar reasons is Michael Nyman's *1–100*, which was recorded on Eno's own Obscure label.[34] "In this piece, four pianists each play the same sequence of 100 [mostly relatively consonant] chords descending slowly down the keyboard. A player is instructed to move on to his next chord only when he can no longer hear his last."[35] As in the Cardew piece, these instructions produce not a specific result but a range of possible results, and the performers must be actively involved in creative listening throughout; also, the technical level of ability of the pianists need not be high, although they must be able to cope with the basics of musical notation and a considerable number of ledger lines.

Cardew's "Paragraph 7," Nyman's *1–100,* and Gavin Bryars's *Jesus' Blood Never Failed Me Yet* (another piece Eno treats briefly) share a quality that was beginning to surface in Eno's own music around the time this essay was published: they give the sense of being music that "is a section from a hypothetical continuum [that is] not especially directional—it does not exhibit strong "progress" from one point (position, theme, statement, argument) to a resolution."[36] One cannot imagine a movement from a Beethoven symphony ending halfway through with a fadeout ending, but one can imagine any number of modern experimental pieces ending this way, since they give no sense of driving inexorably into the future along a developmental line.

Eno does not wish to go too far in his classification and judgment of types of composition and performance practices. Rather, he proposes that every type of music can be placed somewhere along a "scale of orientations" based on the extent to which it tends to subdue or encourage variety in performance. A free-jazz improvisation would be placed toward one end of the scale, a classical symphony toward the other. However,

> virtually any example will show that aspects of *each* orientation exist in any piece. What I am arguing for is a view of musical development as a process of generating new hybrids. . . . A scale of this kind does not tell us much about the music that we place on it, but its function is to remind us to think in terms of hybrids.[37]

"Generating and Organizing Variety in the Arts" is primarily an essay about *process;* Eno does not broach questions of aesthetics as such. Although he declares that the most important characteristic of Cardew's "Paragraph 7" is its calm, meditative quality, and directs one small barb toward the modern music establishment (Nyman's *1–100* "is extremely beautiful to listen to—a factor which seems to carry little critical weight at present"),[38] the focus of the essay is on the ways music is made. Eno does not discuss the large quantities of aleatory (partially improvised) and indeterminate (chance) music composed during the 1950s and 1960s by Pierre Boulez, Cage, Lukas Foss, and others, much of whose non-tonal sounding surface clashes so radically with his own aesthetic preferences and commitments. To Eno, the product is ultimately at least as important as the process.

It is probably fair to say that, under the sway of the image of the authority of the musical score—and for someone who does not read music, that image must seem all the more oppressive—Eno underestimates the importance of "process" during the rehearsal and performance of classical pieces. Orchestral players may be forced to subdue some of their natural variety, but the whole regimen of musical training is nothing if not a process and a discipline; such discipline may appear less interesting to an outsider than spontaneous playing, but certainly a worthwhile product is rarely if ever achieved by mindless music-making in any situation.

Furthermore, the classical tradition is somewhat more open to expressive variety than Eno, with his military image of the orchestra, seems to allow. The orchestra may or may not be "the paradigm of classical organization," as Eno puts it, but in any case he chooses to ignore the role of improvisation in art music—which, though admittedly it has been almost in total eclipse for over a century and a half, has begun to be resuscitated by musicians concerned with authentic historical performance practices. Improvising over a ground bass, realizing a Baroque figured bass or a French unmeasured prelude (types of music composed in notational "shorthand," leaving many rhythmic and textural choices up to the player), extemporizing a set of variations on a theme, elaborating a melody through creative selection from an array of embellishments: certainly in each of these cases one can speak of a process that aims for a range of possible results rather than for a single, entirely predictable result.

But in the cybernetic concept of the adapting, intelligent, complex, heuristically directed organism finding its way among a pleroma of environmental and evolutionary alternatives, Eno has found a striking analogy for the workings of a kind of music-making process that today is to a great extent ruled out by traditional institutions. It was a process in which he had participated through his performances of experimental pieces, and in a different way, as we shall see, it was a process that he was trying to encourage with the making of his own progressive rock and ambient music albums.

6 The Compositional Process

EQUIPMENT

Composer/non-musician Brian Eno's domain or arena of operation has always been that of the recording studio and tape recorder, both of which he has referred to as his "real instruments." As we have seen, many of his comments about pieces of music focus not on what a musicologist might be inclined to call their "purely musical" qualities—melody, harmony, rhythm, and so on— but rather on aspects of production and engineering, on how the recording studio was used to produce a particular kind of sound texture.

As Eno himself has pointed out, his musical work is so heavily dependent on technology that it could not have existed in any previous age.[1] When he speaks of himself as a painter of sound, or a constructor of sonic landscapes, he is being more than metaphorical: for in a very real sense, magnetic tape is his canvas, and he applies his sound substances to that canvas, mixes them, blends them, determines their shape, in specific "painterly" ways. He has just enough instrumental technique to give him his "pigments" to begin with; in the previous chapter we saw how he finds it much more difficult to work with initial recorded materials that already have a complexity of their own. His claim to be not so much a composer as a sound-painter is reinforced by his statements to the effect that the way he works with light in his video pieces is identical to the way he works with sound in his music.

Eno wrote a lecture, entitled "The Studio As Compositional Tool," which he delivered at a number of places in England and the United States during the late 1970s and which was eventually published in *Down Beat* magazine in 1983.[2] The first part of the lecture presents an informal, sketchy history of sound recording, while the second part presents an overview of the structure and components of the modern studio, with examples of how Eno has taken advantage of this layout in his own work. But even when Eno is talking about the nuts and bolts of history, his point of view—his interpretation of history —is clear. A philosophical point on which he lays particular stress is how the act of recording has radically changed the nature of music. Before the advent of sound recording,

The piece disappeared when it was finished, so it was something that only existed in time. The effect of recording is that it takes music out of the time dimension and puts it into the space dimension. As soon as you do that, you're in a position of being able to listen again and again to a performance, to become familiar with details you most certainly had missed the first time through, and to become very fond of details that weren't intended by the composer or the musicians. The effect of this on the composer is that he can think in terms of supplying material that would actually be too subtle for a first listening.[3]

Eno's history of recording touches on other philosophical points, some of which I have already described: recording makes music available to any location that has playback equipment; the early emphasis on faithful reproduction of musical performances has yielded to a realization that the medium has its own unique potentials; the development of magnetic tape was decisive in that it made recorded sound vastly more manipulable, through experimental processes of splicing, looping, reversing, and variable-speed playing; and the development of multi-track recording and mixing makes possible whole new ranges of use and abuse of technology. While many recordings today still have as their purported purpose the most faithful possible reproduction of a musical performance, Eno's emphasis is always on innovative ways the contemporary composer can approach the new technology should he choose to do so. What Eno calls "in-studio composition" is the result of the multi-track idea "that composition is the process of adding more." With in-studio composition,

> you no longer come to the studio with a conception of the finished piece. Instead, you come with actually rather a bare skeleton of the piece, or perhaps with no starting point. Once you become familiar with studio facilities, or even if you're not, actually, you can begin to compose in relation to those facilities. You can begin to think in terms of putting something on, putting something else on, trying this on top of it, and so on, then taking some of the original things off, or taking a mixture of things off, and seeing what you're left with—actually constructing a piece in the studio.[4]

Eno makes much of the "transmission losses" from composer to score, from score to performers, and from performers to audience; and inasmuch as his records sound the same every time they're played, while Beethoven's symphonies do not, he has a point. Perhaps, however, Eno's assumption that any given record of his "is going to be the same every time it's played"[5] underestimates the significant differences in playback equipment on which his records are played. Having heard Eno pieces on several different sets of speakers in different rooms, as well as through various kinds of headphones, I have noticed quite different balances, frequency spectrums, and relationships between elements in the different "performances" of the same piece; manipulation of the playback amplifier's tone controls or graphic equalizer likewise surely constitutes a kind of "transmission loss." These transmission losses, to be sure, are of a different, more subtle type than those that occur along the traditional composer-performer-audience path.

Eno composes on tape; the traditional composer composes on paper. But how different, really, is in-studio composition from traditional on-paper composition? Could it not be argued that the traditional composer has an equal opportunity to do his work "empirically," adding parts, erasing them, trying out different combinations at leisure? The recent vogue of musicological sketch studies attests to the empirical working methods of many composers. Composer/ conductors like Gustav Mahler have indeed even used their orchestras as a sort of playback facility, changing their scores having once heard what the results sounded like. To this extent, Eno's claim that he is working with an entirely new way of composing seems a bit extreme, or a bit naive; and it is entirely possible that, having had no experience with musical notation himself, he underestimates the degree to which a traditional composer can hear his score in his head as he writes it out.

Despite such reservations, we must acknowledge that Eno's claim for the different quality of in-studio composition is not without substance, with regard to the production of popular music in general and even more with regard to Eno's own work. As he said in the second part of his lecture, ". . . many different rock records, in my opinion, are predicated not on a structure, or a melodic line, or a rhythm, but on a sound; this is why studios and producers keep putting their names on records, because they have a lot to do with that aspect of the work."[6] In rock, the same band playing the same songs in the same arrangements may sound completely different when recorded by two different producers; harmonic, melodic, and rhythmic analysis would reveal nothing about this difference, which, however, might determine the difference between a hit record and a flop. As the complexity of the recording process has increased, the producer has become a vitally necessary link between the artist and the technology.

In his solo music, Eno has combined the roles of composer, lyricist, arranger, producer, engineer, instrumentalist, and singer; his taking on the responsibility of all of these functions has given him a control over the product which is rare in either the classical or popular music worlds. But the most important point to be made in connection with Eno's concept of in-studio composition is that Eno's music—his progressive rock to some degree, and his ambient music to a very great extent—is a music in which timbre and sound texture are accorded an extremely high level of importance. Much of the meaning of Eno's music hinges on very subtle factors having to do with the vertical spectrum of tone color; the exact hues of a sound, down to almost imperceptible shifts in overtone structure, are for Eno the substance of the music itself. Seen in this perspective, his claim to be working in an "empirical way that the classical composer never was" makes sense. Much has been made of the expansion of the timbral palette by nineteenth- and twentieth-century composers working with new combinations of traditional orchestral instruments, with new additions to the orchestra or ensemble, and occasionally with newly invented instruments. Eno and other electronic composers, however, create the sounds as they work, and indeed they have a control over the timbral aspect of music that the traditional composer writing for instruments does not. One might say that whereas most Western art music is a music of notes, intervals, and rhythms, Eno's is a music of timbres and textures; rather than being a matter of working with a limited and fixed set of instrumental colors that are applied to musical (melodic, harmonic, formal) ideas, to a large extent Eno's compositional process consists in exploring the properties of sound itself. A traditional composer writing an orchestral work may begin by making a piano score that he subsequently orchestrates; Eno would see this procedure as working backwards, since he often experiments with tone colors in the studio until themes, forms, and other musical elements suggest themselves. In 1979 he said:

> People think that you sit at home and you have a melody and the chord sequence in mind, and then you think, "Well, what instruments would be good for this?" You know, that kind of idea of having a *goal*, which you then build towards. I don't think anyone works like that, or very rarely. Sometimes there will be a melody at the beginning, or a particular rhythmic configuration, but generally there's a sense of, "Well, I'm going to set this process in motion. Where will it lead me? And furthermore, do I *like* where it leads me?" Because if you don't, you abandon it; you start again.[7]

Although the traditional composer may experiment with timbral qualities to some extent, and may not know exactly what his piece is going to sound like until he has finished writing it or until it is played, it is probably fair to say that in the "serious" musical world such uncertainty tends to be frowned upon, regarded as a sign of insufficient technique: one is supposed to have a clear idea of where one is going from the outset, and the compositional task is to get this idea down on paper as accurately as possible. Eno, on the other hand, transforms the "uncertainty principle" into an integral part of his total method:

> Each thing you add modifies the whole set of things that went before and you suddenly find yourself at a place that you couldn't possibly have conceived of, a place that's strange and curious to you. That sense of mystery, learning to live with it and make use of it, is extremely important.[8]

In 1981 Eno offered a metaphor to describe the difference between his in-studio compositional approach and that of the traditional composer. The traditional composer works like a modern architect planning a building, he said, "specifying all the dimensions and all the materials and where all the pipes go." The empirical in-studio composer, on the other hand, gets a hold of a few bricks and maybe some mud, and just starts building a hut by trial and error, guided by no particular plan but by his evolving sense of what the result might be: his image of the hut may well undergo significant changes by the time the hut is finished:

> Of course modern architecture looks the way it does because it has to be done that way. It's naturally going to look extremely regular and inorganic, because you can't specify an organic thing in advance. It's too complex. You couldn't specify a mud hut with an architect's drawing. It's too complex an entity.[9]

In the second part of his lecture "The Studio As Compositional Tool," Eno describes some of the components normally found in the modern recording studio. The twenty-four-track tape recorder, with its twenty-four sets of recording and playback heads, and its massive, two-inch wide reels of tape, is one of the main pieces of equipment. If one is making a live recording of a rock band, every instrument and vocal part can be recorded on a separate track; frequently, drums come in for particularly elaborate miking, with separate microphones on the bass drum, snare drum, high hat, and so on. "You can end up with this two-inch piece of tape with 24 distinct signals, and once you're in this position, you have considerable freedom of what you can do with each of these sounds."[10]

Recording is only the first step; the next step is mixing, in which the producer decides on the overall balance of sound that is desirable, and makes decisions on how to mix the twenty-four recorded channels onto two-track (stereo) tape. As Eno has said, "The mixer is really the central part of the studio":[11] it is the large "board" with as many as nine hundred knobs in neatly arranged rows. Each row of knobs controls one of the twenty-four recorded tracks, and with these knobs, it is possible to control, individually for each track: the volume; the "pan," or where the sound will be located (anywhere from far left to far right) in the final stereo image; the degree of echo (for Eno, echo is a particularly important element, for "it enables you to locate something in an artificial acoustic space");[12] the equalization, or balance between high and low frequencies of the recorded sound (it is possible to bring out or suppress the strength of the sound in any of the audible frequency bands, each being typically about an octave in extent); the compression (when a sound signal is compressed, its loud parts will sound softer and its soft parts will sound louder; compression is typically used when one wants to hear all the nuances of a particular track, nuances that would be otherwise lost against the dynamic level of the other tracks); and the limiting (a limiter is a kind of envelope shaper, capable of altering the attack, sustain, and decay characteristics of the input sound).

Use of this array of controls on each track varies from producer to producer, from group to group, from record to record. Sometimes a producer's characteristic settings will be a well-kept secret. More and more, producers are hired for the particular kinds of sound they are able to coax out of the mixing board; with the producer's know-how, a raw garage band can be made to yield music of the utmost delicacy or pomp, of minimalistic or symphonic proportions. Of course, if an *"audio-verité"* approach is deemed appropriate, that is still possible too.[13] But for composer/producers like Eno, control over the mixing board provides a practically infinite number of sound-controlling possibilities, from a subtle echo enhancing a particular track to radically altered tonal spectrums and sound envelopes—where the original instrumental sound source is often unidentifiable. As he has put it, the controls on the mixing board "allow you to rearrange the priorities of the music in a large number of ways."[14]

The result of the mixing process is a two-channel stereo tape that is then taken to the pressing plant, at which point it leaves the in-studio composer's control. In producing the final stereo mix, Eno tries the music out on at least two sets of speakers—usually medium-priced speakers that are likely to resemble those used by most of the record's buyers in their homes. As he says, "It's the very naive producer who works only on optimum systems."[15]

In his lecture Eno points out some large trends in the history of the use of the mixing board. During the 1950s, producers tended to mix melodic information very loudly, while putting the rhythmic information in the background; frequently the bass line was almost inaudible. "As time goes on you'll find this spectrum, which was very wide, with vocals way up there and the bass drum way down there, beginning to compress, until at the beginning of funk it is very narrow, indeed. Things are all about equally loud."[16] And, as we have already seen, Eno credits groups like Sly and the Family Stone with actually reversing the 1950s concept of sound priorities: on Sly's records, "the rhythm instruments, particularly the bass drum and bass, suddenly become the important instruments in the mix."[17]

When Eno entered his first modern twenty-four-track recording studio, he already had many years of experience with tape recorders, which had always exercised a "magical" influence on his imagination. Having wanted one since he was "tiny,"[18] he finally got access to one at age fifteen:

> I knew it was something I'd never get bored with and I never did. It's still magic to me. By the time I was 20 I had 30 tape recorders. Each had its own characteristic. I'd just collect any piece of rubbish I could find that would turn a piece of tape. Each machine could do something interesting, specific to one task. For example the motor might not be stable so the sound would oscillate. Only one worked properly.[19]

> I thought it was magic to be able to catch something identically on tape and then be able to play around with it, run it backwards; I thought that was great for years.[20]

In 1973, Eno said: "Nothing I've ever done with a tape recorder is brilliant . . . it's just obvious if you think of what the true function of a tape recorder is—if you think of it as an automatic musical collage device."[21]

Few people would speak of the "true function of a tape recorder" as "an automatic musical collage device." But inspired by a powerful personal vision of the untapped potential of this piece of technology, Eno built his non-musician's career around it.

Of musical instruments proper, the one Eno has probably played more than any other is the synthesizer. Although voltage-control synthesizers had been commercially available since the mid-1960s, Eno had never laid hands on one until he was called in by Roxy Music in 1971 to make some demo tapes for them. A synthesizer was sitting in the room, and Eno began to fool around with it; the sounds he produced were so impressive that the band asked him to join on the spot. As he has said, "I'm very good with technology. I always have been, and with machines in general. They seem to me not threatening like other people find them, but a source of great fun and amusement, like grown up toys really."[22]

Since Eno is among the most acclaimed synthesizer players in rock, interviewers have often asked him about his equipment and about the vast array of synthesizers available for the modern musician to choose from. He often claims to know actually very little about the synthesizer market, and what he says on the general subject frequently takes the form of an argument for the virtues of "low" technology: he prefers inexpensive synthesizers with a limited number of features, as opposed to state-of-the-art machines like the Synclavier or Fairlight. This appears to be a deliberate strategy on his part to limit the possibilities with which he is faced, and to develop as complete an understanding as possible of the instruments he works with. He appears to experience genuine revulsion toward the unthinking, unlistening more-is-better approach that seduces so many contemporary musicians who use electronics. In 1983, he said:

> I've been moving more in the direction of very low technology—found objects and other things that have some kind of interesting inherent sound to them— just anything lying around, really. I spend a lot of time around Canal Street [a long stretch of junk shops and flea markets located in downtown New York] hitting things and listening to what this little bolt might sound like or this metal pot or whatever. As for high technology, all of the work I've heard from those machines [the Synclavier and Fairlight] is so unbelievably awful to me.[23]

The main synthesizers Eno has worked with are the EMS Model AKS, Yamaha CS-80, Yamaha DX7, Arp 2600, Korg Micropreset, and the Yamaha YC-45D organ.[24] The EMS was Eno's workhorse during the 1970s and early 1980s. He found it extremely flexible because it allows the user to set up any desired signal path: the standard path of the signal from oscillator to filter to envelope shaper, which is fixed on many synthesizers, could be bypassed completely and a variety of unusual patches set up. Eno enjoyed using the EMS's joystick, and also lauded the machine for the versatility of its controls, which enable the musician to adjust each function by potentiometer knobs, rather than simple on/off switches. The Yamaha CS-80 was one of the first polyphonic synthesizers (capable of producing more than one note at a time) on the commercial market, and Eno admired it for its simplicity: "It's perfect for me. I'd rather have six beautiful sounds from a synthesizer than a possible infinity of mediocre sounds."[25]

By 1985 Eno had gotten a Yamaha DX7 and was calling it his favorite syn thesizer. The DX7 is a completely digital synthesizer, which means that sounds are produced and manipulated not by variations in an electrical current (as in analog synthesis) but rather by computerized mathematical operations on num bers in binary code. The commercial success of digital sound synthesis tech nology has been one of the big stories in the music industry of the 1980s, for the digital method offers cleaner sound and potentially more precise control for the musician than earlier analog systems. Learning to program, or create, one's own original sounds on a digital synthesizer like the DX7, however, is notoriously difficult and, as Eno notes, many musicians simply use the factory-preset sounds that come with the instrument. For Eno, the DX7 opened up a new world of tone color to investigate: "I would be doing things on the DX7 and I would notice that certain number relationships were interesting. So then I started getting books about acoustics to find out what I was doing, and how that related to ordinary instruments."[26]

Eno's method of getting to know his electronic equipment is unorthodox, simple, and creative:

> With devices my technique is always to hide the handbook in the drawer until I've played with it for a while. The handbook always tells you what it does, and you can be quite sure that if it's a complex device it can do at least fifteen other things that weren't predicted in the handbook, or that they didn't consider de-sirable. It's normally those other things that interest me.[27]

This slightly irreverent attitude toward technology's cornucopia extends to the matter of getting his machines serviced. By and large, Eno does not:

> I know a lot of people are into the inhuman cleanness of a synthesizer, but I don't like that, and I subvert it number one by laziness: I never get my instruments serviced, so they start to become a little bit more idiosyncratic, and I also use a lot of auxiliary equipment, which I also don't get serviced. Now this sounds flippant, this not getting things serviced. I actually do get things serviced some-times, but a lot of the faults that develop are rather interesting, so I leave those alone.[28]

For Eno, synthesizers have three main functions. The first involves using the machine as a conventional keyboard instrument: he programs it to produce a certain tone color, and then plays melodies or chords on the organ-like keyboard controller. The second function is to produce "non-musical" sounds—that is, sounds of which steady tone or pitch is not a primary characteristic; such sounds range from whooshing, wind- and ocean-like effects based on filtered and oth-erwise altered white noise, to a vast array of percussive sounds, to a similarly vast array of complex, muffled yet punctuated background sounds, to a variety of variably lifelike and mechanical-sounding "animal and insect noises, at which I'm now, I'm sure, the world specialist."[29] The synthesizer's third function for Eno is to control and alter the sound output of other instruments, whether electric or acoustic. The signal path in a synthesizer normally starts with its own tone or noise generator, and can be channeled through various circuits that alter the signal; but by bypassing the tone or noise generators, a signal can be fed in from an outside sound source, which can then be "treated" like the synthesizer's own. This sort of processing is one of the most exciting things about the synthesizer for Eno. He has explained that, in effect,

> what you do is create a new instrument. You create an instrument that has all of the interesting idiosyncracies of a natural instrument, but also some of the special features of a synthesizer. . . . When I'm recording I nearly always have something going through the EMS. It's a way of giving a character to the track, from a very early stage, that takes it away from being just another bass and drums and blah, blah, blah.[30]

Eno has a paradoxical relationship to technology. While he seems to exult in the fact that he could not be a composer without it, he levels much of his harshest criticism against other musicians who use it, and sometimes against the machines themselves. In 1981 he complained that synthesizers lacked "a sound that is idiosyncratic enough to be interesting." This has been a common lament among musicians ever since the development of the synthesizer. It is difficult to match electronically, for instance, the subtlety and complexity of an acoustic piano tone color, which is slightly different for every note of the keyboard. Instruments made of natural materials like wood have quirks that synthesizer designers have taken pains to eliminate. "A guitar sounds slightly different at each fret, and it has oddities, which are undoubtedly a large part of the interest of the instrument. A good player will understand and make use of those oddities."[31]

Similarly paradoxical is what Eno the "non-musician" has said about the need for synthesizers that are more responsive to the physical activity of the player. In spite of the low premium he places on the manual craft of musicianship, he wishes synthesizer designers would exercise more imagination in coming up with ways for enhancing the physical player/instrument interface, for instance with pedals, touch-sensitive keyboards, joysticks, control wheels, and possibly other, as yet unimagined, devices.[32] Thus, while he has expounded an elaborate philosophy which accomodates his lack of digital dexterity, some sort of direct physical contact with his instruments is an important part of the music-making process for him.

If Eno values the controls of the mixing board and the synthesizer for the infinite variety of sounds they are capable of producing, he occasionally needs the solace and simplicity of traditional instruments. In 1978, exhausted after the grueling process of making *Before and After Science,* the weary Eno told an interviewer:

> I have a guitar that makes only one sound. It's refreshing to play. With a synthesizer you have 14,000 choices. Sometimes it's nice to know that the instrument has made that decision for you.[33]

Although one might imagine that Eno would have experimented with many different kinds of electric guitar, he was content to limit the range of his options by using a single one consistently throughout the 1970s, getting to know its unique and evolving characteristics intimately. It was a small Starway model, and Eno deliberately let it deteriorate gradually over the years: he never changed the strings, and when the top one broke he decided not to replace it. The older the remaining five strings got, the more closely their sound approximated that of a pure sine wave; and consequently "the more I could do with the sound afterwards," running it through synthesizers, fuzz boxes, and so on.[34]

By 1983 Eno was using mostly a Fernandez guitar, a copy of a 1957 Fender Stratocaster[35] (Stratocasters have been among the most popular models with rock guitarists since the 1950s), and he also has a 1963 Gibson bass guitar. He uses the guitar primarily as a kind of synthesizer and mixing-board controller, analogous to the keyboard controllers that most synthesizers come equipped with. Thus Eno employs the electric guitar not as an instrument with an essential, characteristic tone color of its own—the closer his Starway got to producing the bland, faceless tones of a sine-wave oscillator, the better—but as a physical interface with his larger "instrument," the whole synthesizer/recording studio complex.

Other important components of Eno's mega-instrument are the innumerable electronic boxes or devices that can be added to a circuit, usually between the guitar or keyboard and amplifier, to alter the tone color and sound envelope characteristics. Typical effects from these linking machines include echo, reverb, (intentional) distortion, flange, phase shift, chorus, and wah-wah. Some of these effects can also be produced at the mixing board, but it often makes a difference where in the total electronic circuit the sound-altering device is located: echoed fuzz may have a different sound profile than fuzzed echo. Possibilities multiply; as Eno has said, "The whole point of using effects devices is to try to reintroduce those idiosyncrasies into the sound, to take the sound out of the realm of the perfect and into the realm of the real. I'll put any amount of junk in a long line after my synthesizer to see what will happen to it [the sound]."[36]

Where possible, Eno likes to work with devices that make use of a foot pedal—again, to give him a sense of physical control. He has no standard "line of junk": his configurations of sound-altering devices are always changing. He sees graphic equalization as being "totally essential" in most of the circuits he puts together; echo effects are almost as important, and he is liable to use two

or even three echo devices at once, normally at the end of the chain nearest
to the tape recorder.[37] Echo and reverb are in a sense in a different class than
other effects, since they create the illusion that the music is taking place within
a physical space. The same instrument can be made to sound as if it is located
in a small room, a large room, a concert hall, a stone cathedral, or even the
Grand Canyon. Echo and reverb effects "can evoke a whole geography."[38]

Example 1 (see following page) may make the whole studio complex easier
to visualize. In this hypothetical recording situation, four sound sources (voice,
electric guitar, piano, and rhythm box) are sent through different chains of
timbre-altering equipment, recorded on twenty-four-track tape, and finally
mixed down to the stereo version which the listener will ultimately hear.

Although certain timbres recur from time to time in Eno's music, many of
his electronic sound-producing chains are unique: constructed empirically, they
are dismantled after being put to a particular use. If the chain is important
enough, he will remember it; but he has been reluctant to fix such chains in
writing, for fear of stultifying his creativity. "I made a rule very early on, which
I've kept to, which was that I would never write down any setting that I got
on the synthesizer, no matter how fabulous a sound I got. . . . If I had a stock
of fabulous sounds I would just always use them, I wouldn't bother to find new
ones."[39] Thus, specifications for many of the total circuits Eno has used to
produce his dazzling array of timbres are apparently lost forever; the exact
process is gone, but the product remains. Often his complex chains of sound-
producing and -altering equipment include multiple instruments and electronic
devices that interact in unpredictable ways. He describes one such situation
that arose when he was working in a studio in Canada with producer Daniel
Lanois. The studio happened to contain a Fender Rhodes electric piano and a
rattly old amplifier/speaker. Eno put the speaker on the piano's sustain pedal
so that all the notes were free to ring, fitted a long plastic tube onto a microphone
which was plugged into the speaker, then experimented by playing various
notes at the keyboard:

> One note—just one note—made the whole system come to life. It made the
> speaker shake with a beautiful purring sound, like a huge foghorn. The piano was
> ringing away, and the pick-up through the tube particularly resonated around
> that frequency and all the harmonics.[40]

SYSTEMS OF COMPOSING

Although when he gets to the studio he may work in an empirical way, without
much conscious idea of what is going to happen next, general ideas for projects
take shape in Eno's imagination over fairly long periods of time, and it seems
he is constantly toying with a multitude of ideas about creative situations, many
of which never come to fruition. In a sense, the first steps in the compositional

Example 1
Flow of Electronic Signals
in a Hypothetical Studio Situation

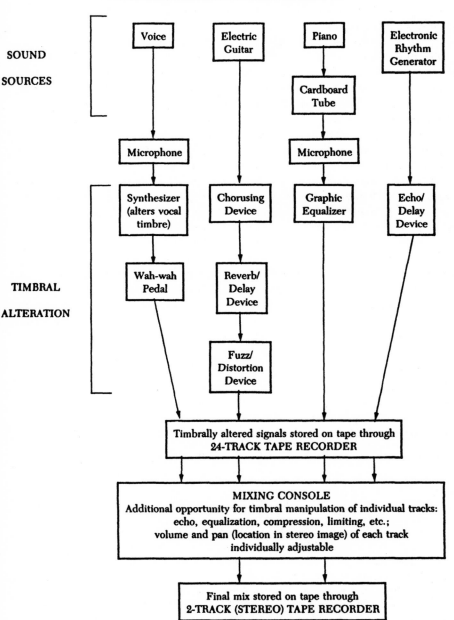

process involve the decision to work on a piece in a general way, the decision of whether or not to use other musicians to generate raw material, and some concept of the form of the final product (through the 1970s and early 1980s, normally a record album).

Eno has a reputation for being extremely busy all the time; even when not in the studio, he is likely to be experimenting with instruments and tape recorders at home, tapping and banging on found objects to see what they sound like, or recording environmental noises on a portable cassette recorder. The vast majority of the music he has made has never been released on record; in 1983 he estimated that he had about seven hundred pieces stored away on tape, some of which he'd made alone, some of which were leftovers from studio sessions with other musicians. "People would probably be surprised to know my own rejection rate of my work. I must produce a hundred times the amount of music I release."[41] Evidently putting sounds on tape is far from enough; judgment has to intervene at some stage of the game. One reason Eno saves so many of his sketches, however, is that he is aware that his judgment may change at some point in the future, or that his ear will pick up something on an old tape of which he had not been aware at the time: "Later on you may suddenly realize that there was a secret concern that you weren't consciously dealing with, but which actually dominates the piece, and that concern might be the most interesting one." On the other hand, he says, "Sometimes I do things and I know they're just absolute crap. There's no point in wasting storage space with those, so those go."[42] In some sense, then, composing is a near-constant process for Eno—a process that is not always suffused with inspiration. In 1985 he said:

> It quite frequently happens that you're just treading water for quite a long time. Nothing really dramatic seems to be happening. . . . And then suddenly everything seems to lock together in a different way. It's like a crystallization point where you can't detect any single element having changed. There's a proverb that says that the fruit takes a long time to ripen, but it falls suddenly. . . .[43]

Moments of true inspiration are rare, and their arrival cannot be predicted; Eno has been no more successful than others in trying to coerce his muse to speak to him, but he has found it worthwhile, during the long periods of the muse's silence, to maintain a state of preparedness:

> The point about working is not to produce great stuff all the time, but to remain ready for when you can. There's no point in saying, "I don't have an idea today, so I'll just smoke some drugs." You should stay alert for the moment when a number of things are just ready to collide with one another.
>
> A lot of factors go toward creating a work: technological considerations that suddenly are a little exciting to you, some feeling or mood, a nice day, you just had a talk with a friend. All sorts of things will coincide—and that moment doesn't last for long. It's like things in orbit; they'll move away again.

> The reason to keep working is almost to build a certain mental tone, like people talk about body tone. You have to move quickly when the time comes, and the time might come very infrequently—once or twice a year, or even less.[44]

For Eno, then, there is much that can be done at a conscious, day-to-day level to enhance one's chances of coming up with good creative work. In 1980 he stated his belief that imagination and the ability to think independently were things that "you can work at developing," mentioning that he'd read several books by Edward DeBono and William J. J. Gordon on the subject of ways of prompting creativity. Eno contends that "the process of creating isn't largely spontaneous . . . there are lots of ways that you can interfere with it and make it more efficient."[45] Although Eno's music does not depend on a high level of instrumental musicianship, his conceptual and practical mastery of the resources of the recording studio and the synthesizer constitute a different kind of craft. He puts it succinctly: craft "enables you to be successful when you're not inspired."[46]

Eno is unusually aware of the ebb and flow of his creative energies, and often does specific things in order to influence them one way or the other, such as taking a break from a taxing project:

> The difficulty of always feeling that you ought to be doing Something is that you tend to undervalue the times when you're apparently doing nothing, and those are very important times. It's the equivalent of the dream time, in your daily life, times when things get sorted out and reshuffled. If you're constantly awake workwise you don't allow that to happen. One of the reasons I have to take distinct breaks when I work is to allow the momentum of a particular direction to run down, so that another one can establish itself.[47]

Even with the application of various techniques of promoting the creative process, it is a day-to-day struggle:

> There are some days when my confidence level is so high that I can make anything work. Particularly if you work without a group, as I do, you really need a lot of energy to push something through those first stages, where it's just a rhythm box going "bump-titta" and a piano going "dum, dum, dum." I mean, that doesn't sound terribly interesting, so maintaining the conviction to keep going, in the hope, or in the trust that it's going to turn into something does require a lot of application. And some days I just don't have that.[48]

The sensation of being engaged in an interesting process, and the attitude of expectant attention as to where it might lead, are central to Eno's experience of composition. He occasionally puts the whole matter in simple terms: "Nearly all the things I do that are of any merit at all start off as just being good fun."[49] As for specific methods of composing, or making individual pieces of music, he articulated his most systematic statement on the subject in 1978, when he outlined five distinct approaches. The first requires keeping a microcassette tape recorder on hand at all times and recording any stray ideas that hit him out of the blue—a melody, a rhythm, a verbal phrase. Periodically, Eno will browse through the thousands of fragments to "see if any of them fit together." Those that do may be worked into a preliminary "demo" and stored in his tape library for future use. The second approach is entering the recording studio with no particular ideas, taking stock of the available instruments and equipment, and perhaps hiring a couple of instruments he has a yen to use. "Then I just dabble with sounds until something starts to happen that suggests a texture." At some point during this process, the overall sound texture may suddenly suggest a geographical location or evoke a childhood scene to Eno, and from that point on the image guides the development of the composition.

A third way of working is from deliberate non-musical constraints, for instance by saying, "Well, this piece is going to be three minutes and nineteen seconds long and it's going to have changes here, here, and here, and there's going to be a convolution of events here, and there's going to be a very fast rhythm here with a very slow moving part over the top of it." Sometimes Eno uses graph paper when working like this, since it tends to be a visual process for him. The fourth approach is the kind that characterized the studio sessions for his progressive rock albums: Eno would "gather together a group of musicians who wouldn't normally work together" and generate ideas from the unexpected interactions between them. Finally, Eno says he has "also worked from very mathematical and structural bases, but in general that hasn't been so successful."[50]

When asked in 1985 what were his first steps in beginning a piece, Eno approached the issue from a different angle, outlining three forms of motivation. The first is practical: if he has accepted a commission, for instance, he has to start worrying about the piece because he is obliged to. "The second is arriving at it from an intellectual position of considering what I've done, sifting through and rearranging it, and trying to include more. That's designing a piece of work and saying *this* is the kind of method I'm going to use." The third way to initiate work on a piece is to play around with something specific, whether that be something concrete like a new piece of equipment or a more abstract entity like a particular modal scale.[51]

Images of partaking in a natural process—of watering a garden daily, of riding on the dynamics of the system, of letting oneself be led rather than pushing, of writing music by interfering as little as possible—abound in Eno's discussions of his creative work. Clearly this whole idea owes much to Cage and his chance operations, his ideal of letting the sounds be themselves; but it stops short of the Cageian ideal of writing music that is completely untainted by history and personal psychology, for as we have seen, Eno has quite specific compositional aims, specific emotions he wishes to arouse in the listener, specific geographies to evoke. Active judgment and discriminatory listening are very much part of Eno's approach, no matter how much he simultaneously tries to adopt the attitude of an onlooker. His is an active interaction with the growing work of art, but in this interaction the artist's will and aggressively creative intentions do not predominate. In most of his creative work, Eno perceives two phases, pushing and letting go:

> Once phase two begins everything is okay, because then the work starts to dictate its own terms. It starts to get an identity which demands certain future moves. But during the first phase you often find that you come to a full stop. You don't know what to supply. And it's at that stage that I will pull one of the cards out.[52]

This brings us to one of Eno's most curious inventions, the deck of *Oblique Strategies*, subtitled *Over one hundred worthwhile dilemmas.*[53] The deck, which Eno developed and produced in collaboration with his painter friend Peter Schmidt, is a set of oracle cards modeled philosophically on the ancient Chinese *I Ching*, or *Book of Changes.*[54] While still in art school, Eno had taken to formulating aphorisms to aid him in the creative process, to give him a new perspective on working when he got bogged down in specific details, was unable to maintain a large perspective on what he was doing, and was thereby losing a sense of his creative options. During the Roxy Music period, he wrote these aphorisms down on cards he placed around the recording studio. His random selection of a card and reflection on its message often provided fresh and unexpected resolution of a compositional quandary. It subsequently developed that Schmidt had been doing much the same thing, with a little notebook he kept for the purpose. When Eno and Schmidt compared notes, it turned out that many of their aphorisms were essentially identical. They decided to put the aphorisms on stiff paper the size and feel of playing cards and to market a limited edition of 500 copies in 1975. Several thousand were sold in revised editions in 1978 and 1979, after which they decided not to produce any more. The deck comes in a handsome black cardboard box with gold-embossed lettering, and contains the following description and instructions:

> These cards evolved from our separate observations of the principles underlying what we were doing. Sometimes they were recognized in retrospect (intellect catching up with intuition), sometimes they were identified as they were happening, sometimes they were formulated.
> They can be used as a pack (a set of possibilities being continuously reviewed in the mind) or by drawing a single card from the shuffled pack when a dilemma occurs in a working situation. In this case the card is trusted even if its appropriateness is quite unclear. They are not final, as new ideas will present themselves, and others will become self-evident.

The short messages on the cards are varied, evocative, and often intentionally cryptic. Some examples, randomly chosen from the deck: "Would anybody want it?" "Go slowly all the way round the outside." "Don't be afraid of things because they're easy to do." "Only a part, not the whole." "Retrace your steps."

"Disconnect from desire." "You are an engineer." "Turn it upside down." "Do we need holes?" "Is it finished?" "Don't break the silence." "What are you really thinking about just now?"

The aphorisms are remarkably well-crafted in the sense that it is easy to imagine how each is applicable to any stage of or particular problem arising in the course of the creative process. Eno consulted the *Oblique Strategies* extensively during his creative work of the mid- and late 1970s, and may have continued to do so into the 1980s, though he has not talked about this in recent interviews.

The *I Ching* was a partial inspiration for the deck of *Oblique Strategies;* Eno called the latter "an attempt to make a set that was slightly more specific, tailored to a more particular situation than the *I Ching,* which is tailored to cosmic situations, though I suppose that with sufficient skill one could use the *I Ching* in the same way."[55] Eno pointed out that it was not necessary to believe that anything supernatural or paranormal was taking place in the use of the *Oblique Strategies* in order to derive creative benefits from using them: "You can believe that they work on a purely behavioral level, simply adjusting your perception at a point, or suggesting a different perception."[56] The concept behind the *Oblique Strategies* fits smoothly into Eno's overall empirical, in-studio compositional approach: the aphorisms enabled him to get beyond his linear thinking process, especially during the early, formative stages of a work, and provided the sensation that he was indeed riding on the dynamics of some greater system that logic alone could not penetrate.

VERBAL EXPRESSION AND LYRICS

As the quotations from his interviews have demonstrated, Eno is well-practiced and accomplished at the art of verbal expression. He uses interviews deliberately as opportunities to verbally straighten out and refine his thinking. When he has a point to make, he is capable of making it in general, abstract terms, of citing specific pertinent examples, and of constructing elaborate, often striking metaphors to illustrate his train of thought. His published essays and lectures offer further proof that Eno knows what verbal logic and exposition are all about. Yet, when he was called upon to discuss painter Peter Schmidt's watercolors and his own reasons for including them on the cover of his album *Before and After Science* for the journal *Arts Review,* he prefaced his remarks with a disclaimer:

> Because art criticism is a verbal activity, I write with the consciousness that my language is being evaluated in that context, and knowing that certain words and phrases will assume overtones that were not intended. I choose to ignore this hazard by reassuring the reader that art-criticism is not my primary (or even secondary) occupation in life, and that my intention is to write about these works

simply, and because I want to. I hope that by doing this I can assume a level of trust on the part of the reader that might otherwise not be afforded me.[57]

Even if this boils down to Eno's nervousness at the prospect of his thoughts appearing in the context of a critical journal, it is his "consciousness of the hazard" of his language being misinterpreted or overinterpreted to which I would like to draw attention here. Elsewhere as well, Eno has shown signs that he is all too aware of the ways that language, even ordinary spoken or written prose, can work on a multitude of levels, not all of which were intended by the speaker or writer. This is especially true when it comes to historically, emotionally, and conceptually loaded words—big words like "art," "music," and "God." In 1978, after discussing what he and others mean by the term "art band," he said:

> Art—and artist—are words that are very hard to use. I use them all the time because I'm not frightened of them anymore. I just decided that there's nothing else to describe what I want to say, so I have to use them. But I know, at the same time, that it evokes the most awful ideas in other people's minds—so I use the terms rather judiciously.[58]

As we have already noted, "music" is a word that Eno increasingly finds inadequate for the products of the recording studio. In 1983 he put it this way:

> I think the word "music" has become difficult to describe. Traditionally music was written down and given to a conductor, who then translated it for the performers. It was necessarily ephemeral. Once the performance was finished it ceased to exist except in code on paper or in people's memory. Now music is anything but ephemeral. When you make a record it exists forever and it exists in space.[59]

Here Eno cuts to the core of a problem with which ethnomusicologists, scholars of popular music, and musicologists concerned with the performance of early music have begun to grapple during the last few decades. If, as Marshall McLuhan said, "the medium is the message," then when we are dealing with "music" in entirely different media—live, written, recorded—do we perhaps not need entirely different words for each medium, or different sets of concepts to understand what message is being presented in each case? Modern recording technology has developed to the point where the sound heard can be "larger than life," an intensification of reality, in the same sense that a Hollywood film, through quick cuts, panning, music, use of multiple locations, slow motion, color distortion or enhancement, and other techniques, presents a sequence of events to the viewer that are impossible to duplicate in a theater situation with live actors. Music teacher Andrew Buchman of Evergreen State College told an amusing anecdote at a conference I attended recently: one of his students, writing a report on a live concert, enthused that "the *sound* was great —almost CD quality!"

If Eno is wary of the ambiguities of language in ordinary speech and prose, it is precisely such ambiguities that he has attempted to exploit in his song lyrics. The idea that in terms of the conveyed meaning the sung word stands somewhere between the specificity of the spoken word and the abstract emotional language of music is not new, of course. In rock music, the first self-conscious experiments in the use of song lyrics for their purely phonetic and evocative qualities, rather than for their verbal meanings, were undertaken during the 1960s by Bob Dylan—many of whose songs, especially on his 1965–6 masterpieces *Bringing It All Back Home*, *Highway 61 Revisited*, and *Blonde on Blonde*, appeared to be chaotic jumbles of fantastic images without much connection to left-brain, linear, linguistic reality. The influence on Dylan of the French symbolist poets of the nineteenth century, Rimbaud in particular, and of the zen/beat poets of the 1950s, like Allen Ginsberg, was more than superficial: to Dylan, such poets offered a concept of the use of song quite different from the one that had been current in the world of popular song for over a century.[60]

After Dylan, almost anything was possible in rock lyrics, and songwriters, some under the influence of psychoactive drugs and the psychedelic movement of the late 1960s, poured out streams of unprocessed visual, sensuous, and conceptual imagery. John Lennon credited Dylan directly with showing the Beatles that song lyrics didn't have to make sense, and indeed the Beatles' lyrics after *Help* of 1965 took an entirely different direction. Lennon said, for instance, "You don't have to hear what Bob Dylan's saying, you just have to hear the way he says it."[61] Other rock groups and songwriters who explored the realms of free association and "meaninglessness" in their work included the Grateful Dead, the Jefferson Airplane, Jimi Hendrix, and Yes.[62]

It was after the psychedelic efflorescence had faded considerably, during the early 1970s, that Eno began writing and recording songs. Four of his solo albums between 1973 and 1977, *Here Come the Warm Jets*, *Taking Tiger Mountain (By Strategy)*, *Another Green World*, and *Before and After Science*, consist mostly of songs, with an occasional instrumental piece; since then he has written lyrics only rarely. Eno's lyrics stand directly in the tradition of painting with words in rock music that begins with Dylan and runs through the psychedelic songwriters of the late 1960s and early 1970s; and it was his lyrics, as much as his music, ideas, and personal image, that were behind the critical excitement that accompanied his appearance on the scene. But Eno stands apart from most of the songwriters of the era in the deliberation and rationality with which he approached his task. For him, presenting as art the unprocessed contents of consciousness and of the unconscious was not enough: there was a distinction to be made between the vision and the form in which it was presented, and the working-out of the form was as important as the vision itself.

Another important influence on Eno's concept of lyrics was the phonetic poetry of Hugo Ball, Kurt Schwitters, Ernst Jandl, and Richard Huelsenbeck. Shortly after getting out of art school, Eno went through a period of about six months during which he experimented with sequences of words selected solely for their phonetic, "musical" qualities, without any regard for their denotational or connotational meanings. He integrated his ideas about phonetic poetry with his experiments with tape recorders: phonetic poetry

> was the first musical area that I was interested in [as a composer/performer]. It was a kind of music in disguise, so I allowed myself to be interested in it. At the time I'd been listening to music for a long time, and since I couldn't play any instruments and could scarcely control my voice, I considered that I really didn't have a future in that area. . . . [Doing phonetic poetry] was important in that it started me using tape recorders in an interesting way because shortly after I had begun doing work with my own voice, I'd begun building up backing tracks of lots of other voices on top of which to do my poems, so that I was starting to work with multi-tracking if you like at that stage.[63]

In the song lyrics of his solo albums, Eno rarely indulges in pure phonetic poetry; rather, he treads a careful line between nonsense and sense, between connotation and denotation, between the explicit and the implicit. When, in 1985, he and John Cage were talking about their shared distaste for music that comes too heavily laden with intentions, Eno added, "I have the same feeling about lyrics. I just don't want to hear them most of the time. They always impose something that is so unmysterious compared to the sound of the music [that] they debase the music for me, in most cases."[64] This disinclination to deal with the concreteness of verbal meanings played a large part in Eno's turn away from songwriting after having finished *Before and After Science* in 1977.

The process of writing song lyrics has always been "peculiar and convoluted" for Eno; to write them at all he had to "trick" himself into doing it. He felt writing lyrics was embarrassing because of the way words can expose the mind's thoughts and feelings. To write words, he had to search for ways to throw the inner critical voice off guard:

> With the lyric writing, I tend to begin by just shouting to a backing track, gradually building up a system of syllable rhythm, then getting the kind of phonetics that I want and gradually beginning to fill in words to the types of sounds my voice is making at this stage. . . . It works from sound to words and from words to meaning, so it works quite the other way around from the way people normally think lyrics are written, I think.[65]

Eno used this "backwards" technique to write the lyrics to the songs on all of his solo progressive rock albums. He would very infrequently, if ever, begin to work on a song with any concrete idea of what it would be about in the verbal sense. "The lyrics are constructed as empirically as the music,"[66] as unselfconsciously as possible, with a "What would happen if . . . ?" attitude.

Eno has likened his lyric-writing process to "automatic writing, the way you scribble until words start to appear."[67] Frame of mind is all-important in this sort of creativity: while the negative critical judgment, or censor, which tends to inhibit the free play of musical and verbal association, must be turned off, positive judgment of other kinds must at some point be exercised to determine whether the words fit the music and have suitable musical colors in themselves, whether the words are indeed capable of evoking a rich enough fabric of meaning—whether, in short, the words are any good. In effect, Eno's lyric-writing technique represents a way of probing the unconscious mind, systematically mining it for images and meanings—meanings tied up with images that, once found, may still be somewhat obscure. Eno is not interested in trying to strip off the final layers of ambiguity; the final results of such a stripping might resemble the dream interpretations of psychoanalysis, and hence indeed have a pronounced "embarrassing" effect. Eno is content to give the listener the dream without the interpretation, the more so since this gives the *listener* the opportunity to be creative, through trying to work his or her own thoughts and emotions around the images presented. He said in 1981:

> It's as if you've discovered a very dusty inscribed stone somewhere, and you're trying to scrape off all the muck to find out what's underneath it, and you keep coming up with one word here, another one there, and you're trying to imagine what might be in between those words. So in that sense I'm in the same position as the listener. I'm looking for the meaning of it as well. The only temptation to resist is the temptation to fall into a simple meaning. It's a tantalizing process, you know?[68]

Eno's image of cleaning the dusty old stone in search of its inscription is strikingly reminiscent of analogies used in analytical psychology to describe the process of trying to discover the contents of the unconscious. A Jungian might amplify Eno's image by saying that such a stone was inscribed ages ago by a "civilization" with which we no longer have direct contact (the archetypes of the collective unconscious); the inscribed surface bears some message of great importance to us now, if we can only make it out. Eno may not find the whole message; some of the letters may be worn away with age, and he may have to fill in some of its words through guesswork. And he is not intent on *interpreting* the message in a personal way, at least not in public; he is content to let it speak for itself, for it might have a different meaning for different listeners.

Ultimately, this reluctance to actively interpret the contents of the unconscious, to risk the embarrassment that might accompany such interpretation, must be considered a limitation in Eno's song lyrics. His words, for all their ingenuity, evocative power, and phonetic sensibility, often lack the sense of real moral commitment that comes with the best rock lyrics, like those of Dylan or Lennon. Eno's lyrics are strong in their aesthetic impact, and occasionally in their mysterious, quasi-spiritual quality; they have less to say about the realm of the ethical, the realm of human realities and relationships. They are not so self-indulgent as some of the spacey cosmic tableaux of early psychedelia and later progressive rock, and yet one senses that Eno sometimes is indeed holding back too much, is perhaps *too* nervous about making a real statement. But at least he seems to be aware of his intentions, and his lyrics do accomplish what they set out to do, which is to force the listener to forge some kind of meaning out of them.

chapter 7

The Musician as Philosopher

The content of Eno's ideas and his consistently stylish, eloquent way of expressing them make him the most articulate theorist to emerge from the world of rock musicians. Along with all his other activities, he has devoted considerable time to reading. Considering his love of systems and his tendency to see things in abstract terms, it is no surprise to learn that his favorite books—books he not only reads but rereads—are about ideas: for instance, H. G. Barnett's *Innovation: The Basis of Cultural Change*, Gregory Bateson's *Steps to an Ecology of Mind*, Chogyam Trungpa's *Cutting through Spiritual Materialism*, and C. H. Waddington's *Towards a Theoretical Biology*.[1] Through such studies, Eno has linked himself to some of the most compelling trends in modern intellectual history.

ULTIMATE REALITIES

An interviewer asked Eno in 1981, "Do you think there's a God?" After pausing for a moment, he replied, "I don't ever use that word."[2] In spite of, or more likely because of, his Catholic background, Eno has systematically avoided using Christian mythology as a conceptual framework, at least in public. On the other hand, he has been open to certain oriental religious ideas. If he rejects the idea of God in the abstract, the idea of a spiritual aspect of life is not entirely foreign to his way of thinking:

> Spiritualism is not the promise of a better life but the highest level of discussion one entertains in life—an agreement to partake of a discussion of the largest and most difficult problems. My main problems are, "What is really happening? How inaccurate am I? How inadequate am I?" I realize my map doesn't fit the real world. Spiritualism is the agreement to deal with this problem.[3]

Eno characteristically poses the question of personal "inaccuracy" as a "spiritual" one. The tone of his language when discussing such matters is decidedly cool and detached. Indeed, "fervor" is a word that one would find singularly inadequate to describe most of Eno's music; the phrase he prefers, when considering his more agitated progressive rock music, is "idiot energy." Yet Eno has come close to expressing something similar to the conventional religious image of awakening to a greater reality:

> All the musical experiences that have had an important effect on me have prompted the same feeling, of being faced with this strange connection of familiarity and mystery embodied in the same source, as if a door has unlocked into a whole universe of feeling that exists somewhere deep inside. It's the feeling of being awake, rather than automatic. You get hooked on that feeling; everybody who has once felt it wants it for the rest of their lives.[4]

Eno's attachment to a religious viewpoint goes no further than this. He is decidedly unsuperstitious, and his philosophical stance in general is probably best described as that of a freethinking agnostic. In accordance with such a stance, he takes a curious yet cautious view of paranormal phenomena. When an adventurous interviewer asked him what he thought about flying saucers, Eno lamented the lack of a "serious investigation . . . that wasn't conducted by crackpots," and at the same time revealed that he had seen one as a child with his sister, and had written to her years later to confirm his memory:

> She wrote back and described it exactly as I had remembered it, so I figured that I had actually seen it unless we mutually manufactured this myth. So I'm prepared to believe in their existence, or in a phenomenon strong enough to create the impression of their existence in your head.[5]

If Christian philosophy and mythology have had little impact on the formulation of Eno's conscious and public world view, the impact of oriental ideas is pronounced and explicit, although he has apparently never made a systematic study of Eastern religions. He has mentioned repeatedly the childhood influence of his uncle Carl, who was a painter and gardener who had lived in India for about fifteen years, coming "back from the East with a number of very exotic theories about reincarnation and so on and so on which struck the Suffolk farmers as extremely odd." Eno was transfixed by Uncle Carl's tales; they gave him "an impression of how strange the world was outside our small town."[6]

Reading Cage's *Silence* also contributed to his growing awareness of Asian ideas. In 1986, Eno spoke of his interest in "the Chinese point of view," and of its direct impact on the way he works. He singled out two of its aspects as being particularly important to him. The first is the idea "that every moment is a concatenation of hundreds of forces which just meet at that instant, and will never come together in the same way again—synchronicity."[7] In much of his ambient music, but especially in his audiovisual installations of the 1980s, this concept is given a direct artistic embodiment, with multiple tape-loops of different lengths running simultaneously, never overlapping in precisely the same way twice, and producing a series of unique moments or events. The second is the Eastern view of the passage of time:

Our mental model is that we look *into* the future; the past is behind us. I was told that the Chinese see things quite differently: they look at the past, and the future washes over them, which seems to me to be much more sensible. There's a kind of peacefulness in that attitude that I appreciate. You're standing in one place, or treading water in one place, and meanwhile the drift of things is coming past you from behind. As the events recede, they cluster into bigger groups and become generalities, so you have this nice transition of specific events to a background of generalities.[8]

Again, this philosophical point of view has found musical expression, particularly in the solo album, *On Land*, of 1982.

Eno's interest in cybernetics was the focus of his article, "Generating and Organizing Variety in the Arts." In the context of another discussion of cybernetics, Eno dismissed two other twentieth-century Western disciplines or practices as being of little use to him. Cybernetics, which acknowledges the complexity of systems, points (as does quantum theory) toward certain classes of results, rather than toward specific outcomes; and "in that sense it's an inexact science, and it's the first inexact science that actually can do something. As far as I'm concerned, those other ones, like sociology and psychology, are *very* inexact and they really don't seem to work."[9]

Eno has made a number of intriguing remarks that can be grouped loosely together under the rubric of epistemology—remarks that reveal his curiosity about the nature of knowledge. One concerns a hierarchical concept which he uses to explain the creative process:

Ideas are the result of meta-ideas, which are the result of meta-meta-ideas. I sometimes think I could put together all the ideas I've ever had that led to interesting things in about 20 seconds. . . . An idea can generate a host of other ideas, which in turn will generate a host of pieces of work.[10]

In musical terms, Eno's meta-meta-ideas have been two: a certain approach to rock music involving harnessing of his "idiot energy," and a certain approach to musical materials that resulted in the creation of the ambient style. Each of his solo albums springs from one of these, and can be seen as revolving around a meta-idea—a specific approach to specific problems of style, of group organization, of musical theory and presentation.

The limits of understanding are acknowledged by Eno in his rephrasing of a Socratic aphorism: "You can never understand anything totally. But when you begin to understand something, you realise how much more there is that you don't understand."[11] The context for this remark was his close study of paintings of Ron Kitaj. Reading criticism of the paintings, Eno said, had not lessened his appreciation of the painter's work; on the contrary, he found it more fascinating the more he learned about it. A final facet of Eno's thinking about knowledge is the idea that one's sum total of knowledge remains the same, as if one had a maximum available at any given moment, though its contents might shift:

> Luis Buñuel said that in a film every object obscures another object. That's a great maxim for me. I have another version of that: Every increase in your knowledge is a simultaneous decrease. You learn and unlearn at the same time. A new certainty is a new doubt as well.[12]

CULTURE AND INFORMATION

Since the early 1980s, Eno has been preoccupied with working out a theory of "culture as a system of knowledge . . . as a system of evolution in the same way that you might talk about genetics as a system of evolution. . . . But since this is practically all I ever think about, since it occupies practically all of my serious thinking time, I don't have any simple comments about it."[13] He mentioned in 1981 that he hopes to publish this theory in one form or another, but as yet all we have is a handful of typically Enoesque, thought-provoking fragments. He sees all human culture as a system for the transfer of information, directly analogous to genetics, in the sense that "all creatures transmit information about their environment genetically."

> Culture is all human behaviour, outside of pure instinct. Everything we do is cultural: gardening, cooking, different fashions, architecture.
> What artists do a lot, in music in particular, is look at culture in the world. Music doesn't depict something, it's about other music. So quite a lot of the business of "culture merchants" like myself is studying how culture works—how it changes and how it changes us.[14]

One view of the history of culture, and of specific art forms such as music, holds that the primary role of the creative artist is to innovate, the result being a sort of linear progress or evolution in what one hopes is a positive direction. Eno finds this view old-fashioned and outmoded. The artist, according to Eno,

> "re-mixes"—he *perpetuates* a great body of received cultural and stylistic assumptions, he *re-evaluates* and re-introduces certain ideas no longer current, and then he also innovates. But the "innovation" part might be a much smaller proportion than we usually think. Consequently, I started to suspect that the palette of the painter or artist was incredibly broad—that it was the whole history of art. There's nothing linear about evolution at all: it is a process of trying to stay in the same place, of trying to maintain an identity in a changing landscape.[15]

All of this is strikingly reminiscent of Leonard B. Meyer's interpretation of twentieth-century music as having entered a period of stasis, following centuries of what was perceived as evolution.[16] In fact, Eno's musical career itself can be seen as a first-rate example of Meyerian stasis in microcosm: many kinds of music and ideas *exist* and are available to him as a composer, and although people change and their interests shift, the effort to define their development in terms of evolutionary steps is not especially relevant.

The Masculine and the Feminine

During the last few decades Western society seems to have undergone a profound change in sexual orientation in the broadest sense. We are familiar enough with many of the outward manifestations of this change: the liberation movements of the 1960s and 1970s, when traditional attitudes toward sexual relationships shifted dramatically; the decay of the institution of marriage; the rise of movements dedicated to the acceptance of homosexuality; and, in general, the questioning of very old and ingrained socio-sexual roles, with more women than ever before entering the labor force and (perhaps) more men than ever before taking on aspects of the traditional female roles of domestic responsibility and nurturing. Some of the most incisive insights into these changes come from Jungian psychologists such as Edward Whitmont, who in his challenging book, *Return of the Goddess*, argues, through interpretation of past and present cultural symbols, that the age-old myth of the supremacy of the male deity (representing the triumph of [male] consciousness and will over [female] unconsciousness and instinct), is losing its ability to guide mankind's collective fate in the age of science and the thermonuclear bomb.[17] The last few years have seen the inevitable swing of the pendulum: a conservative backlash seems to be gaining ground, with calls for renewed commitment to traditional family values and sexual mores; yet it seems clear that during the decades and centuries ahead, new masculine and feminine roles will have to be forged and taken on by men and women in order for society to attain a new psychic balance and indeed to avert the catastrophes bound to occur when a society continues to live by a myth that is no longer supported by reality.

The role of rock music in contemporary sexual politics is not easy to summarize, since it is played out on many levels. The rise of rock and roll in the 1950s was seen by moralizing critics from the right as a threat to traditional values: the physical movements of the some of the performers were notoriously suggestive ("Elvis the Pelvis"); the lyrics to some of the songs were openly provocative about sex, not euphemistic and sentimental as they had been during the era of Broadway and Tin Pan Alley; the music was loud, hypnotic, and mesmerizing, supposedly encouraging teenagers to lower their conscious defenses; and even the term "rock and roll" itself was taken from a black slang expression for the sex act.

Since those early and, in retrospect, seemingly innocent times, popular music has been the forum for the testing-out of many different sexual self-images, even if the dominant image continues even today to be that of the macho male youth, or "cock-rocker," to borrow an expression from Simon Frith.[18] The 1960s saw the "girl-group" phenomenon (which Barbara Bradby has argued was *not* merely a cover for male pop creativity and marketing strategies),[19] and also the cosmic androgyny of the hippie movement and acid rock, in which fashions of dress and of music were nearly interchangeable between the genders; the 1970s saw the emergence of the "sensitive" male singer/songwriter, epitomized by James Taylor, as well as various female roles, from the acute musical intelligence of Joni Mitchell to the 'wildly visionary, proto-punk posturings of Patti Smith, who didn't bother to change the gender of the person she was forcibly to seduce in singing Van Morrison's "Gloria" on her 1975 *Horses* LP. In the 1970s and 1980s the women's movement found in song an outlet for the expression of new modes of femininity, notably through singer-songwriters like Holly Near.

In the early 1970s one of the most radical of all sexual images surfaced in England—that of the totally feminized male. Stars like David Bowie, Elton John, and Marc Bolan (of T. Rex) appeared onstage and on album covers in partially or completely feminine attire, or at least in the attire of a particular male fantasy-image of the female. In the whirlwind of dyed hair, exaggerated makeup, platform shoes, and glittery costumes, "glam rock" seemed pointedly to question male identity. How much of this was truly significant role-questioning at a deep collective level, and how much was simply "the latest fashion fad, encouraging an escape from immediate concerns and obvious commitment," is an issue that has been probed by Iain Chambers, the writer who probably more than any other has focused on the connotational importance of visual aspects of rock performance.[20]

It is against the backdrop of glam rock that we may situate the androgynous public image Eno presented to the public in his work with Roxy Music and subsequent onstage appearances during the early 1970s. According to Eno, that image resulted in part from "a deliberate decision by all of us to dress interestingly as well as to be aurally interesting."[21] In a sense, Eno was simply in the right place at the right time, able to capitalize on his image's shock effect for publicity purposes while "glam" was at its peak. But, at the same time, there is no reason to doubt the sincerity of his subsequent explanations of why he wore such things as lipstick and mascara, peacock and ostrich plumes, leopardskin shirts, and a soft beret over cascading blond locks. In 1978, after the release of his solo album *Before and After Science*, he discussed the matter not only in terms of artistic self-expression but in terms of probing the essence of life through the archetypal duality of the masculine and the feminine:

> The conditions before and after science are identical in terms of how people will relate to each other. McLuhan's global village and tribal village are the same thing. Right now, although you may have your personal oases of before or after science, the world is in science. I use that word in a limited sense: deification of rational knowledge. . . . Before I ever joined Roxy, I got interested in wearing clothing that would have been considered effeminate. I didn't like masculine

clothes. The Western version of masculinity opposes rational man against intuitive woman. The part of my being that interests me has always been my intuition. . . . I don't bother to question my intuition. If I feel like doing something, I do it, and figure that I'll understand it later. If I had questioned my intuition, I would probably be a bank clerk. In any person's life, the most important decisions are indefensible.[22]

Paradoxically, Eno's visual persona changed from "feminine" to "masculine" during the same period around 1975 that his musical style underwent a marked shift from "masculine" to "feminine" values. Since that period he has kept his thinning hair relatively short, and has been photographed in utterly "male" jeans and slacks, T-shirts and sneakers or sandals. His disarmingly normal appearance may be indeed motivated, as one writer has suggested, by a desire "to enjoy the thrill of anonymity."[23] But whereas his work with Roxy Music and on his first three solo albums utilized, at least to a considerable extent, the arguably masculine musical qualities of a thrusting, pulsating rock beat, and a dynamic level that was frequently aggressive and even strident, since his 1975 album *Discreet Music* Eno's solo music has embraced and embodied the more feminine qualities of containment, being, and spaciousness.

Eno has been explicitly aware of the change. An interviewer asked him in 1981 whether he thought *Discreet Music*, *Music for Airports*, and *Music for Healing* (an album that was never released) contained "unmasculine music." He responded, "I think it's pretty bisexual, that's what I think." The interviewer pressed on: "Do you feel like you're moving even further into the feminine area?" Eno said:

These are interesting questions. My own perspective on what I do is that my work started out as being very distinctively masculine. My look was ahead of the music. Then the music moved away from that position. I'm now working in the opposite direction of just cramming the song with thrills, sharp or harsh things. I'm trying to get *rid* of things now. Every event either obscures another event or obscures silence, so you may as well leave as much out of everything as you can.[24]

POLITICS

Eno has never been a political musician in the sense of someone who believes in and tries to put across in music a certain specific program for social change. Even his solo album *Taking Tiger Mountain (By Strategy)*, which is loosely based on a set of picture-postcards of a Chinese revolutionary drama, is not so much a political statement as it is an aesthetic response to a strange, exotic culture—reminiscent of Debussy's pentatonic *chinoiserie* in "Pagodas" and other works. As we have seen, Eno was attracted to Cardew's experimental piece "The Great Learning"; but Cardew's later, more overtly political music left him nonplussed: "My personal opinion is that the Maoist thing for him is a very big mistake, and it significantly reduced his music." When musicians become overtly political, according to Eno, they inevitably begin relying too heavily on language, which is in effect a denial of their real mission.

> Normally, when people become politically conscious in the way that Cardew did, they . . . say, "The job of the artist is to radicalize society," for example, and they say, "How do you do that?" And so then they start thinking, "Well, you do it by this and this and this"—and suddenly, the music becomes like an advertisement for a doctrine.[25]

Eno believes that "serious political change is always personal."[26] In spite of his enthusiastic work with punk and new wave groups during the late 1970s and 1980s (and most recently with U2), Eno rejects the more aggressive political overtones of those movements. In 1982, he criticized "post-new-wave" music for its excessively narrow view of human experience, and in so doing directed a barb or two at Marxist sociologists of rock:

> It's such an outmoded view, that grows out of that Western academic idea of reducing everything to economics. There is this terrible spurious socialism that affects so many groups but the music actually belongs to another political stand-point altogether—it's almost a thuggish, power, *me, me* position which is the real politics of that music, the real message.
> To me, my decision to work in the way I do has political resonances. The decision to stop seeing yourself as the centre of the world, to see yourself as part of the greater flow of things, as having limited options and responsibility for your actions—the converse of that "me" generation, "do your own thing" idea—that is political theory: and it's what the music grows from.[27]

Eno puts little store in the dominant contemporary ideology of materialism and acquisitiveness. When an interviewer posed the unwieldy question, "What's the most overrated idea currently held by western culture?," Eno responded:

> Oh god. Well, in my opinion it's the idea of the free individual. That's a very overrated aspiration and American society is full of its symptoms. There's a very limited sense in which people differ from one another and those differences seem to me to be fairly superficial. There are many more ways in which people are similar but the whole accent of this culture has been to stress those differences and understress the similarities. People are encouraged to want their own this and their own that, and led to believe that those external things are all attributes of their individuality and they aren't complete without them. And such is the basis of a consumer culture.[28]

For the most part, specifically political issues are avoided in Eno interviews; when they come up, Eno is liable to put them into some much broader context, or, occasionally, to take a point of view that is detached almost to the point of being chilling. He showed interviewer Frank Rose a scrapbook of newspaper clippings he had been keeping; one headline read "The War of the Satellites: Pentagon Is Developing Defense Measures Against Soviet Hunter-Killer Space-craft." This "sets him off," according to Rose, "on a 15-minute discussion in which he terms the idea of ritual wars in space involving unmanned craft 'quite interesting.' "[29] Taken out of context, such a remark gives an impression that Eno did not likely intend, but it is not difficult to guess what he found intriguing about the prospect of Star Wars: space exploration itself, to which his 1982 album *Apollo: Atmospheres & Soundtracks* is a tribute; the idea of interaction between vast, impersonal, computerized systems which are likely to produce completely unexpected results; and the idea of ritualized conflict itself, which he had probed, albeit obliquely, in *Taking Tiger Mountain (By Strategy)*. Eno is constantly seeking underlying patterns and principles to gain perspective on the facts and occurrences of human and nonhuman existence.

METAPHORS AND IMAGES

In the foregoing I have attempted to sum up some of Eno's ideas on a variety of subjects, in order to demonstrate the broad scope and content of his world view. The style of his verbal discourse frequently relies on metaphor and simile—and on sometimes fanciful, sometimes profound conceptions of cross-connections between diverse fields of knowledge and experience.

Eno has acknowledged on several occasions that he is more inclined to think in visual or spatial terms than in a strict linear fashion. We have already seen how he thinks of his creative products as ultimately stemming from a few "meta-ideas," which in turn spring from a very few "meta-meta-ideas," in a sort of hierarchical web or matrix. He has been known to doodle incessantly while being interviewed, often producing diagrams that he believes express his thinking better than linearly ordered sentences. He has filled volumes of notebooks with diagrams, sketches, lists, tables, ideas, expressions, and what he calls "amateur mathematics." Reproductions of a number of these notebook pages were published in 1986,[30] and he has occasionally hinted that he would like to assemble a collection of his sketches, ideas, lectures, fragments, and graphs into a book intended to be read not from beginning to end but by choosing various possible "pathways" from one section to another.

A particularly good example of the way in which visual and spatial images and patterns compose the substance of Eno's way of thinking is provided by his account of walking past "an enormous rubber plantation in Malaysia":

> It was a chaos of trees, thousands of them. I thought it strange that they should be planted so randomly. Then I reached a point where I realized they were in absolutely straight rows. Only at one point could I see that.
>
> Particular ideas create a point of view that organizes something that, from any

other angle, is chaotic. The same is true of memories. You think of your past as a kind of jungle. Suddenly you'll have what I call a crack in time, where you can see right through the gap to the field at the other end.[31]

Eno has used an elaborate visual metaphor to illustrate the contrast between the mechanical noises frequently produced by musicians using synthesizers and the kinds of sounds he tries to draw out of them. The typical sounds produced by synthesizers, he says, are like the synthetic designer material formica: elegant from a distance, but rather boring and regular from close up. Acoustic instrumental sounds, and synthesized sounds properly treated, are more like a forest, which is beautiful and complex at any degree of magnification: viewed from miles above; from the level of the treetops; each individual tree and leaf; and the microscopic, molecular structure of the plants themselves. "The thing permits you any level of scrutiny. And more and more, I want to make things that have that same quality . . . things that allow you to enter into them as far as you could imagine going, yet don't suddenly reveal themselves to be composed of paper-thin, synthetic materials."[32] Indeed, one of the things that distinguishes Eno's best ambient music from the vast majority of superficially similar electronically-based pieces in the "space music" genre is precisely this sense of depth and complexity at any number of audible structural levels. (We shall return to this point in Chapter 10.)

Another striking and even more extended metaphor is what has been called Eno's "hologram theory of music." He begins by describing Samuel Beckett's *Company*, a book about ninety pages long and printed in very large type. In typical Beckett style, *Company* contains a few phrases that are endlessly repeated, permutated, said over and over again in slightly different ways. "Once you've seen the first two pages, you've effectively read the entire book." This reminded Eno of the Catholic doctrine he learned in school, to the effect that the host—the bread wafer received at Holy Communion—"could be broken into any number of minute parts and . . . each part was still the complete body of Jesus Christ." Later Eno learned about holograms, the specially engineered plates that reproduce a three-dimensional image. Holograms, he discovered, were a concrete, physical analog to the doctrine of the host, for when a hologram is shattered, each piece still contains an image of the whole, though it is indistinct and fuzzy. He observed something of the same phenomenon in his study of a series of Cézanne paintings: "You could take a square inch of one of those Cézanne paintings and somehow there was the same intensity and feeling and style within that one piece as there was within the whole picture." Eno's conclusion from all these observations was simple, yet it has affected much of his music: "I thought, this is really how I want to work from now on. I don't want to just fill in spaces anymore. . . . I want to be alive every stage of doing any project.[33]

Eno relied on a more down-to-earth metaphor in responding to an interviewer who said to him, "As somebody who is so frequently 'borrowed from,' I would think you'd have mixed feelings about new artists doing something that really isn't new art":

> I think of it as compost. If you think of culture as a great big garden, it has to have its compost as well. And lots of people are doing things that are . . . not dramatic or radical or not even particularly interesting; they're just digestive processes. It's places where a number of little things are being combined and tried out. It's like members of a population. We're all little different turns of the same genetic dice. If you think about music in that way, it makes it much easier to accept that there might be lots of things you might not want to hear again. They happen and they pass and they become the compost for something else to grow from. [Laughs.] Gardening is such a good lesson for all sorts of things.[34]

Another image which Eno has drawn upon in explicating his ideas is that of a surfer riding the waves:

> I don't just want to see a good idea or a clever use of materials. One of the motives for being an artist is to recreate a condition where you're actually out of your depth, where you're uncertain, no longer controlling yourself, yet you're generating something, like surfing as opposed to digging a tunnel. Tunnel-digging activity is necessary, but what artists like, if they still like what they're doing, is the surfing.[35]

The image of the surfer resonates with Eno's creative philosophy of "riding on the dynamics of the system" as opposed to making up rigid theories and taking ineffectual actions in attempts to control.

part II

Eno's Music

8 Taking Rock to the Limit

Although the varieties of rock are legion, certain musical characteristics remain more or less constant. Among these are: song forms deriving largely from blues and the American popular song tradition; a melodic technique most often based on short phrases of text whose musical embodiment is intimately matched with the natural cadences of speech; a harmonic idiom based on the traditional major/minor tonal system in terms of chord content (but not necessarily in terms of chord progressions); and a complex of rhythmic archetypes in which 4/4 meter with displaced accents (on beats two and four instead of one and three) predominates. Rock is also based on a set of textural norms involving a prominent vocal line with an accompaniment in which electric bass and drum kit are indispensable, electric and/or acoustic guitars are nearly indispensable, and other instruments such as keyboards (acoustic and electric piano, organ, synthesizer, and other electronic keyboards such as the mellotron), brass, woodwinds, and assorted percussion, are prevalent but not indispensable. In musical terms, the most important style characteristic for determining whether a piece is or is not "rock" is the instrumental format in conjuction with a set of musical patterns set up by the rhythm section of drums, bass, and guitar. To "rock" a piece of classical music, it usually suffices simply to add a rock rhythm section to the tune. Conversely, a rock piece can be "classicized" or "de-rocked" by re-orchestrating it and subtracting the rhythm section, as is frequently done in canned music.

If rock music is thus seen not as a genre determined by the demographics of record consumption, the verbal content of the songs, or the political stance of the musicians, but is seen rather as a complex of musical style characteristics, how far can those characteristics be diluted or extended before the music ceases to be rock? Many answers to this question have been proposed, not in abstract musicological terms, of course, but in actual pieces of music.

A number of rock's leading musicians have taken rock to the limit, only to pull back to more traditional positions. During their most innovative period, from *Rubber Soul* to *Magical Mystery Tour* (or roughly 1965–67), the Beatles extended the musical definition of rock through their textural experimentation, drawing freely on the instrumental resources not only of the rock and jazz traditions, but of Western classical music, Indian music, and electronic music; in later efforts such as the 1968 "white album," *The Beatles*, they largely abandoned such non-rock trappings in favor of a back-to-basics approach. The Rolling Stones' development followed a similar path, their pinnacle of experimentation being reached in *Their Satanic Majesties' Request* of 1967 and in *Beggar's Banquet* of the following year. Throughout their entire subsequent career, the Stones drew back into the rock mainstream and reaffirmed its attendant stylistic norms. The progressive rock group Yes, adding synthesizers and expanding rock's harmonic palette beyond most previous limits, broke out of rock's formal conventions with compositions like the nineteen-minute "Close to the Edge" of 1972; when Yes regrouped in the 1980s, however, it was with a more frankly commercial sound operating within considerably streamlined formal dimensions.

Many groups have extended the language of rock by attempting a fusion of genres, notably jazz and rock. Blood, Sweat & Tears and Chicago approached such a fusion from the direction of rock, while Miles Davis, Herbie Hancock, and Chick Corea approached it from the direction of jazz. A few remarkable musicians, such as Frank Zappa and Robert Fripp, have made repeated forays beyond the bounds of rock styles, but they have tended to return to rock as if it were a relatively stable home base.

Eno, on the other hand, is among the few prominent musicians from a rock background who has taken rock to its stylistic limits, gone beyond them, and stayed beyond. His last major solo effort in a rock-related style was in 1981, when he made the strange, unique album *My Life in the Bush of Ghosts* with David Byrne—an album that owes at least as much to Eno's assimilation of world music influences as it does to rock proper. Up to that point, Eno had worked with essentially two musical types, progressive rock and the ambient style, moving back and forth between them for individual projects, or, in a number of highly interesting experiments, combining elements of the two; since 1981, his solo music has been strictly ambient. In this chapter and the following ones we shall examine Eno's progressive rock and ambient music in turn, concentrating on those albums in which Eno is listed as the primary composer or co-composer.[1]

The Albums

For his first solo album, *Here Come the Warm Jets* (1973), Eno brought some sixteen musicians into the studio (several of whom he had worked with previously) and assembled a set of ten songs that in some respects were derivative, in some respects were experimental, and in other ways strikingly anticipated developments in the punk and new wave rock of the late 1970s. The album's title turned out to be a poetic reference to urination. The credits, which, as on all of Eno's progressive rock records, meticulously list who played what on which tracks,[2] note that "Eno sings . . . and (occasionally) plays simplistic keyboards, snake guitar, electric larynx and synthesizer, and treats the other instruments." "Snake guitar" and "electric larynx" are the first of many such whimsical terms that Eno coined to describe given sounds either by their timbral character or their means of production. Although the songs are composed by Eno, Eno/Manzanera, Eno/Fripp, and Eno (arr. Thompson/Jones/ Judd/Eno), Eno was the controlling force behind the album's creation, as well as its producer. In the music of *Here Come the Warm Jets*, references, probably both intentional and unintentional, to the history of rock abound: in Eno's vocal style, which in some songs is directly modeled on the idiosyncrasies of Roxy Music's Bryan Ferry; in the standard formal outlines and harmonic structure of many of the songs; and in specific sound types such as the neo-'50s tinkling piano and falsetto "ahs" of "Cindy Tells Me" or the characteristic drum rhythms of "Blank Frank" (modeled on Bo Diddley's classic "Who Do You Love" which had been covered by several groups). Eno's own musical personality emerges, however, in the highly varied uses of texture and instrumentation, in the formal experimentation (for instance, in "On Some Faraway Beach," in which the vocal melody enters, tacked on almost as an afterthought, only after several minutes of an instrumental set of variations), and in the special attention paid to timbre (as in the hymn-like vocal and electronic keyboard sonorities of "Some of Them Are Old"). All in all, *Here Come the Warm Jets* is refined ore from the same vein of quirky, intentionally mannered progressive rock mined by groups like Roxy Music and Gentle Giant.

Here Come the Warm Jets was recorded in twelve days, a short span of time by modern studio standards. Eno's role was as much instigator and manipulator as composer. Describing his studio technique at the time, he said that he listened to what the musicians were playing (the chord and rhythm changes presumably having been established beforehand), and "then I'll take what they're doing and say, 'What position does this put me in?,' and 'how can I justify the musical idea to suit?'"[3] With his progressive rock albums, Eno was interested in assembling

> groups of musicians because they're incompatible and not because they're compatible. I'm only interested in working, really, with people I don't agree with or who have a different direction. Particularly on *Here Come the Warm Jets*—I assembled musicians who normally wouldn't work together in any real-life situation. And I got them together merely because I wanted to see what happens when you combine different identities like that and you allow them to compete. My role is to coordinate them, synthesize them, furnish the central issue which they all will revolve around, producing a hybrid. . . . [The situation] is organized with the knowledge that there might be accidents, accidents which will be more interesting than what I had intended.[4]

So much, it would seem, for the overriding authority and pre-existence of a definite compositional intent. Albums like *Here Come the Warm Jets* are somewhat like group improvisation within certain limits. Or, to put it metaphorically, the residues of the group improvisation furnish the block of marble whose properties—grain, shape, size—Eno the sculptor then contemplates and carves out according to an empirically-derived idea of what the end result should look like—though this process itself is subject to change at any stage. Eno's actual role in the making of albums like *Here Come the Warm Jets* was thus obviously not that of the traditional composer, who conceives and writes out a score from which parts are transcribed and which musicians then play, or even that of the popular songwriter, who is often less concerned with arrangement, performance, and recording than simply with crafting melody and harmony. Eno's role was somewhat paradoxical: although he retained complete artistic control over the final product, he was at pains not to suppress the spontaneous creativity of his musicians.

What did Eno actually tell or ask his musicians to play? Apparently he gave them verbal suggestions, often with the help of visual images or body language. "I dance a bit, to describe what sort of movement it ought to make in you, and I've found that's a very good way of talking to musicians. Particularly bass players, because they tend to be into the swirling hips."[5] Many if not most rock musicians, in the absence of a written, notated form of communication, get their ideas across to each other through body language, singing, making other kinds of percussive and pitched noises, and through mixtures of verbal and nonverbal communication. Eno is particularly adept at this kind of thing, on the receiving end as well as the giving.

After the actual work of collective or individual recording was done and stored on twenty-four-track tape, Eno himself carried out a further process of mixing, refinement, and condensation, frequently giving form to a piece that bore little resemblance to what the musicians heard themselves play in the studio. Eno arrived at the lyrics to most of the songs on *Here Come the Warm Jets* through the process described in Chapter 6, playing back the backing tracks, singing whatever nonsense syllables came into his mind, and eventually working these syllables or phonetic motives taken from them into actual words and phrases.

Reviews of *Here Come the Warm Jets* were for the most part favorable. Lester Bangs called the record "incredible" and stressed Eno's penchant for the bizarre and avant-garde, as did most reviewers.[6] Robert Christgau gave the record a "B plus."[7] Ed Naha honored it by making it one of *Circus* magazine's "Picks of the Month," and wrote: "Dwelling in an eerie realm fluctuating somewhere between [Walt Disney's] *Fantasia* and early Sixties British pop, Eno dabbles in a musical world untouched by human hands . . . so far, anyhow."[8] The editors of *Rolling Stone* had Cynthia Dagnal write a feature article on Eno; she called the album "a very compelling experiment in controlled chaos and by his own self-dictated standards a near success."[9] A month later, however, Gordon Fletcher, reviewing *Jets* in the "Records" section of the same magazine, sounded one of the few sour notes in the general acclaim for Eno's approach and results. Eno, he wrote,

> writes weird songs but their weirdness is more silly than puzzling. Lacking any mentionable instrumental proficiency, he claims he "treats" other musicians' instruments—though the end product of his efforts would have to be classed as indiscernible. His record is annoying because it doesn't do anything. . . . In fact the whole album may be described as tepid, and the listener must kick himself for blowing five bucks on baloney.[10]

Using a core band of five instrumentalists (keyboards, guitars, bass, drums, and percussion), *Taking Tiger Mountain (By Strategy)* of 1974 further explores the stylistic territory mapped out by *Here Come the Warm Jets:* sharply etched, texturally varied, imaginatively produced rock songs with lyrics full of wordplay, irony, and half-emerging meanings. Although Eno may never have had a gift for writing the popular song hook (if record sales are any indication), his melodies here are well-crafted, perfectly matched to the rhythms of the lyrics, and they vary sufficiently between stepwise directional motion, jumpy leaps, and "recitation tone" delivery to offset the increasingly bland color of his voice and the narrowness of its dynamic range. The overall impression given by the collection of ten songs on *Tiger Mountain* is of a conventional rock idiom, but with everything slightly off-center: in one song it might be a stripped-down minimalistic texture with a lot of space between the notes; in another, a guitar timbre that has been electronically treated to give it a peculiar, exotic tone quality; in another, a vocal part delivered deadpan in Eno's colorless low register; in another, the scratchy, out-of-tune string section of the Portsmouth Sinfonia. In the middle of "The Great Pretender," the last song on Side One, an electronically produced chorus of chirping crickets enters and remains sounding all the way into the wind-off grooves, after the rest of the music has faded out. Thus, whereas certain elements of the album's music—form, harmony, melody, rhythm, and instrumentation—remain rooted in rock conventions, other elements—most notably texture and timbre—become vehicles for experiments in sound.

Eno had come across a set of colorful picture postcards depicting scenes from the Maoist revolutionary drama "Taking Tiger Mountain by Strategy," and was captivated by the evocativeness of the title:

> I nearly always work from ideas rather than sounds. . . . I'm not Maoist or any of that; if anything I'm anti-Maoist. Strategy interests me because it deals with the interaction of systems, which is what my interest in music is really, and not so much the interaction of sounds. One of the recurrent themes of rock music is a preoccupation with new dances. And it's taken by intellectuals as the lowest form of rock music, the most base and crude. So I was interested in combining

that very naïve and crude form of basic expression with an extremely complex concept like "Tiger Mountain."[11]

The combination of elements works only on a very abstract level; there are a few references to China in the lyrics, notably in the song "China My China," but only very considerable reading between the lines could make this record a statement about China or Maoism. The song "Taking Tiger Mountain" itself is almost completely instrumental, and the lyrics consist of a single verse, "We climbed and we climbed / Oh how we climbed / Over the stars to top Tiger Mountain / Forcing the lines to the snow." Eno explained his idea of what the album's title meant:

> It typifies the dichotomy between the archaic and the progressive. Half *Taking Tiger Mountain*—that Middle Ages physical feel of storming a military position —and half *(By Strategy)*—that very, very 20th-century mental concept of a tactical interaction of systems.[12]

Tiger Mountain received even more attention in the rock press than had the previous year's *Here Come the Warm Jets*, and once again most notices were highly favorable. Robert Christgau upgraded his estimation of Eno's efforts to an "A," writing that "for all its synthesized, metronome androidism, Eno's music is more humane than [Roxy Music leader] Bryan Ferry's . . . and it's nice that in his arch, mellow way the man (or even android) is willing to hide some politics behind the overdubs."[13] Henry Edwards called the album "a gleeful combination of wit and insanity,"[14] while Pete Matthews enthusiastically played up its conceptual nature.[15] A reviewer in *Circus* magazine wrote: "Sick! Sick! Sick! But, oh-h-h, it feels so good! . . . guaranteed to be put on the 'Most Wanted' list by psychopaths everywhere. . . . [Eno] takes you on a dada-ist's musical tour-de-force, lampooning and integrating every type of music conceivable."[16] Wayne Robins, while vacillating a bit in his judgment of Eno's eclecticism, wrote that "the future is a sonic Disney named Eno, who makes music you can live with."[17] Ed Naha found *Tiger Mountain* disappointing compared to *Here Come the Warm Jets:* "Much of the Wonderlandish magic found on Eno's first LP is lost on this rocky terrain, being replaced by a dull, repetitive aura that is annoying as all hell."[18]

Eno's next solo album, *Another Green World* (1975), is his progressive rock masterpiece, and, appropriately, it is the first album on which he is listed as composer of all the pieces. The sequence of tracks is carefully planned, the album being distinctly divided into two halves, with Side One representing the timbral and textural manipulations of Eno's previous solo work carried to new heights, and with Side Two consisting of slower, sometimes virtually pulseless, softer-edged music that hints strongly at the decisive step Eno was to take in his next solo album, the ambient *Discreet Music.*

Another Green World represents a turning point in Brian Eno's career and compositional output. His previous solo albums had contained songs in a quirky, idiosyncratic progressive rock idiom in which the lyrics and vocal delivery, however thoroughly they were worked into the total texture, remained the prime focus of interest. In *Another Green World*, by contrast, only five of the total of fourteen pieces have lyrics at all; of the nine that do not, seven are pieces in which Eno himself plays all the instruments, predominantly electronic and non-electronic keyboards, guitars, and percussion. These instrumental pieces tentatively explore a new kind of sound world that is quiet and restful, forming a bridge between Eno's earlier progressive rock songs and his later, wordless works in which texture and timbre are the most important musical elements. Later, in 1983, Eno acknowledged the transitional nature of *Another Green World* in the following terms:

> The idea of making music that in some way related to a sense of place—landscape or environment—had occurred to me many times over the last 12 years. My conscious exploration of this way of thinking about music probably began with *Another Green World* in 1975. Since then I have become interested in exaggerating and inventing rather than replicating spaces, and experimenting with various techniques of time distortion.[19]

One could characterize *Another Green World* as a "concept album" in the sense that it presents a sequence of pieces clearly arranged with a view to the whole. Side One is the rock side, with several songs having the straightforward rhythmic accents and overall sonorities of the popular rock song; Side Two, on which only two pieces have lyrics, is the more thoroughly experimental: drums are entirely lacking, tempos are slower, the pulse is sometimes nonexistent, and the prevailing mixed sonorities follow no rock conventions.

Another Green World was recorded at Island Studios in London during July and August of 1975. As on Eno's other solo albums, the backup musicians were friends of Eno, and every piece uses a different combination of instruments. Instrumental credits are conscientiously listed for each track. Phil Collins plays drums and percussion; Percy Jones plays fretless bass; Paul Rudolph plays "anchor bass," snare drums, "assistant castanet guitars," and guitar; Rod Melvin plays Rhodes piano and acoustic piano; John Cale plays viola and "viola section"; Robert Fripp is credited with "Wimshurst guitar," "restrained lead guitar," and "Wimborne guitar"; Brian Turrington plays bass guitar and pianos; and Eno himself plays synthesizer, "snake guitar," "digital guitar," "desert guitars," "castanet guitars," "chord piano," tape, Farfisa organ, Hammond organ, Yamaha bass pedals, synthetic percussion, treated rhythm generator, "Peruvian percussion," "electric elements and unnatural sounds," "prepared piano," "Leslie piano," "choppy organs, spasmodic percussion, club guitars," and "uncertain piano."

The sometimes fanciful designations used to identify some of the instruments allow the listener to distinguish exactly who is contributing what to the textures, which are often complex but usually lucid and transparent. "Castanet guitars," for instance, are electric guitars played with mallets and electronically treated to sound something like castanets; a "Leslie piano" is an acoustic piano miked and fed through a Leslie speaker with a built-in revolving horn speaker (or through an electronic apparatus designed to produce this effect); "chord piano" distinguishes this instrument from the "lead piano" on the same song. "Snake guitar" was so named "because the kind of lines I was playing reminded me of the way a snake moves through the brush, a sort of speedy, forceful, liquid quality. Digital guitar is a guitar threaded through a digital delay but fed back on itself a lot so it makes this cardboard tube type of sound." Before recording the "Wimshurst guitar" solo on "St. Elmo's Fire," Eno asked Fripp to visualize a Wimshurst machine, which is "a device for generating very high voltages which then leap between the two poles, very fast and unpredictable."[20]

Eno viewed the making of *Another Green World* as an experiment. In order to put to the test the flexibility and intelligence of his musicians and himself, he walked into the recording studio with nothing written or prepared. "I fed in enough information to get something to happen and the chemical equation of the interaction between the various styles of the musicians involved—who were intelligent enough not to retreat from a situation which was musically strange—took us somewhere that we would have been unable to design."[21] The result of such an experiment could easily have been an overproduced, self-indulgent mish-mash, but Eno was able to shape the final product into a re-markably economical musical statement:

> Twenty-four-track technology encourages you to keep adding things. But there comes a point where adding simply obscures what's already there, and toward the end of that album [*Another Green World*] I listened to the tracks to see what I could take away. The more you supply, the less you demand of a listener.[22]

There is a simple organizational reason why *Another Green World* makes a stronger overall impression than Eno's other progressive rock albums: it has six pieces on Side One and seven on Side Two; the other three albums all have only five pieces per side, and some of the pieces tend to run on a bit, with long fade-outs or inner instrumental sections that add little musical substance. *Another Green World* is a model of musical concision that benefits from the high proportion of purely instrumental tracks and from the extraordinary di-versity of the music.

Henry Edwards's review of *Another Green World* called the album Eno's "most accessible to date" and went on to declare: "mostly instrumental, the disc features a great many melodic themes, some of which are classically ori-ented."[23] The theme of the accessibility of *Another Green World* was echoed by Tom Hull, who in his ideological treatment of Eno's work up to 1976 wrote, "It wouldn't be fair to say that *Another Green World* is Eno's best album, but certainly it is his easiest to love."[24]

Charley Walters, who in 1976 could still write that "Eno's eccentric music doesn't stray beyond rock's accustomed borders so much as it innovates within those parameters," did find in *Another Green World's* nine instrumental numbers Eno's "most radical reshapings of the [rock] genre," and called the album as a whole "perhaps the artist's most successful record." Walters pinpointed Eno's "imaginative, even queer arranging" as the factor that saved the music from the monotony of "merely pedestrian" melodic lines and rock chord structures. The record's main fault, in Walters' view, had to do with the pieces that rely too heavily on the rhythm box: "synthetic percussion always seems like a cocktail-lounge drum machine—a frustrating, though by no means disastrous, distraction on several cuts." Writing in 1976, it would have been difficult for Walters to predict that electronic drum machines, otherwise known as rhythm boxes or rhythm generators, would become, in the decade ahead, a staple addition to the percussion batteries of many popular acts ranging from disco, soul, and rap to mainstream rock and on to jazz-rock fusions and performance art (Laurie Anderson). Today, the drum machine, whose range and quality of sounds have been vastly expanded and improved through digital technology, has completely shaken off its "cocktail lounge" associations, and Eno stands out as an early pioneer of its creative use. Walters' review was placed, with a large headline, at the beginning of the "Records" section in the issue of *Rolling Stone* in which it appeared—an indication of the editors' perception of its importance. Walters sums up: "Eno insists on risks, and that they so consistently pan out is a major triumph. I usually shudder at such a description, but *Another Green World* is indeed an important record—and also a brilliant one."[25]

Alexander Austin and Steve Erickson, in an article on rock during the 1970s, called Eno

> nothing less than one of the three or four most important pop artists [of] this decade. . . . Eno's records are filled with vitality and fun, shimmering like the sun on a lake at dusk, creating atmospheres of shadow and occasional glimpses, such as in his masterpieces *Taking Tiger Mountain (By Strategy)* and *Another Green World*. His music is as much akin to Debussy or Satie in their impressionistic periods as to any current pop avant-gardist, and yet pop his music certainly is.[26]

Arthur Lubow noted that "Like many Eno compositions, 'Another Green World' [the song] has the pictorial vividness of program music. As it opens, the scientific smoke is blowing away, permitting the outlines of a new Eden to come into sharper focus. *Before and After Science* [Eno's next progressive rock album] amplifies the picture."[27] Lubow hit on an important point here: Eno's compositional process, even in purely instrumental works, relies heavily on visual imagery, and he chooses his titles with great care, believing they cannot but influence the listener's perception of the music. Stephen Demorest called the album a potpourri of haunting sounds, living aural landscapes populated by grating noises dubbed sky-saws and by delicate, fleeting fragments—the musical equivalents of haiku. Several of the tracks seem like unfinished arrangements, far more interesting than the more traditional pop tunes on the LP. . . . Their most charming common element is minimalness, a spare, floating quality that shows Eno moving directly contrary to conventional rock's thickly layered, tyranically thrusting "grooves."[28]

Mikal Gilmore observed that *Another Green World* "lacks [the] demonic cutting edge [of Eno's previous solo albums] (the brilliant 'Sky Saw' is the one exception)." Gilmore writes with rather a greater command of musical terminology than most reviewers; here, in a review that characterizes Eno as "an atypical rocker, clearly an artist first, and a pop figure only in the extension of an artistic gesture," he noted that

the best of the instrumentals bear comparison to Ornette Coleman's prescription (in *Skies of America*) for music that can begin or end at any given juncture, a formula that necessarily belies traditional conceptions of progression and resolution. . . . Utilizing a corral of keyboards and tape loop systems, Eno builds broad, overlapping levels of interrelated chord structures and simple melodic motifs, which could (and do) repeat indefinitely. Movement is limited to a gradual addition and subtraction of layers, and Eno's tendency to favor such spacious harmonic support often negates the impression of chord changes, imparting a modal illusion.[29]

Jon Pareles, who subsequently wrote a number of more extended critiques of Eno, was initially puzzled by Eno's new direction on *Another Green World*. His short review is given here in its entirety: "This ain't no Eno record. I don't care what the credits say. It doesn't even get on my nerves."[30] The implication is that Pareles missed the raw, abrasive, progressive rock sound of Eno's first two solo albums, which had served him as a kind of mental stimulant; he found the more poppish tunes and non-rock electronic excursions of *Another Green World* less challenging.

Lester Bangs had a similar reaction:

I found much of it a bit too, well, "Becalmed," as one of its precisely programmatic titles declared. Those little pools of sound on the outskirts of silence seemed to me the logical consequence of letting the processes and technology share your conceptual burden—twilight music perfectly suited to the passivity Eno's approach cultivates. . . . Me, I'm a modern guy, but not so modern I don't still like music with really heavily defined *content* that you can actively *listen* to in the foreground.[31]

Bangs's difficulty with pieces exhibiting little distinction between foreground and background is a theme that runs through portions of the published criticism, representing one kind of subjective reaction to an important feature of Eno's music, and, one might add, of much of the music of the last two decades that has been labeled "minimalism."

Eno's final solo progressive rock album, *Before and After Science*, was two years in the making. At the time, Eno was involved with a number of other projects, including his ambient-style records *Discreet Music* and *Music for Films*, but he was also faced with, and a bit intimidated by, the acclaim for *Another Green World*: he wanted to produce another landmark in rock innovation, but was afraid of repeating himself, and did not want to stop short of perfection. Over a hundred songs and soundscapes were recorded, fiddled with, remixed, and rejected. Ultimately Eno had to put a stop to this painful process—it is said that an artist never completes a work, only abandons it—and released a sparkling yet somewhat brooding set of ten pieces manifesting a broad stylistic spread, made with the help of fifteen backup musicians. There are a couple of hard-driving rock songs whose words Eno spits out forcefully; "Kurt's Rejoinder" is a small-scale jazz piece in something like an electronic be-bop style; "Here He Comes" is a soft ballad; the percussionless "Julie With . . ." uses broad, reverberating cascades of synthesizer colors that evoke the seashore scene the lyrics are about; "By This River," a collaboration with members of the German synthesizer group Cluster, uses only piano, electric pianos, voice, and a melodic synthesizer line, in a stripped-down texture that anticipates the prevailing sonorities of *Music for Airports* (1978); "Through Hollow Lands" is entirely instrumental, and "Spider and I," the last song on the album, is a grand synthesizer hymn, moving through harmonic progressions in solemn stateliness, with a short enigmatic lyric placed in the middle. Like *Another Green World*, the order of pieces was planned with a view to the whole, and also like the earlier record, the conceptual progression here runs from rock frenetics to calm, contemplative music.

The music of *Before and After Science* drove some reviewers in the rock press to new extremes of metaphor. Joe Fernbacher wrote: "Brian Eno is mechanized anathema. The sounds of Eno are the collected sounds of some sentient alien seltzer busily digesting a greasy heart that's too big for its own cogs." He liked the record, though, calling it "the perfect Eno album."[32] The "alien" image, which had been growing around Eno since his first solo album, was used once more by Mitchell Schneider: "Brian Eno is an agent from some other time and some other place who seems to know something that we don't but should. . . . I can't remember the last time a record took such a hold of me—and gave such an extreme case of vertigo, too."[33] Russell Shaw enthused: "What a wonderland of a zoo, a cross between steaming smoke, atonal mystery and hanging, frothy ditties. . . . This is another typically awesome, stunning, numbing Brian Eno album—the record Pink Floyd *could* make if they set their collective mind to it."[34]

In 1977 Eno was at the height of his esteem in the rock press. A few writers criticized individual works, but as to his overall approach and the resulting music, it seemed he could do no wrong. He had pushed back the limits of rock, had established a secure place in the music industry, had collaborated with some of rock's greatest innovators, and had charmed the critics with his endless stream of theorizing about rock and art. By this time, though, he had already established the bases of his ambient style with the records to be discussed in Chapter 10. As his interest in non-rock styles increased, his feeling for the primacy of rock as a medium decreased, and many critics in the press, bound to their readerships and to the canonical musical principles of rock itself, were unable or unwilling to follow him into the new territory he had opened up.

chapter 9
Eno's Progressive Rock: The Music

The pieces on Eno's four solo progressive rock albums are of five basic types. The early albums feature "assaultive" songs that bowl over the listener with a hard rock attack—distorted electric guitars, a hard, driving beat, an almost saturated acoustical space, and a strident, shouted vocal quality—and with lyrics that feature aggressive, futuristic, sexual, bizarre, or surrealistic imagery. The second type of song, never dominating but always present in each of these albums, is best described as "pop," involving lighter textures, less distorted timbres, a more relaxed vocal delivery used in conjunction with suaver melodies—in a word, a more Top-40 sound. To view these pieces merely as pop songs, however, would be misleading, for Eno's intent is frequently ironic: by combining light music with ambiguous or sarcastic lyrics, he achieves a peculiar clash of contexts.

A third class of song, embracing a considerable variety of musical approaches, is the "strange." These are songs in which Eno allows his imagination free reign to play with elements of rock, pop, and jazz, resulting in unique combinations of textures and timbral qualities, frequently in conjunction with dark, irrational verbal imagery. Some such songs evoke our sense of the weird, the demonic, the grotesque, or the frightful; others are wistful, vaguely menacing, or dream-like. The quality of "strangeness" in other songs results from a clash of contexts, for instance a puzzling, enigmatic text over a deceptively carefree (though not exactly "pop") musical accompaniment.

The fourth type of song is characterized by simple, slow vocal melodies and broad, diatonic, harmonic textures played on synthesizers programmed to sound like church organs or string sections; I call this type "hymn-like." The aesthetic of these songs points forward to the nonvocal ambient style Eno was working on from the time of his collaboration with Robert Fripp on the 1973 album *(No Pussyfooting)*; it also refers back to the player piano hymns of Eno's childhood.

The final type of piece is the instrumental. More a generic than a stylistic category, Eno's instrumentals on these albums may be classed as pop, strange, and ambient. These pieces are forerunners of Eno's systematic explorations of non-vocal musical textures on later albums like *On Land* and *Apollo*.

In Chart 1 (below) the pieces on each album are listed by type, and thus the overall character of each record can be seen at a glance. Particularly striking are the preponderance of assaultive songs on the first two records, the total absence of such songs on *Another Green World*, and the tendency to close out each album with hymn-like songs and instrumental pieces: Eno was evidently seeking something of an "Amen" effect for each of the four cycles.

Chart 1
COMPOSITIONAL TYPES ON ENO'S SOLO PROGRESSIVE ROCK ALBUMS

Here Come the Warm Jets (1973)

Side One
Needles in the Camel's Eye—assaultive
The Paw Paw Negro Blowtorch—assaultive
Baby's on Fire—assaultive
Cindy Tells Me—pop
Driving Me Backwards—strange

Side Two
On Some Faraway Beach—pop/strange
Blank Frank—assaultive
Dead Finks Don't Talk—strange
Some of Them Are Old—hymn-like
Here Come the Warm Jets—(instrumental) pop

Taking Tiger Mountain (By Strategy) (1974)

Side One
Burning Airlines Give You So Much More—pop
Back in Judy's Jungle—pop
The Fat Lady of Limbourg—strange
Mother Whale Eyeless—pop
The Great Pretender—strange

Side Two
Third Uncle—assaultive
Put a Straw Under Baby—pop/strange
The True Wheel—assaultive
China My China—assaultive
Taking Tiger Mountain—hymn-like

Another Green World (1975)

Side One
Sky Saw—strange
Over Fire Island—(instrumental) strange

St. Elmo's Fire—pop
In Dark Trees—(instrumental) strange
The Big Ship—(instrumental) strange
I'll Come Running—pop/strange
Another Green World—(instrumental) ambient

Side Two
Sombre Reptiles—(instrumental) strange
Little Fishes—(instrumental) strange
Golden Hours—pop/strange
Becalmed—(instrumental) ambient
Zawinul/Lava—(instrumental) ambient
Everything Merges with the Night—strange
Spirits Drifting—(instrumental) ambient

Before and After Science (1977)
Side One
No One Receiving—assaultive
Backwater—assaultive/pop
Kurt's Rejoinder—strange
Energy Fools the Magician—(instrumental) ambient
King's Lead Hat—assaultive

Side Two
Here He Comes—pop
Julie With . . . —strange
By This River—strange
Through Hollow Lands—(instrumental) ambient
Spider and I—hymn-like

ASSAULTIVE ROCK SONGS

Assaulting the audience with a barrage of very loud distorted sound and violent lyrics is part of the rock tradition. The real target of the assault, of course, is not the audience itself, but the musicians' and audience's "other": those aspects of reality—whether this means the older generation, the political establishment, rival youth cultures, or a lover/enemy—whose negative influence is deemed to be irreconcilable with the attainment of selfhood. The electric guitar itself, with its potential for a lacerating, buzz-saw sonic attack, can be a phallic weapon wielded against those who would squelch the individual's aggressive, defiant gestures toward absolute freedom and dominance.

The history of rock has seen waves of assaultive sound types crash against and wear away the shore of the musically acceptable, each wave seemingly more violent, more absolutely noise-like than the last: the electric guitar so-norities of black musicians like Chuck Berry and Muddy Waters during the 1950s; the fuzz-tone menace of mid-1960s songs like the Rolling Stones' "Sat-isfaction"; the bass-heavy, cavernous, earsplitting heavy metal sound pioneered by Led Zeppelin during the late 1960s and early 1970s; and the vengefully, violently, deliberately anti-musical cacophony of late-1970s punk.

Eno's adoption of the assaultive sound-ideal was not an unpremeditated, instinctive act, as it has been for so many rock musicians. Even early in his career he was making music about music: his pieces are part of a process of distancing; they are removed from the unreflected level of everyday rock real-ities and myths. He has never promoted violence except at the artistic level, and it is just at this level that the images and textures of his assaultive songs play themselves out.

The lyrics of the assaultive Eno song tend to be macabre and disturbing, evoking a generalized malaise not directed at anything in particular, and thus lacking the confrontational, us-against-them dialectic of much assaultive rock. "The Paw Paw Negro Blowtorch" (*Warm Jets*), in Eno's words, "celebrates the possibility of a love affair" with a man "who emerged from the forests around Paw Paw, Michigan with a strange ailment—his breath caused things to ignite."[1] "Baby's on Fire" (*Warm Jets*) is a bizarre fantasy about a photography session involving a burning infant and unthinking, laughing onlookers—possibly re-ferring to the napalm tragedies of the Vietnam War. "Blank Frank" 's (*Warm Jets*) hero, in the words of the song, "is the messenger of your doom and your destruction [like Dylan's "Wicked Messenger" on *John Wesley Harding*]. . . . His particular skill is leaving bombs in people's driveways." Birds of prey, headless chickens, zombies, dead finks, opium farmers, suicidal Chinamen, deadly black waters, fallen meteors, dark alleys, guns, weapons, satellites, black stars, and burning fingers, toes, airlines, uncles, books, and shoes: such evil images restlessly prowl through Eno's assaultive rock songs, often disconnected from any logical or comprehensible sequence of events, shadowing the barely controlled logic of the musical presentation.

Here Come the Warm Jets opens Eno's solo career with a sonic assault, though the lyrics to "Needles in the Camel's Eye," if ambiguous and vague, evoke a spiritual quest with overtones both Christian and Taoist (Eno's "All mysteries are just more needles in the camel's eye" derives from Jesus' words, "It is easier for a camel to pass through the eye of a needle than for a rich man to enter the Kingdom of God," while "Those who know don't let it show" rephrases Lao-Tzu's "He who knows, speaks not; he who speaks knows not")[2] more than a tormented expressionistic journey to the hell of the unconscious. Layers of distorted electric guitars (which point directly back to the early Who and straight forward to punk), the shouted, plunging vocal, and the use of a single chord progression throughout (: I | IV V | I | IV V | I | V | ♭VII | IV :|) set up a continuous river or lava flow of sound that is broken only in the instrumental middle section of the song. The aggressive nature of the musical setting works effectively to counterbalance the earnest sentiment of the lyrics. Characteristically, if unrealistically, Eno tries to dissuade us from reading too much into the lyrics: the words were "written in less time than it takes to sing. The word 'Needles' was picked up from the guitar sound which to me is reminiscent of a cloud of metal needles. . . . I regard [the song] as an instrumental with singing on it."[3]

Another assaultive "instrumental with singing on it," whose lyrics probably *can* be ignored, or at least left uninterpreted, is "Third Uncle" (*Tiger Mountain*). Here the words were undoubtedly arrived at through free phonetic and linguistic association, Eno singing nonsense bits along with the instrumental tracks: they consist of litanies of randomly chosen words set to formulas like "There are tins / There was pork / There are legs / There are sharks / There was John / There are cliffs / There was mother / There's a poker / There was you / Then there was you," delivered like a spoken magical chant in a tone of voice that takes on menace through its very lack of coloration. "Third Uncle" is an example of Eno restricting himself to minimal harmonic materials (‖: I |♭VI :‖ throughout the five-minute duration) in order to bring melodic, textural, and rhythmic elements to the fore. (There is one slight harmonic complication: toward the middle, the bass begins playing the note A♭ while the guitars are playing their C major tonic, creating the suggestion of an augmented chord; when the guitars switch to A♭ major, the bass moves to C. The whole-tone feel is further heightened by Phil Manzanera's animated guitar solos, which have a motive that rotates the notes C, E, and F♯.) As the song goes on, the interest shifts from the back-and-forth rapid strummings of the two rhythm guitars to the increasingly noise-like careenings of the lead guitar. Although such repetitive songs, in which fixed elements alternate and vie for attention, may be worlds apart from Eno's later ambient music in terms of sound (being loud and abrasive rather than soft and yielding), they are not really so very different in concept.

Eno adopted three basic approaches to form in his songs. "Needles in the Camel's Eye" and "Third Uncle" both use theme and variations form, in which an unchanging harmonic progression is repeated with vocal and/or instrumental textural variants. The second approach is that most frequently used in rock and pop: a strophic structure with or without refrain, and with some kind of contrasting instrumental or vocal "bridge" or "B section" placed typically between the second and third verses. The third formal approach is best described as through-composed: formal units, though they may be repeated altered or unaltered, follow one another in a design unique to the given work. (In traditional classical music, pieces that have no standard set form such as the sonata, theme and variations, etc., are said to be "through-composed.")

"King's Lead Hat" (*Science*), a song whose title is an anagram of "Talking Heads," is of the strophic type, built around a pattern of sectionalized verses, with an instrumental middle section:

Example 2
FORM OF "KING'S LEAD HAT"

A: | V | ♭VII | I | I |

B: | I | I | vi | vi |

C: | I | I | I | I |

D: | V | IV | I | I |

AAAAAA: Instrumental fade-in
BBBBAA: Verse 1 with refrain
BBBBAA: Verse 2 with refrain
BBBB: Instrumental with guitar solo
CC: Instrumental with guitar solo
BBBBAA: Verse 3 with refrain
AA: Refrains repeated
DDDDDD: Instrumental fade-out with synthesizer
solo

"King's Lead Hat" is the last manic screamer that Eno put out on his solo albums; although it is convincing enough as a rock piece, the aesthetic of chaos implicit in the verbal and musical attack was something he saw no point in taking further. How much further, after all, could it be taken? This song, though well crafted in its way—Robert Fripp's syncopated, pitch-restricted minimalistic guitar solo adds an element of cerebrated discipline to the Dionysian mayhem, while Eno's synthesizer solo at the end represents the last word in "funny" electronic sounds in an assaultive rock medium—says little that "Needles in the Camel's Eye" did not say four years earlier with somewhat greater economy. "King's Lead Hat" is more *complicated* than the earlier song, both lyrically and musically, but complication in this genre is difficult to reconcile with the primal force that gives it life.

Nevertheless, it is true that what I am calling the assaultive rock idiom has a great deal of expressive musical potential that Eno, precisely because of his lack of instrumental expertise, and because of his limited knowledge of music theory, was disinclined to explore. Heavy metal groups, with the possible exception of Led Zeppelin, have not fared much better in this regard, though one suspects that in many cases both commercial pressures and lack of imagination have contributed to the musical stagnation of the genre. The pinnacle of intelligence and imagination in the assaultive rock medium remains Robert Fripp and King Crimson's album *Red* (1974): working with a peerless guitar technique, a command of music theory that enabled him to draw freely on whole-tone and other unusual scales (and to construct large-scale tonal structures outside the conventional major-minor idiom), and an adventurous rhythmic sense that integrated odd meters based on five and seven beats per measure, Fripp pushed the assaultive medium far beyond where Eno had taken it. Like Eno, however, he abruptly dropped it and went on to a variety of other musical projects in an assortment of styles. For both musicians, it is unlikely that the decision to cut off further experimentation in the genre was a purely musical one: heavy metal during the late 1970s and 1980s became increasingly associated with cynically commercialized satanic symbolism and with a very young, loud, and primarily male audience, with whom neither Fripp nor Eno were especially keen on cultivating a continuing relationship.

POP SONGS

"Pop" is a term that has been used with many different shades of meaning. It does not translate well to or from languages other than English; it carries different connotations whether used in reference to Anglo-American visual art or to music; and in England, the conceptual split between pop and rock seems somewhat more pronounced than in the United States. A workable definition of "pop" for our purposes, however, is provided by the reference work endorsed by one of pop/rock's enduring publishing institutions, *The Rolling Stone Encyclopedia of Rock & Roll*:

> Pop is the melodic side of rock—the legacy of show tunes and popular songs of the prerock era. Pop's standards of what makes a well-constructed song still apply to much of rock, which strives for memorable tunes and clear sentiments; the tension between pop virtues (such as sophisticated chord structures and unusual melodic twists), and incantatory, formulaic blues elements animates much of the best rock, like that of the Beatles. "Pop" also connotes accessibility, disposability and other low-culture values, which rockers have accepted or rejected with varying degrees of irony.[4]

There is a further stylistic distinction to be made between pop and rock: pop songs tend to be based on more "realistic" instrumental sounds than rock—that is, sounds less manipulated or distorted through electronic processes. In terms of production values, the equation rock-equals-dirty while pop-equals-clean may be oversimplified, but it has a certain validity. While absolute volume levels can be determined by the listener on his or her stereo system, pop will sound psychologically softer than rock played at the same level. Rock is aggressive, sometimes even assaultive; in pop, the tendency is toward a more intimate, confidential tone. Obviously the potential for irony is high if what is being confided by the singer is of an impersonal, incomprehensible, ambiguous, or even slightly perverted nature.

Some such irony is usually what Eno was after in the pop songs on his progressive rock albums, an effect evident even in some of the titles of deceptively innocuous music: "Burning Airlines Give You So Much More," "Back in Judy's Jungle," "Mother Whale Eyeless." One is reminded once more of Satie, with his penchant for absurd titles.

"Cindy Tells Me" (*Warm Jets*) by Eno and Manzanera is a Beatlesque example of musical irony. While a poppish backing track replete with falsetto "oohs" and a tinkling piano runs through a clichéd set of chord changes slightly spiced with a treated electric guitar, the singer tells a sad story of modern times in which affluent housewives cannot cope with "their new freedoms"; although they have supposedly chosen their fate, it turns out that it is just a "burden to be so relied on." The British pop/rock tradition of lightly lampooning the middle class was well established when Eno wrote this song, going back to songs like the Kinks' "Well Respected Man," about a punctual personage whose daily routines never change, and the Rolling Stones' "Mother's Little Helper," in which prescribed drugs help the housewife "minimize her plight." At three and a half minutes, "Cindy Tells Me" fits neatly into the smallish duration requisite of a pop song, and its form—sung and instrumental verse sections alternating with a bridge—is likewise conventional.

"Put a Straw Under Baby" (*Tiger Mountain*) is incomprehensible until one realizes that the title refers to the Catholic practice Eno was induced to carry out in his childhood of doing homage to the infant Jesus by placing a piece of straw under an icon. The song is not so much satirical as it is intent on suggesting the mixed effect such rituals are likely to have on a child's consciousness. The kindergarten innocence of the musical setting—highlighted by the organ, which evokes images of church and fairground—is belied by the bizarre content of some of the lyrics, in which the child has taken Christian symbols and dogma which he doesn't understand and woven them together with stories he has been told into a surrealistic personal mythological tapestry: "There's a place in the orchard / Where no one dare go / The last nun who went there / Turned into a crow . . . There's a brain in the table / There's a heart in the chair / And they all live in Jesus / It's a family affair." Eno used the (intentionally out-of-tune) Portsmouth Sinfonia string section and his own slightly cracked falsetto in this song to add to the atmosphere of childhood foreboding.

"St. Elmo's Fire" (*Green World*) is the most unblushingly poppish song Eno has ever committed to record. It was doubtless prominent in the minds of those critics who called *Another Green World* Eno's most accessible album; and it is a considerable puzzle why he did not release it as a single, as it seems to have most of the ingredients of a popular hit: conventional verse/refrain form, a lively beat, simple major tonality, pleasant and unobjectionable though original instrumentation, a dynamic guitar solo, suave falsetto harmonies on the refrain, and—most importantly—a genuine melodic/lyrical hook in the refrain (the words "In the blue August moon / In the cool August moon"). If the song lacks one crucial element for the hit parade, it is the earthiness and sensuality of explicit romantic interest: "St. Elmo's Fire" is a love song of a sort, but its imagery is too rarefied for the Top 40, telling of a couple's metaphorical journey through moors, briars, endless blue meanders, fires, wires, highways, and storms ("Then we rested in a desert / Where the bones were white as teeth sir / And we saw St. Elmo's fire / Splitting ions in the ether"). "St. Elmo's Fire" is a beautiful pop song that accepts and embraces the limitations of the medium.

Only two musicians took part in making the song. Eno plays organ, piano, Yamaha bass pedals, "desert guitars," and synthetic percussion (including tom-tom-drum-like and woodblock-like effects, whose driving rhythms compensate for the lack of actual drums), while Robert Fripp adds the "Wimshurst guitar" solo whose genesis has been described previously (see page 104). Overall, the texture of "St. Elmo's Fire" is more dense than usual for Eno, but this is in keeping with the song's more popular nature. At three minutes, it does not overstay its welcome. The song's form is easily schematized:

Example 3
FORM OF "ST. ELMO'S FIRE"

—Introduction (cumulative entrance of instruments)
—Verse 1 (over major tonic chord)
—Refrain (over ‖: vi | V | IV | IV :‖ progression)
—Verse 2
—Refrain
—Verse 3 (Wimshurst guitar warms up in background)
—Wimshurst guitar solo (over Refrain chords)
—Refrain
—Fade-out over tonic chord

Straightforward as it is harmonically, rhythmically, melodically, and formally, Eno was correct in pointing out that songs like this cannot be reductively analyzed in such terms alone: "You can't notate the *sound* of "St. Elmo's Fire.""[5] (Emphasis mine.)

Perhaps Eno's most soothing song of the pop variety is "Here He Comes" (*Science*). An endless stream of tonics, dominants, and subdominants wash across the listener while muted drums, basses, guitars, and synthesizers contribute their pastel tone colors to the mix. Once again, the ambiguity of the lyrics, about "the boy who tried to vanish to the future or past," who "is no longer here with his sad blue eyes," takes this song out of the realm of unreflected pop; but this type of song does have clear precedents, such as the Beatles' "Nowhere Man," written a decade earlier. "Nowhere Man" and "Here He Comes" have the same tempo and harmonic similarities, and share the idea of a wistful masculine antihero. While the Lennon tune is based on a descending melodic sequence, however, Eno's is a prolongation or embellishment of essentially one note. Whether, at five and a half minutes, "Here He Comes" must be judged too long depends on the receptivity of the listener and the mode of listening. In the linear, horizontal mode, little or nothing seems to "happen" for the piece's duration; but listened to vertically, the song reveals a perpetual play of timbral and motivic elements: strip away the drums, voice, and steady pulse, and we are not far from the ambient style.

STRANGE SONGS

It was probably Eno's proclivity for creating specialized "strange" songs that more than anything else led to the congealing of his public image as the "cadaver we've all come to love and recognize . . . the scaramouche of the synthesizer."[6] Lester Bangs could describe him as "the real bizarro warp factor for 1974," in an age of rock star transvestitism, glam, and glitter.[7] There was more to Eno's penchant for transgressing the bounds of taste and custom than dressing and grooming himself like a woman: his strange pieces are arguably the most original of all his songs, since in them he felt most free to experiment with the elements of musical style.

Eno did not exactly create the strange genre. Precursors of a sort can be found in that perennial presence on the pop charts, the novelty song, of which may be cited examples as diverse as Bobby "Boris" Pickett and the Crypt-Kickers' "Monster Mash" (1962), Arthur Brown's inimitable "Fire" (1968), and Bob Dylan's "Rainy Day Women #12 & 35" (1966) with its punning "Everybody must get stoned" refrain. There is even a specific "demented" tradition in rock—catalogued, popularized, and celebrated by Dr. Demento for his syndicated radio show, featuring such immortal monuments to musical bad taste and kitsch as "Little Puppy" and "Living with a Hernia." Analogs to Eno's strange genre might also be found in nineteenth-century compositions like Liszt's *Totentanz* ("Dance of Death") or in the horrors of expressionist pieces like Schoenberg's *Pierrot lunaire* or *The Book of the Hanging Gardens*—pieces whose utterly humorless sense of dread in some respects parallels Eno's strange contributions more closely than does the slapstick grotesquerie of the novelty or demented song.

"Strange" in the sense the term is used here may carry the connotation of the conceptually weird, or it may simply mean highly unusual, highly individuated in a musical sense, the total sound texture owing little to specific generic compositional precedents. It is in the same sense that much of the material on such progressive rock albums of the same period as Gentle Giant's *Octopus* or King Crimson's *Larks' Tongues in Aspic* may be classed as "strange." The conceptually weird and the musically individuated, however, often overlap in the same piece.

Such is the case in "Driving Me Backwards" (*Warm Jets*). A near-psychotic din is created by Eno's relentless hammering on a piano that is out of tune (or electronically treated to sound so), by the double-tracked vocal (widely used in rock since the early 1960s to add depth and coloration to a single singer's voice, double tracking here serves as an almost literal metaphor for the schizophrenic personality), by the thudding, boomy bass, and by Fripp's metallically treated electric guitar machinations. The lyrics consist of inexplicable, tormented expressionistic outbursts: "Ah Luana's black reptiles / Sliding around / Make chemical choices / And she responds as expected / To the only sound / Hysterical voices." Eno's own exegesis of "Driving Me Backwards," written some dozen years after the song itself, is a model of rationality. He called the song

> a mixture of a series of thoughts about controlled existence—the desirability of being stripped of choice if you like. . . . [The song] has a combination of qualities that would not have been arrived at by anyone else, since it is the product of my musical naïveté on the one hand, and my ability to manipulate extant ideas on the other. In this track as in most of the others [on the album], the musical idea is very simple—there are only three chords, each different from the other by only one note [C minor, A diminished, and A♭ major], there are no tempo changes and the tempo [*sic*] is simply 4/4. I enjoy working with simple structures such as these for they are transparent—comparable to a piece of graph paper and its grids. The grid serves as the reference point for the important information—the graph line itself.[8]

We are fortunate to have an artist so willing and eager to take us into his workshop, though in this case the contradiction between the strict rationality of the process and the overpowering irrationality of the product may seem extreme to the point of absurdity. Music history, however, shows us numerous composers who have been able to explain and articulate at a very rational level the logic of their techniques—techniques used, however, in the service of a powerfully expressive intent. Alban Berg, with the formidably logical forms and pitch structures of his nevertheless almost wantonly expressionist opera *Wozzeck*, may serve as an example.

Not so ferocious as "Driving Me Backwards," but strange in its way, "The Fat Lady of Limbourg" (*Tiger Mountain*) is Eno's contribution to the "spy song" genre that has produced such classics as "Peter Gunn," "Goldfinger," and "Secret Agent Man." Eno establishes an air of tongue-in-cheek mystery and spookiness through an economical, airy, minimalistic texture in which every isolated musical event can be clearly heard. Single blows on a gong establish a conceptual connection to the "China" theme of the rest of the album, while understated saxophone breaks add to the low-life atmosphere.

Some of the basic premises of *Another Green World* as a whole are set out on the first track, "Sky Saw": active, yet clearly distinguishable instrumental parts, making for sparkling clarity of texture; few words; a simple repeated harmonic framework (‖: I | V |♭VII | IV :‖),[9] using the inverted circle-of-fifths progressions common in rock music at least since Jimi Hendrix's "Hey Joe" of 1968;[10] and in the area of tone color, a combination of the familiar and the electronically exotic.

In "Sky Saw"'s overall texture, despite the rock-like rhythmic drive, nothing actually remains constant except for Paul Rudolph's "anchor bass," which hits the chord roots regularly in a simple rhythmic pattern. On top of this, the other parts are striking for their constant changes, Percy Jones's fretless bass playing melodic arabesques, Phil Collins's drumming never falling into a real "groove," Rod Melvin's Rhodes piano hitting notes that are panned rapidly back and forth between left and right stereo channels, John Cale's violas entering late in the song with downward-careening glissandi, and Eno's own "snake guitar" and "digital guitar" supplying the indescribably rich, overtone-flexing "melodic" grating sounds that represent the "Sky Saw" of the song's title.

"Sky Saw" is essentially in variation form, the theme being the four-measure harmonic framework, and the variations consisting of timbral and textural elaborations. Within this scheme, additional formal articulation is provided by the cumulative addition of instruments, rising dynamics, and complication of melodic and timbral interest, all contributing to a crescendo of musical density. Finally, after five instrumental variations, comes the belated entrance of the lyrics: "All the clouds turn to words / All the words float in sequence / No one knows what they mean / Everyone just ignores them." These words, which comprise the totality of the coherent text, indicate Eno's growing dissatisfaction with lyrics in general (he was to abandon them in his solo work after one more album of songs, *Before and After Science* [1977]), while simultaneously embodying his philosophy of lyric-writing, which valued the sheer *sound* of the words over the semantic meanings of their combinations. In the context of "Sky Saw," Eno highlights the equivalence of words and music by singing, "All the clouds [of sound] turn to words . . .," phrases emerging out of what the listener had suspected would be an all-instrumental piece; and, as if to confirm the idea, the text proper is accompanied by background voices singing strings of phonetic, free-associative nonsense poetry: "Mau mau starter ching ching da da / Daughter daughter dumpling data / Pack and pick the ping pong starter / Carter Carter go get Carter," etc. After the verse are four more instrumental variations. Thus the whole is very nearly symmetrical:

Example 4
FORM OF "SKY SAW"

Five instrumental variations
One vocal variation
Four instrumental variations (song fades out toward end of fourth)

The variation principle, here used in almost classical purity, is one that informs much of Eno's work; given his overriding concern with color—the "vertical" aspect of musical sound—it is natural that he should find in the variation technique a suitable framework for the working-out of his ideas: the variation form does not get in the way, but readily accepts the content poured into it, sometimes (as here in "Sky Saw") even proving amenable to the grafting of a quasi-developmental symmetrical form on top of it.

One of Eno's compositional techniques is to select material from his vast library of tapes of his recording sessions and private experiments and work it into new pieces. The "Sky Saw" tapes came in for this kind of treatment:

> There are two pieces of mine, "Sky Saw" from *Another Green World* and "A Major Groove" from *Music for Films* which are exactly the same track, mixed differently, slowed down, and fiddled about with a bit. I also gave it to Ultravox for one of the songs on their first album. It's been a long way, this backing track. Listen to all three, and you hear what kind of range of different usage is possible.[11]

A completely different approach to the realm of the strange—the realm of the highly individuated composition—is found in "Everything Merges with the Night" (*Green World*), a song that adopts the harmonic framework of the eight-bar blues, which is repeated six times (the fourth and sixth times without words). And yet there is little else in the song that suggests the blues, either the original Afro-American varieties or their rock derivatives (though in a sense, of course, this piece is precisely a—very—"white" blues!). The sparseness of texture suggests that this is one of the songs Eno composed as much by subtraction as by cumulation of instrumental tracks. The texture is clear, light and airy, with the various layers working together in contrapuntal fashion without any one overwhelming the others. The elements in this simple yet satisfying counterpoint of layers are: Eno's voice; Brian Turrington's bass guitar line, which sometimes doubles the vocal part; Brian Turrington's piano line and Eno's strummed guitar chords, which play a few motives heterorhythmically; and two electric guitar parts played by Eno, consisting of long held notes that move rhythmically in tandem with one another, setting up a series of harmonic intervals. The almost childlike simplicity of this succession of different intervals succeeds remarkably in establishing a musical setting of variety within unity. The screeching tone color and sliding attack of the guitar lines is ingeniously offset by the restfulness of the actual lines they are playing: Eno may have been inspired by the guitar work of Procol Harum's Robin Trower, who often used a similar paradoxical technique—something like Jimi Hendrix in slow motion.

It is probably songs like this that led some critics to speak of a certain "unfinished" quality in *Another Green World*: to "finish" this song, how easy it would have been to make the guitar and piano strumming continuous instead of stop-and-start, add a drum track, add instrumental solos over the wordless verses. The result of such finishing, though, would have been a typically cluttered, undifferentiated, more faceless pop song, and not the economical, justly proportioned, and delightfully minimal piece that "Everything Merges with the Night" in fact is.

HYMN-LIKE SONGS

Hymn-like sonorities are far from rare in rock; once more, Eno can be credited not so much with creating as with developing a particular idiom. The Beatles used organ sounds both ironically and sincerely (in "Dr. Robert" and "Let It Be," by Lennon and McCartney respectively); the quintessential "Bach rock" group Procol Harum used the Hammond organ as one of the main constituents of their early sound, their 1967 hit "Whiter Shade of Pale" containing a stepwise descending bass line and organ obbligato derived from Bach; and Emerson, Lake & Palmer came up with a synthesizer-rock version of the Anglican hymn by William Blake, "Jerusalem."

"Spider and I" (*Science*) is a good example of an Eno "hymn": utterly consonant, stately and majestic; electronically produced but evocative of a Baroque organ in a vast cathedral; its words both incongruous with and strangely linked to the religious connotations of the music. Again, one reason Eno stopped writing songs with words was so that he could allow himself and the listener to bask in such glowing sonorities without being simultaneously forced to activate the verbal, analytical part of the brain. Be this as it may, the images he chose for this song manage to evoke an air of grand mystery, in spite of—or even because of—the inexplicable reference to the geometrical arachnidan universe.

INSTRUMENTAL PIECES

Nine of the eleven instrumental pieces on Eno's progressive rock albums occur on *Another Green World*, giving that record a very special character. Of the remaining two, "Here Come the Warm Jets," which closes out the album of that title, is a set of instrumental variations in a pop/rock style in which distorted electric guitar sounds saturate the acoustical space without much textural variation (if some of Eno's songs were "instrumentals with words on them," this piece could have benefitted from some verbal interest); and "Energy Fools the Magician," from *Before and After Science*, is a short discreet jam on one basic chord.

The diverse instrumentals on *Another Green World* link Eno's progressive rock style to the ambient style he was to evolve in the years to come. The instrumental pieces can of course be categorized, in a similar way to the vocal ones, for instance as "strange," "hymn-like," "rhythm-box," "improvisational," but each of them is so distinct that I shall discuss them in the order in which they appear on the album.

"Over Fire Island" is a miniature gem, lasting under two minutes, with such a stripped-down texture that one suspects it is one of those pieces whose final form was arrived at through a process of subtraction in the final mixing stages. Phil Collins's drums and Percy Jones's fretless bass together produce a sort of pointillistic, neo-be-bop "middleground" matrix: normally such a texture would serve a rhythm-section function, a backdrop for foreground activity, but here Eno finds its understated punchiness interesting enough in itself, and occasionally alters the tone color of a group of drum beats electronically. If there is a foreground, it is Eno's occasional dabs of synthesizer and guitars. The melodic fragment for synthesizer (C-B-A-F-C-B, descending) that drops into the texture now and then in various rhythmic relationships to the steady 2/4 beat is the only melodic activity as such, though a two-note motive also appears briefly (B♭-G descending, E♭-G ascending). The pitches emphasized by the bass's improvisatory roulades are B and C. Thus, taken as a whole, the pitch material of "Over Fire Island" suggests a mode on C, C-E♭-F-G-A-B♭-B, though the emphasis on B (in the bass and in the synthesizer melody) implies a B-Locrian twist that makes a straightforward modal interpretation impossible. Technicalities aside, what all this amounts to is Eno the non-musician playing with notes and melodies in a way that many a musician trained in standard tonal and modal theory might not have thought of.

A number of subtle touches make this piece more interesting than verbal description of its bare-bones framework might suggest. There are the (sometimes barely audible) alterations in the drum kit timbre which I have already mentioned. Midway through the piece, an indefinite electronically produced wave of sound, reminiscent of the dense, complex sounds of aggregational natural phenomena like flocks of birds in flight, moves across the aural horizon from left to right, only to recede as quietly and inexplicably as it came. A bit later, the sound of the drum kit splits into two parts, the second part mixed at a lower dynamic level than the first and playing slightly off the beat of the first, which creates a kind of audio 3-D, a fleeting sense of phase-shift spaciousness and overlapping rhythmic planes. The most remarkable touch, though, is the brief "coda": the synthesizer plays its first chords of the piece, C and B (without fifths), twice; then, as the backing tracks are faded out, and before fading out itself, the synthesizer intones a majestic (if understated), tonally suggestive yet ambiguous succession of major chords—an almost Brahmsian modulation—in free rhythm, | B (implied) | G | E ‖: C♯ | F♯ :‖, with a shimmering, oscillating tone color that is the antithesis of the preceding be-bop-like texture. Touches like this occur in much of Eno's music spontaneously, inexplicably, and without apparent pattern or precedent. They can seem like random and almost pointless surface glosses until one realizes that they are the stuff of the music itself.

"In Dark Trees" is the first of seven cuts on *Another Green World* on which Eno is credited with playing all the instruments. And, like the others, this piece uses primarily electronic and electronically treated sounds to weave a unique sonic tapestry. The opening is composed of blunt, almost palpably shaped and contoured masses of sound that have little to offer in the way of conventional melodic and harmonic motion, formal articulation, or developmental processes; rather, the passage may be characterized, as Xenakis characterized his electro-acoustic piece *Bohor I* (1962), as music that is "monistic with internal plurality."[12] Another way of putting this would be to say that nothing much "happens," though there is always a lot to hear.

Eventually, specific layers of sound become identifiable, repeating in a certain pattern: electric percussion and treated rhythm generator define a fast duple background pulse and a tenor-range ostinato (repeating pattern) on C♯, with unpredictable accents (played on echoed, synthetic "wood blocks"); an electric guitar motive consisting of a downward glissando between E and D♯, with an A held above (and below, in the bass synthesizer); an electric guitar melodic motive comprised of descending sixths, | C♯/A♯ | D♯/G♯ | A/F♯ | G♯/E | (pitches accountable to C♯-minor/Dorian); and occasional deep bass synthesizer tones that alternate between the pitches A, E, and F♯ (the tonic C♯ is significantly lacking). The result is a kind of layered counterpoint, or a counterpoint of layers, with shifting harmonic interpretations resulting from the interaction of the various pitches. It is probably pieces like this that Frank Rose had in mind when he spoke of the "peculiar dynamic between . . . two beats. It is not simply a case of two rhythms working in tandem; it is more like two metabolisms grappling with each other."[13] The "two metabolisms" of "In Dark Trees" are the fast duple background pulse of the rhythm generator and the ultra-slow temporal articulations of the bass synthesizer.

As is the case in many Eno compositions of this general type, the music fades in at the beginning and fades out at the end. This befits the nature of the music, which is not linear or teleological but rather spatial or, as it were, spherical. Pieces like this do not have a beginning or an end in the traditional sense: what happens when we hear them is that we perceive a terrain with certain characteristics that stretches without boundaries in all directions. Eno has outlined the genesis of this piece in the course of a discussion on his compositional procedures in general:

> I can remember how that started and I can remember very clearly the image that I had which was this image of a dark, inky blue forest with moss hanging off and you could hear horses off in the distance all the time, these horses kind of neighing, whinnying.
> [INTERVIEWER:] Was this an image from your personal experience?
> [ENO:] No, it was just what the rhythm box suggested.[14]

Like "In Dark Trees," "The Big Ship" is a piece on which Eno plays all the instruments, in this case synthesizer, synthetic percussion and treated rhythm generator, and like the previous song, the percussive pulse is provided by the repeated rhythm (here triple) coming out of the rhythm box, which probably suggested the title of the song and its musical means to Eno. Unlike "In Dark Trees," though, "The Big Ship" is a hymn-like piece, and has a beginning and a cumulative structure, if not a real end (it fades out): it can be considered a composition of the ground-bass type, beginning with a few synthesizer tones that suggest the harmonic structure or two-part theme:

Example 5
HARMONIC PROGRESSION OF "THE BIG SHIP"

‖: I | IV | vi | IV |
| I | V | vi | IV :‖

The sound of the rhythm generator is faded in during the second part of the first statement of the theme, and in what follows, new layers of synthesizer are brought in over every four-measure phrase, slowly filling out the texture until a rich, complex, full-bodied sonority is achieved, at which point the fade-out begins. Each layer of harmonious sound is distinguished from the others by registral and timbral factors, but the final result is homogeneous. Although "The Big Ship" has some of the cumulative effect, diatonic grandeur, and simplicity of conception of Pachelbel's famous Canon in D (which Eno admired and used later in the same year as the basis of a long piece on *Discreet Music*), it lacks the Baroque composition's inner melodic differentiation and is somewhat the worse off for it.

It is perhaps worth pointing out that, so far, we have not heard a dominant-tonic (V-I) cadence on *Another Green World*; "The Big Ship" may be totally diatonic, but such harmonic cadences as exist in it are of the plagal (IV-I) and deceptive (V-vi) varieties. A plagal or subdominant orientation runs throughout most of Eno's pieces that use conventional chord root progressions at all; it calls to mind the studied avoidance of dominant-tonic relations in the music of another twentieth-century composer concerned with color as a primary means of musical expression—Claude-Achille Debussy.

The title track of the album, "Another Green World," is remarkable for its brevity and for its almost self-effacing quality. It is the third of the seven all-Eno, all-instrumental pieces, and in its repetitive nature bears some resemblance to the first two. Here a two-chord progression, | IV7 | I |, provides the structure for a short set of variations which rely on familiar timbres: acoustic piano, Farfisa organ, and "desert guitars"—really an imitation of Robert Fripp's favored electric guitar tone color, with heavy fuzz-tone and indefinitely long sustain characteristics.

"Another Green World" may strike the listener as a piece without much musical content, and without even much in the way of Eno's usual zest for exploring texture and timbre. A more generous assessment of the piece's meaning, however, would allow it a two-pronged significance. First, in the overall formal scheme of *Another Green World* it occupies the closing moments of Side One; if it lacks content, it nevertheless fulfills a formal rounding-off function, perhaps analogous to those of Mozart's transitions and codas that Wagner criticized for lack of "melody." Second, if we consider it in the context of Eno's musical output as a whole, "Another Green World" may be seen as an experimental prefiguration of the types of music he was to produce on such albums as *Discreet Music* and *Music for Airports*—music with a slow pulse and soft dynamics, using a minimum of materials and realizing an aesthetic which encourages the music's qualities of depth and psychological resonance to emerge in inverse proportion to the amount of surface activity.

The second side of *Another Green World* begins with two more wordless pieces in which Eno is credited with playing all the instruments. "Sombre Reptiles" is the last of the rhythm-box-type pieces on the album, although Eno did not use an actual rhythm generator here, unless the cryptic designation "Peruvian percussion" indicates a rhythm-generator-generated sound. To achieve the dark yet rather cartoon-like brooding sound structure of "Sombre Reptiles," Eno played Hammond organ, guitars, "synthetic and Peruvian percussion," and "electric elements and unnatural sounds." The composition has a certain monolithic quality not in keeping with Eno's best work, and yet the originality and strangeness of the sound-world of this experiment cannot be denied. The piece takes its inspiration from familiar rock sources (such as the timbre of the electric guitars and the persistent beat) as well as, apparently, ethnic music sources (the "Peruvian percussion" again). Yet the result can be called neither a rock song nor a real attempt at fusing world-music elements with Western music and technology (as Eno later attempted with David Byrne on *My Life in the Bush of Ghosts*): "Sombre Reptiles" is typical of a large number of idiosyncratic Eno compositions that have no real stylistic antecedents or parallels.

In terms of pitch relations and formal layout, the basic premise of "Sombre Reptiles" is an eight-measure theme highly suggestive of the following harmonic structure (although I can hear no bass instrument as such): (v) ‖: i | i v | i | i | v | v | iv | v :‖.

This theme, melodically articulated chiefly through simple two-part counterpoint between an electric guitar and a synthesizer in the tenor range, is repeated five times before the piece fades out, with little or no textural or timbral variation. Aside from the chugging of the percussion in the background, the other main element in the overall sound consists of pulsating chords on a Hammond organ in the soprano register.

"Sombre Reptiles" leads without a break into "Little Fishes": just as the former is fading out, the latter fades in. Thus Eno highlights the contrast between the two pieces. Within the unassuming dimensions of "Little Fishes"—another instrumental piece taking living forms as its inspiration—we get the clearest glimpse yet of the kind of music that increasingly occupied Eno during the years to come, culminating in *Ambient 4: On Land*, an album Eno thought of as containing his best work up to 1982.[15] This new kind of music has no pulse, or a very slow or uncertain one at best; it abandons functional harmony (although it may use a pitch collection and triadic structure accountable to one or two major or minor modes). The new style has a light, airy quality, with a relatively large amount of open space between and around the notes and other sounds (unlike, for instance, "Sombre Reptiles," where the rhythmic space is virtually filled up). The prevailing dynamics are soft, and the music abandons developmental and variational processes as such in favor of a compositional ideal of continual flux. Unpitched, complex multi-pitched, or noise-based sounds of uncertain origin and great variety replace or at least complement traditional pitched sounds and unpitched percussion.

In "Little Fishes," Eno plays prepared piano and Farfisa organ. There are three timbral layers; in each layer, sound events transpire unpredictably, though within a certain range of possibility. One layer is occupied by a slowly revolving cycle of slowly arpeggiated chords played on unprepared piano strings, with the sustain pedal held down:

Example 6
PIANO CHORDS OF "LITTLE FISHES"

C major (sometimes C dominant seventh)
G major
F major (sometimes with an added B-flat)

The alternation of B-flats and B-naturals results in a sense of tonal ambiguity: the listener's sense of functional harmony, should he or she attempt to bring it to bear on the successions of chords, is constantly thwarted.

The prepared piano sounds as such comprise the second timbral layer. We hear, on and off, some of the types of sounds familiar since the experiments of John Cage during the 1930s—rattlings, ringings, buzzings, and bell-like tones, mostly of indefinite or complex pitch makeup. The final layer of sound events consists of little melodic fragments and isolated tones on the Farfisa organ, some with a "straight" tone color and others with an extremely wide and rapid vibrato and slight downward glissando. Sometimes these organ sounds coincide in pitch with the piano arpeggios, and sometimes they have their own independence. The odd, fleeting sonorities that result from the interaction of these three layers add up to the concept of an active yet static sonic frieze which Eno explored thoroughly during the years ahead.

"Becalmed" (to the chagrin of Lester Bangs—see page 106) captures perfectly the mood of its title. It is another of Eno's unique soundscapes, in this case without the potentially mechanical (or "cocktail-lounge") ambiance of the rhythm box that was a prominent part of "In Dark Trees," "The Big Ship," and "Sombre Reptiles." Unlike the similarly percussionless "Little Fishes," however, "Becalmed" is an entirely pitch-oriented composition. In fact, it uses the same chord progression as Side One's "The Big Ship"—the piece I compared to the Pachelbel Canon:

Example 7
HARMONIC PROGRESSION OF "BECALMED"

‖: I | IV | vi* | IV |
| I | V | vi | IV :‖

(The * denotes a thirdless chord.)

The difference, though, is profound: whereas "The Big Ship" seemed to be a too densely layered exercise in diatonic grandeur, "Becalmed," with its less pulsative rhythm, more focused synthesizer sound shapes, and clear formal boundaries, succeeds in establishing and maintaining an atmosphere of serenity and calm from beginning to end.

Eno plays the only instruments listed in the credits, Leslie piano and synthesizer. "Becalmed" opens with a soft swooshing, wind-like sound that soon gives way to a few harmonically suggestive notes on the Leslie piano. Commonly used for variable-speed tremolo effects with an electronic organ, the Leslie speaker produces a slight pulsation of volume and pitch; here the pulsation takes place at a very low speed, making the effect very subtle. After this indefinite introduction, the synthesizer enters with the chord progression of Example 7, which is repeated four times before ending, with a subdued, paradoxical sense of rest and mild anticipation, on the subdominant.

Several subtle factors determine the aesthetic success of "Becalmed." The lack of rigid synchronization between piano and synthesizer contribute to it. So does the languishing, almost non-existent pulse itself. A seemingly minor detail—the lack of a third in the first vi in the succession of chords—provides an unexpected spatial opening which, had it been filled, might have made the piece's simple, consonant harmonies too sweet, closed, shut-up. In a similar way, the melodic appoggiatura (a note not belonging to the background harmony), creating a dissonant interval of a second at the appearance of each tonic chord, provides a mild element of tension that offsets the general celebration of consonance.

"Zawinul/Lava"[16] is a prefiguration of later developments in Eno's compositional career. The repeated acoustic piano motif, D-G-A-D/D-G-A-C (ascending), is almost identical to some of the motives featuring major seconds and open fourths in *Music for Airports* (1978), and the general sound world of this piece has much in common with that of "Little Fishes." Unlike "Little Fishes," however, "Zawinul/Lava" is a collective effort, with Phil Collins on percussion (occasional accents and trills on cymbals and drums), Percy Jones on fretless bass (isolated tones), Paul Rudolph on guitar (one or two notes), Rod Melvin on Rhodes piano (a few notes here and there), and Eno on grand piano (the repeated motif), synthesizer (a few animal- or human-like crying sounds), organ, and tape. A tonic (G) pedal in one or another instrument is present from about halfway through.

"Zawinul/Lava" was doubtless the result of group improvisation within certain limits that Eno specified—an "experiment" whose outcome could not have been completely foreseen. If one particular feature of this piece distinguishes it from similar later experiments, it is the element of drama and development, however understated: "Zawinul/Lava" starts with the piano motif alone, slowly builds to a mezzoforte high point ("climax" is far too strong a word) at the establishment of the pedal point (the long held "drone" notes), and then subsides as it fades out. Later Eno compositions of this general type tend to maintain the established musical premises from "beginning" to "end," the point being that they do not have clear-cut beginnings or endings.

As if to illustrate the "merging" idea of the previous song, "Spirits Drifting" enters before the fade-out of "Everything Merges With the Night" is quite complete. "Spirits Drifting" is another all-instrumental, all-Eno piece: he plays bass guitar, organ, and synthesizer. The harmonies—minor-based and at times extremely dissonant—are unusual for Eno, who normally works within either a relatively consonant diatonic framework or almost completely outside the harmonic realm as such. Like "Little Fishes" (which was, however, major-based), "Spirits Drifting" operates over a structure of bass notes chosen from a fifth-related set of three, in this case D-A-E. The sequence of these bass notes, articulated individually on the bass guitar, is as follows (various octave displacements are used):

Example 8
BASS LINE OF "SPIRITS DRIFTING"

```
A E A E
A E A E
D E A E
A E A E
D E D E
A E A E
D E A E
D E A E
D E A E
A E D E
D E
```

(The E's are preceded by an upbeat "passing-note" D, or sometimes, when approached from a structural D, by the chromatic figure D-D♯.)

The second and fourth roots of each group of four remain consistently E; the first and third appear to vary randomly. On top of this "root structure" move a number of meandering synthesizer and organ lines, predominantly among the pitch-set common to the scales of D, A, and E (natural) minor (D, E, G, A, C), but also among the pitches belonging to only one or two of those keys, and sometimes touching on D♯ and G♯, the contextually very dissonant "leading tones" to E and A. (Eno later returned to similar quasi-serialist procedures in *Music for Airports*. Serialism was an outgrowth of Arnold Schoenberg's twelve-tone method, and a major force in musical composition during the 1950s; serialist composers were fond of using recurring, predetermined sets of notes to form the structural basis of their pieces.)

The quiet, brooding, totally non-rock sonorities of this, the final composition on *Another Green World*, make for a striking formal dénouement, and in themselves form yet another bridge: they look forward to subsequent works in which Eno thoroughly explored the quiet style that emerged on this album.

In the lyrics of the first song on *Another Green World*, "all the clouds turn to words"; in the last song, "everything merges with the night." The final composition, "Spirits Drifting," is the night music itself. Given these framing factors—the long "Sky Saw" instrumentals that precede the entrance of that song's text, which is about the futility of words ("No one knows what they mean / everyone just ignores them"), and the floating instrumental sonorities of "Spirits Drifting"—the content of *Another Green World* as a whole seems to emerge from darkness, crystallize into various forms, and then sink back whence it came. The album represents Eno's greatest artistic achievement in testing the limits of rock.

chapter 10

The Ambient Sound

To John Cage, ambient sounds were the sounds of the environment one happened to be in. To the editors of *Webster's New Twentieth Century Dictionary*, "ambient" meant "surrounding; encompassing on all sides; investing; as, the *ambient* air." Ambient could also be a noun, meaning "that which encompasses on all sides."[1] Ambiance today commonly means the quality or qualities of the surroundings in a specific place, and carries certain almost musical connotations—"the totality of motives, patterns, or accessories surrounding and enhancing the central motif or design."[2] The concept of ambiance is associated with the decorative arts, with places where people gather, with the planning and architecture of urban and suburban spaces. Adding a commercial dimension to the content of the word "ambient," the Japanese electronics company Panasonic began, a few years back, advertising their "miracle ambient sound," an effect which added an aural illusion of spaciousness and depth to music coming out of the small stereo loudspeakers of portable radio/cassette players, by allowing the listener to shift the left and right channels slightly out of phase with each other. "Ambience" has a specific meaning in the recording studio:

> What sound engineers call ambience is a spatial dimension conferred on sound through some degree of echo delay or reverberation. Virtually all recorded and broadcast music is enhanced by some artificial ambience. It is what makes Luciano Pavarotti sound like he's grabbing you by the collar and singing into your face; it makes a Van Halen record sound like it was recorded in St. Paul's Cathedral.[3]

The word goes back to the Latin: *ambiens* is the present participle of the verb *ambire*, to go around, from the prefix *amb-*, around, and the verb root *ire*, to go. The *amb-* prefix is used in words like ambiguous, ambit, ambidextrous, and—a word Eno might particularly relish—ambitendency, "the state of having along with each tendency a countertendency."[4]

When Eno chose the term "ambient" for the kind of quiet, unobtrusive music he began making during the early 1970s, the word's rich connotations must have been prominent in his mind. It was music that could tint the atmosphere of the location where it was played. It was music that surrounded the listener with a sense of spaciousness and depth, encompassing one on all sides, instead of coming *at* the listener. It blended with the sounds of the environment, and seemed to invite one to listen musically to the environment itself, instead of getting annoyed at people coughing or rustling programs during the slow movement. It had a central motif or design, which, however, could be surrounded and enhanced by a glimmering plenitude of accessory motives and sonic patterns. Ambient music was decorative, rather than expressionist; if not completely free of individual taste, memory, and psychology, as in Cage's ideal, it nevertheless lacked the bathos of self-importance and confessional displays of open psychic wounds. It seemed to rotate around certain central issues, never approaching them directly.

Between 1978 and 1982 Eno produced four albums that he called the Ambient series. They make a handsome set, their covers sporting similar artwork, layout, and typography. Of these four, however, only the first, *Music for Airports*, and the last, *On Land*, contain music that is mostly composed by Eno; *Ambient 2: The Plateaux of Mirror* is a collaborative effort between Eno and composer Harold Budd, and *Ambient 3: Day of Radiance* consists of compositions by hammer-dulcimer player Laraaji. These four albums comprise the Ambient series proper, but Eno himself has used the term "ambient" to describe the music of a number of albums released both before and after the Ambient series proper. I shall therefore use the term "ambient music" to denote Eno's broad approach to composition as well as his concept of the music's appropriate mode or modes of reception.

The music to be discussed in this chapter is firmly attributed to Eno alone, having been composed, produced, and arranged solely by him unless otherwise noted. Other musicians do play instruments on some of Eno's ambient pieces, and in the absence of a written score, we are often not quite sure what or how Eno told his musicians to play, or coaxed them into playing. But from *Taking Tiger Mountain (By Strategy)* of 1974 on, statements like "All compositions written by Eno" begin appearing on his solo albums, indicating that he had final authority over and responsibility for the creative decisions leading to the finished product. It is not unreasonable, then, to attempt here an appraisal of Eno's own personal compositional style.

Certain traits characterize most of the pieces that Eno composed in the ambient style: quietness, gentleness, an emphasis on the vertical color of sound, establishment and maintenance of a single pervasive atmosphere, non-developmental forms, regularly or irregularly repeating events or cycles of events, modal pitch-sets, choice of a few limited parameters for each piece, layered textures tending toward an even balance of tone and noise, and a pulse that is sometimes uneven, sometimes "breathing," and sometimes non-existent.

LONG AMBIENT PIECES

The long signal loop pieces that Eno made with Robert Fripp during the mid-1970s (to be discussed in the next chapter), though repetitive in their way, are strongly developmental: things happen in linear time, and these pieces have beginnings, middles, and ends. But Eno was also interested in making non-teleological music, music that would seem to be "just a chunk out of a longer continuum."[5] With his progressive rock music of the early 1970s, he was still engaged in assaulting the audience at musical, visual, and conceptual levels. But simultaneously he was getting tired of "wanting to shock and surprise and take people by the lapels and shake them all the time with music. I decided I wanted to do something that is extremely calm and delicate and kind of invites you in rather than pushes itself upon you."[6]

What finally precipitated the shift in the balance of Eno's musical interests, and what served to crystallize his thoughts about this new kind of music, was an accident: on leaving a studio in January 1975, he was struck by a taxi and briefly hospitalized. This hospitalization set the scene for a musical revelation, which he has described as follows:

> My friend Judy Nylon visited me and brought me a record of 18th century harp music. After she had gone, and with some considerable difficulty, I put on the record. Having laid [sic] down, I realized that the amplifier was set at an extremely low level, and that one channel of the stereo had failed completely. Since I hadn't the energy to get up and improve matters, the record played on almost inaudibly. This presented what was for me a new way of hearing music—as part of the ambience of the environment just as the colour of the light and the sound of the rain were parts of that ambience. It is for this reason that I suggest listening to the piece ["Discreet Music"] at comparatively low levels, even to the extent that it frequently falls below the threshold of audibility.[7]

Such was the conceptual backdrop for the making of *Discreet Music*. The title track, which at thirty and a half minutes fills up just about the maximum space available on a single side of a long-playing record—thus suggesting that the music was indeed taken out of a much larger, even infinite continuum—was composed of "two simple and mutually compatible melodic lines of different duration stored on a [synthesizer with a] digital recall system." One melody consists of the pitches c″ d″ (rest) e′ (rest) g′; the other is somewhat more elaborate: d′ e′ (rest) d′ b g (rest) d (rest) e″ g″ a″ g″. (The designation of octave positions in these examples follows the scheme employed by the *New Harvard Dictionary of Music*; see its article on "Pitch.")

Having composed the melodies and set up a tape-delay and storage system, Eno's activity as a composer/performer was limited to setting the tunes in motion at various points, and to "occasionally altering the timbre of the synthesizer's output by means of a graphic equalizer."[8] The musical result was half an hour of simple, tranquil, repeating and overlapping melodic segments—a kind of switched-on, slow-motion heterophony. (Heterophony is a term often used to describe folk and other music in which the basic melodies are varied or embellished, intentionally, instinctively, or unintentionally, by the performers.)

It would be difficult to notate precisely the rhythmic values of "Discreet Music"'s melodies, as the pulse in the music itself is not metronomic. Though the recurring rhythms of the seven melodic fragments separated by rests imply a pulse of sorts, the two long melodies are not strictly synchronized, so at best there is a sense of overlapping pulses. The word "breathing" seems to describe the rhythm much more accurately than "pulse." Furthermore, the "rests" are invariably filled in by "echoes" of previously heard fragments, occurring approximately six seconds after each fragment itself, so that the music continuously consists not only of fresh new events but of previously heard events that are echoing gradually into the past and into inaudibility. The harmony is static, based on the overlapping of eleven different pitches forming a G-major chord with added ninth, eleventh, and thirteenth—typical of Eno's search for basically consonant sounds with just a bit of spice:

Example 9
HARMONIC CONTENT OF "DISCREET MUSIC"

a''
g''
e''
d''
c''
g'
e'
d'
b
g
d

It is interesting that the lowest note should be the fifth of the chord: a technique that will appear again and again in Eno's ambient music, this prevents the total sound mass from sounding too "rooted," too gravitationally drawn to or stuck around a tonic.

The form of "Discreet Music" is completely accidental, unintentional. Eno was preparing some tapes to be used as background sounds for a live, improvised performance by Fripp and himself. Having set up and turned on the tape-delay system (to be described in the next chapter), and having programmed the melodies into the synthesizer at his home studio, the phone started ringing, people started knocking at the door, and I was answering the phone and adjusting all this stuff as it ran. I almost made ["Discreet Music"] without listening to it. It was really automatic music. . . . Since then I've experimented a lot with procedures where I set something up and interfered as little as possible.[9]

An additional accident that led to the final version of "Discreet Music" was that when Eno played the tape for Fripp, he put it on at half-speed by mistake. It sounded "very, very good. I thought it was probably one of the best things I'd ever done and I didn't even realize I was doing it at the time."[10]

Since Eno was occupied with other business while making this piece, one tends to hear clumps of inputs set in motion periodically and then to hear them all gradually echo away into the distance. The variations in equalization make a surprising amount of difference. When so much in the way of melody, rhythm, and harmony has been stripped away from the music, timbral subtleties loom structurally large. Equalization changes the timbre from round flute- or even foghorn-like sounds to sharper, clarinet-like tones; even the octave position of the melodic fragments can appear to change. In terms of noise versus tone, the timbral predominance leans decidedly toward tone compared to a piece like Fripp and Eno's "An Index of Metals"; yet the equalization changes make one acutely aware of the noise-like content of upper harmonics.

Side Two of *Discreet Music* contains a piece representing a different way of satisfying Eno's "interest in self-regulating and self-generating systems." "Three Variations on the Canon in D Major by Johann Pachelbel" is for

a group of performers [string players] with a set of instructions—and the "input" is the fragment of Pachelbel. Each variation takes a small section of the score (two or four bars) as its starting point, and permutates the players' parts such that they overlay each other in ways not suggested by the original score.[11]

The audible result of this process, gamely played by the Cockpit Ensemble conducted by Gavin Bryars, is some twenty minutes of pandiatonic music operating on several rhythmic levels simultaneously, in three sections that present the familiar melody in strange new guises and disguises. Eno's treatment of the Pachelbel piece is an experiment in conceptual neoclassicism, and the result is not really all that gripping: a process piece with a marginally valuable product. As Eno later said, it does make a difference what the input is. In this case, the input gave Eno too many notes to work with: randomness here created cacophony, whereas on the other side of *Discreet Music,* with the input drastically limited, it produced ambient euphony.

Music for Airports was the first of the four albums in the Ambient series that Eno produced between 1979 and 1982. In the liner notes, Eno described the philosophical and practical program and criticized Muzak, Inc. for its saturation of the background-music market with "familiar tunes arranged and orchestrated in a lightweight and derivative manner." Eno explained that "over the past three years, I have become interested in the use of music as ambience, and have come to believe that it is possible to produce material that can be used thus without being in any way compromised." *Music for Airports*, which was actually piped into the Marine Terminal at New York's La Guardia Airport in 1980,[12] was Eno's initial compositional response to the problem. There are four untitled, numbered compositions on the album, each taking up about half a record side with variously orchestrated studies in sculptured sound and silence. Major-key pandiatonicism and pure, uncluttered tone colors reign supreme in slowly shifting sonic tapestries which, as Eno says of his ambient music in general, "must be able to accommodate many levels of listening attention without enforcing one in particular."[13]

"2/1," the second piece on the first side, is the purest, and arguably the most effective, of the four compositions. The only sound sources are taped female voices singing single pitches on the syllable "ah," with an absolutely unwavering tone production, for about five seconds per pitch. These sung notes have been electronically treated to give them a soft attack/decay envelope and a slight hiss that accompanies the tone. Once again, the pitch material is very limited: seven tones that taken together spell a D♭ major seventh chord with an added ninth. (See Example 10.)

Example 10
HARMONIC CONTENT OF "2/1"

a♭'
f'
e♭'
d♭'
c'
a♭
f

The rhythm of "2/1" is serially organized. As Eno has explained, he recorded each long note onto a separate piece of tape, and made each piece of tape into a loop of a different length. The relationships between the lengths of the loops "aren't simple, they're not six to four. They're like 27 to 79, or something like that. Numbers that mean they would constantly be falling in different relationships to one another." In fact, Eno did not measure the lengths precisely, but simply spun off what seemed like a "reasonable" amount of extra tape for each note. "And then I started all the loops running, and let them configure in the way they chose to configure. So sometimes you get dense clusters and fairly long silences, and then you get a sequence of notes that makes a kind of melody."[14]

Thus Eno deemed unimportant the exact ratios between the cycles of repetition of the seven notes. For the record, the approximate duration of each cycle, determined through measurement with a stopwatch, is given in Example 11; the pitches are given in order of their first appearance.

Example 11
APPROXIMATE DURATION OF PITCH-CYCLES IN "2/1"

c′	e♭′	f	a♭′	d♭′	f′	a♭
21″	17″	25″	18″	31″	20″	22″

It is interesting to note that once again Eno's pitch material adds up to a chord that is not in root position (that is, the theoretically strongest note, D♭, is not the lowest note of the chord). Furthermore, the root D♭, the one note capable of producing a high-level dissonance in the context (a minor second with the neighboring C), has the longest cycle of the whole set, and is thus heard least frequently. The competing "tonics" of D♭ and A♭ exemplify the modal ambiguity found frequently in Eno's music. Such music *suggests* a key, keys, or mode, but does not assert one unambiguously. The melodic, harmonic, and rhythmic cadences so important to the establishment of key in tonal music are completely absent here.

The balance between sound and silence is of the essence in "2/1," and in no other piece of Eno's is silence itself so important. The composition, in its rarefied nature, its systematic use of long notes, and its serial organization, is reminiscent of Webern pieces like the first movement of his Symphony, Op. 21, of 1928, despite the different tonal idioms. Most critics and musicologists would agree, however, that even those initiated souls who numerically have plotted out the complex double canon among tone-row forms in that Symphony's exposition are unlikely to have much success following the canon in real time without a score. In Eno's "2/1," on the other hand, owing to the limited pitch material, the fixed, narrow register, and the slow rhythmic cycles, the informed listener has considerably greater hope of following the serial unfolding, should he or she choose to do so. Between airport ambiance and mental chess game, "2/1" admirably lives up to its professed goal of accomodating different levels of listening attention while offering different kinds of rewards at each level.[15]

Many times in these pages I have remarked upon the spatial and visual qualities of Eno's music. It is easy to imagine how Eno, with his art school background and its emphasis on experimentalism, his continuing interest in the visual arts, and his own "painterly" or "sculptural" approach to music, would become actively involved in a new field of expression—video. He began his video experiments in his loft in downtown Manhattan in 1978, when he turned a monitor on its side and left the camera lying (also on its side) on his windowsill to tape the slowly shifting patterns of light on buildings and clouds in the sky. Since then, he has produced primarily two kinds of video work, which he calls "video paintings" and "video sculptures" respectively. In the former, he treats the video screen as a canvas, in the specific sense that he does not present the viewer with a narrative or story—a sequence of events that must be watched in its entirety to be understood; therefore, the viewer may come to rest for a few minutes in front of the video painting, contemplate it, and leave as he or she chooses. Some of the video paintings use recognizable images; some are abstract. But whether realistic in nature or not, they embody the idea that "light stands in the same relation to images as sound does to words":[16] and if with his music Eno was always more interested in sound than with words, in his visual works he is more concerned with light than with images. The video sculptures are similar in concept, but here the video screens are concealed beneath or behind translucent materials built into various geometrical shapes, so that the viewer confronts a three-dimensional object on whose surface transpires a continuous play of color.

Since 1979 Eno has been setting up audiovisual installations in galleries, museums, at festivals, and in the occasional train station or airport. In these installations, he seeks to create a total environment, a place that emanates the same kind of ambiance as his ambient music, and that, like his ambient music, is able to accomodate varying levels of attention and reward them equally. His ideal installation is "a place poised between a club, a gallery, a church, a square and a park, and sharing aspects of all of these."[17] He wants his installations to provide for urban dwellers an experience "like sitting by a river";[18] a viewer might drop by for repeated observations during his or her lunch hour, using the place whose ambiance Eno has gently crafted as a space in which to think.[19]

> What I like to do with the music is first of all inspect the place where the show is going to be, and then try to make a piece which completely sinks into that environment somewhere. So that many of the sounds are indistinguishable from the traffic outside, the general hum of the city.
>
> I like to have this feeling that people could sit there and think that the music continued out of earshot. I like the notion that you're sitting in this field of sound, and you don't necessarily hear all of it.[20]

The actual configuration and spatial disposition of loudspeakers, tape recorders, video sculptures and paintings, places to sit, and such things as the size and shape of walls and rooms, vary from place to place, and thus each installation is unique. Eno is currently seeking a permanent site for what he calls "The Quiet Club," which evidently will be an ambient environment designed to stay put.[21]

One thing that the audio-video installations tend to share is the kind of cyclic approach to music found in "2/1" from *Music for Airports*. In that piece, seven notes recurred, each according to a different time-cycle. Eno's installations typically use four tape players, each set in motion at a randomly chosen moment, and each playing a different cycle of events, sometimes of very long duration. Auto-reverse cassette decks are employed so that the music can continue playing unattended for an indefinite length of time. The effects of such cyclic music are similar to those of "2/1," but on a much larger scale: rapid clusters of events alternate with more evenly spaced episodes, and even with stretches of complete silence. Unique constellations of events take form, never to recur again.[22]

In 1984 Sony Japan commissioned Eno to create a video and accompanying soundtrack that would be written and recorded specifically for compact disc, to be released only in that medium. Eno made seven video paintings of a nude female model and combined these with a cyclic musical composition. The finished result, called *Thursday Afternoon*, has been shown internationally and took first prize for best non-narrative video at the Video Culture Canada exposition in Toronto in October 1984. The video itself, and a CD of the same title, containing sixty-one minutes of uninterrupted music, were commercially released in 1986.

For Eno, the attraction of writing a piece for compact disc was twofold: it could be much longer than the thirty or so minutes available on one side of a conventional LP; and it probably would not have the background hiss associated with analog mastering techniques. However, although *Thursday Afternoon* was digitally mastered, the music was originally recorded on a conventional twenty-four-track analog machine; Eno explained that he needed the capability of changing tape speeds more than the fifteen percent or so currently offered by digital technology. Slowing down recorded sounds by fifty percent or more "does something to the timbre of sound that I like, by bringing upper harmonics into hearing range," he said.[23]

In the music of *Thursday Afternoon*, very small events take on large proportions in the quiet sonic expanse Eno sets up. A low drone remains nearly constant until close to the end, when it drops out to highlight the other almost ubiquitous element, a high, shimmering major chord on synthesizer. These shimmering timbres seem constant, fixed; and yet, when not much else is happening in the music, one realizes that the sound never stays the same at all, but has an inner richness and vitality in its own right.

Over these background sounds occur a number of distinct kinds of sound events in periodic clusters, that is, appearing for certain stretches of time, then vanishing: very high, bright, bell-like tones with rich harmonics; a melodic-harmonic motive using the overlapping pitches C, B, and F, and timbrally using rapid amplitude modulation; "bird sounds" and "cricket sounds"—high-frequency twittering; a sound like an echoed water drop, which is approximately on the pitch A; long single synthesizer tones with very soft attack and decay; a strange, low-frequency, variably pitched, almost human "sighing" sound with a downward slide and fairly quick attack and decay; and—what the listener is bound to focus on whenever it appears, because its timbre is the most evocative of traditional, known music—an essentially Mixolydian set of pitches played on treated piano in seemingly random rhythm and order. (See Example 12.) All of these sound events have occurred at least once within the piece's first fifteen minutes.

Example 12
PIANO PITCH COLLECTION IN "THURSDAY AFTERNOON"

$$d''$$
$$c''$$
$$b'$$
$$g'$$
$$f'$$
$$d'$$
$$b$$
$$g$$

Except for very occasional short sections when the background shimmering changes to a C-major from a G-major chord, the harmony of *Thursday Afternoon* is essentially static throughout, though with a tendency to throw in and out of relief the rich overtone partials of the equal-tempered tritone, B–F. *Thursday Afternoon* follows no developmental logic; it is a non-temporal painting in sound.

The press's attention to Eno's ambient style peaked between 1976 and 1979, around the time reviews for *Discreet Music, Another Green World,* and *Music for Airports* were coming out. Mikal Gilmore wrote sympathetically of Eno's "ideal of passivity" in *Discreet Music;*[24] James Wolcott bravely tried to "fire public enthusiasm" (that is, the enthusiasm of *Creem's* rock readership) for that album's music: "It's lullingly beautiful, both intimate and distant, like music heard at night from a distant shore, and it has a calming, meditative effect: soon every molecule in the room has been reduced to balletic drowsiness."[25] Some critics were unable to fathom (or stomach) the ambient approach. Michael Bloom, while admiring Eno's level of electronic craftsmanship, and realizing that perhaps such records were intended more as "*gebrauchsmusik,* or utilitarian undertakings . . . environmental sound," wrote bitingly, "As aesthetic white noise, *Ambient 1: Music for Airports* makes for even more dissipated listening than last year's similarly unfocussed *Music for Films.*"[26] Ken Emerson derided Eno's "avant-garde Muzak," in a petulant review of *Music for Airports* that complained, "One man's nirvana is another man's nap."[27] Such reviews, both positive and negative, probably represent a fair sampling of how Eno's music was being received by private listeners: some found it relaxing, beautiful, gently stimulating; others found it boring, faceless, unmusical.

During this same period Eno's music was featured in numerous articles in the music press. Tom Johnson was the author of an attempt to come to grips with the renewed interest, on the part of contemporary composers like Eno, Reich, Riley, and Rzewski, in writing tonal music. Tonality in the new works, Johnson recognized, has nothing to do with functional harmonic progressions supported by bass lines, but is more a matter of free use of a diatonic (major-scale) pitch collection.[28] Johnson also wrote a rambling review of the ten-day festival "New Music, New York," ambitiously attempting to sum up developments in the new music scene of the 1970s, highlighting the growing split between the older generation—Cage-inspired, Eastern-philosophy-influenced —and the younger—electric guitars in hand, performance-art-oriented. Eno appeared at the festival, arguing for the inclusion of a sensuous element in new music to balance what he felt was the overstressed intellectual element.[29] A Marxist critique of Eno's music was offered by Tom Hull, who found in it a response to the post-Adorno challenge to art

> to catch up, to take command of the future and command of its technology. . . . His work is predicated not on the immediacy of the revolution, as Lissitzky's was, but rather . . . on the revolution's inevitability, the real presence of a new world. The drift of history is on his side, awaiting only that New Man to come to seize the possibilities knowledge and technology offer and wield them into a rational society. Eno, as a socially responsible artist, has two basic tasks: to engage our hearing in novel ways, and to provide objects for our new world. He does both, splendidly.[30]

SHORT AMBIENT PIECES

Between 1976 and 1983, Eno released four albums containing mostly shorter pieces in the ambient style. The first of these was *Music for Films*, originally released in 1976 in a limited edition of five hundred copies; it was reissued in 1978 as a single album, and then again turned up in the ten-album retrospective boxed set *Working Backwards, 1983–1973*, in a version Eno said was "identical in content to the first edition released in 1978 but rearranged into what I consider a more satisfactory track sequence."[31] With *Music for Films* Eno was in a sense advertising his music for use by filmmakers; the album included an address to which interested parties could write for synchronization licenses. The fact that he had taken the trouble to rearrange the pieces to make a better sounding whole, however, indicates that he simultaneously viewed the album as an artistic product in its own right—as a conceptual album of music for imaginary films. Some of the music, he wrote, "was made specifically for use as soundtrack material, some of it was made for other reasons but found its way into films; most of it is previously unissued in any form."[32] All compositions on *Music for Films* are by Eno, though two were "arranged" with the help of bassist Percy Jones and guitarist Fred Frith. Ten musicians, mostly veterans of progressive rock album sessions with Eno, contributed guitar, bass, percussion, viola, electric piano, and trumpet parts.

There are eighteen pieces on *Music for Films*, nine per side; Eno is the sole musician on eleven of them. In some respects the sound world is very similar to that of *Discreet Music:* few events, very quiet dynamics, diatonicism, repetition, gentle washes of synthesizer colors, merging of foreground and background, frequent lack of definite pulse, a sense of timelessness. Here, however, the actual duration of each piece is reduced, often to aphoristic proportions of less than two minutes. The effect, then, is to evoke a series of miniature worlds, each with a set of characteristics involving tone color and melodic and harmonic procedures.

Music for Films was largely ignored by the music press, which, one feels, was running out of things to say about Eno's increasingly subtle approach: without any words or performances to write about, and faced with a new musical language that would be inappropriate to describe in technical terms in a popular periodical, reviewers and editors balked. Michael Davis, however, bravely set down his impressions of *Music for Films* for *Creem's* readers:

> Begin with a dazzling quartz crystal. Fade up to soft focus on a warm bed being made warmer. Soft sighs heard from beneath the covers are transformed into space meows somehow sensed through the windows of a 747. The plane glides to earth, eventually disappearing into the Bermuda Triangle, where you are seductively attacked by the stewardess in Jamaican chainsaw rhythm. She is easily eluded, however, and you swim to the surface just in time to see your purple-haired secretary teaching the switchboard nursery rhymes. The typewriter on her desk retorts with a funky clavinet imitation. You walk out the door and are immediately sizzled by a sunshower. When your eyes can focus again, you're back at home, staring at your smiling turntable as the needle returns to play the side over again, refusing to reject the record. . . . If you want logic, go carouse with Kraftwerk.[33]

On Land, the final album in the Ambient tetralogy, released in 1982, contains eight compositions, all but one of them by Eno alone. Five musicians contributed synthesizer, guitar, bass, trumpet, guitar, and "live equalization." What sets *On Land* apart musically from most of Eno's quiet, contemplative music is that here the element of timbre takes over to the point of there being very few pitches in use, and often nothing that could really be called harmony. For instance, consider "The Lost Day," a fairly extensive (nine-and-a-half-minute) piece. Throughout, one hears an ominous, indefinable, very low sound that varies slightly in its color and dynamic intensity. An eerie muted metallic clinking that sounds like ropes hitting the mast of a sailboat at rest in the water comes and goes, as do stray blows on a xylophone, a haunting Phrygian-mode synthesizer melody in the tenor range, and indefinable noises, often reminiscent of collective natural phenomena like swarming insects, the baying of cattle, or the sound of a flock of ducks taking off from a body of water. Sonic edges are blurred, events occur in a non-linear, non-narrative fashion, and electronically generated sounds mingle, merge, and blend with instrumental and found sounds to the extent that the impression is one of a continuous tableau, with no real distinction between human, animal, insect, or mechanical sound-sources.

The critical response to *On Land*—the last Eno solo ambient album to generate much attention in the press—was split along the lines I have already described. Jon Pareles continued his love-hate relationship with Eno's music and ideas, chastizing him for theoretical unoriginality though grudgingly admitting to being impressed by the music, while longing for Eno to return to the progressive rock style.[34] Mark Peel offered the condescending put-down: "Brian Eno's 'ambient music' is certainly ambient . . . but it's certainly not music. . . . I'll bet plants love it. As for me, I'm just going to let it lull me to sleep."[35] George Rush, while rendering an enthusiastic account of Eno's career, thought that at times the music "narrowly escapes schmaltz. . . . In several places he employs the worst B-movie sound effects—the ominous haunted-house drone, bird squawks, and frog croaks."[36] Robert Payes and Glenn O'Brien found *On Land's* enveloping environments powerful and satisfying.[37]

Apollo: Atmospheres & Soundtracks, released in 1983, was played and composed by Brian Eno, Daniel Lanois, and Roger Eno. Given that these musicians appear almost equally to have shared compositional, performance, recording, and production tasks on this album, we are faced with a situation like that of the Bowie/Eno collaborations of the late 1970s, where Eno's work as a composer extends by imperceptible degrees into the area of collaboration with others. It is perhaps in this sense that Eno best exemplifies his own philosophy, spelled out in his article "Generating and Organizing Variety in the Arts," of a more horizontally disposed—rather than heirarchically imposed—creative process. In any case, Eno wrote only two of the twelve pieces by himself; the others are co-written or written by Lanois. *Apollo* was the result of a commission to score the music to director Al Reinert's documentary on the Apollo missions to the moon. The musical style is similar to that of *On Land*, but with rather more emphasis on pitch material, which tends to appear over long, sustained drones. As his Ambient series records were a response to the harshness of commercial Muzak, *Apollo* gave Eno an opportunity to portray his reaction to the dawn of the era of space exploration. He had been discouraged by the TV coverage of the first Apollo moon mission, with its "uptempo, 'newsy' manner, short shots, fast cuts, and too many experts obscuring the grandeur and strangeness of the event with a patina of down-to-earth chatter."[38]

Of *Music for Films, Vol. II*, released in 1983 as part of the boxed set *Working Backwards*, Eno explained:

> I released the first volume of Music for Films in 1978, and it contained samples of my work, spanning the period 1975–78. This second volume picks up where

the first left off, but it is somewhat different in that it contains fewer pieces with a greater average length.[30]

Eno himself wrote five of the thirteen compositions on *Music for Films, Vol. II;* the others are collaborations with Daniel Lanois and Roger Eno. Seven of the pieces were taken from the *Apollo* album. The upshot is that *Music for Films, Vol. II* contains only three new "solo" Eno compositions. It is interesting to note, however, that of the pieces borrowed from *Apollo*, Eno changes the length of all but one. That is to say, since these pieces are of the continuum type, it appears that their actual duration is incidental. With regard to classical compositions, it is sometimes said that the ideal version of a piece exists in the score, not in any particular performance. Of most of Eno's ambient works, it may be said that the ideal versions exist on one or more hypothetical strips of magnetic recording tape that go on forever; what we hear on the albums are arbitrarily truncated sections of the ideal versions.

These four albums of shorter ambient pieces may also represent concessions to the reality of the marketplace. Out of the hundreds of pieces Eno claims to have made and stored away on tape, how many would the public really be interested in absorbing in versions that went on for twenty minutes or more? Eno has chosen a middle path of releasing a few albums of long pieces that afford luxurious stretches of uninterrupted ambience, and a few albums that tip the balance toward variety over unity. Furthermore, regardless of the ideal of indefinite length, it does make a difference how many pieces are on a record. Earlier I argued that one of the factors that makes *Another Green World* Eno's progressive rock masterpiece is the sheer brevity, variety, and number of its individual pieces. With regard to the ambient style, I would argue that an album containing four pieces per side, such as *On Land*, is bound to be heard in different terms than one containing nine per side, like *Music for Films*. The terms of listening may, of course, depend to a great extent on the listener— the mode of receptivity he or she is willing to adopt and the level of concentration he or she is capable of exerting. But the terms of listening also depend on the character and absolute duration of the material being presented. Adopting a vertical mode of listening—a disposition of one's faculties of concentration along the timbral rather than the temporal dimension—is positively encouraged in direct proportion to the length of a piece: only after one has gotten thoroughly used to a piece's surface qualities of tonality, sound types, overall texture, and so on, can one really begin to appreciate the minute deviations that are such an important part of Eno's music. Nevertheless, Eno has shown that the ambient style is able to accomodate not only varying levels of listening attention, but varying spans of musical duration, from the miniature to the "heavenly." Concerned with both grain of sand and expanse of space, the composer has created a highly flexible medium.

Leaving aside for now the question of the effect of duration on perception, let us delve further into the musical characteristics of the ambient style on these four albums. Although the collectively authored compositions share many of the same traits, I shall restrict this discussion to the thirty pieces composed by Eno alone. Texture and timbre may be of the essence in the ambient style, but a few general remarks may clarify the style's use of rhythm and harmony. Although they may appear a bit naked or technical in the abstract, these observations may suggest some of the variety of effects that Eno manages to eke out of a rather severely limited repertory of traditional musical materials.

Of the thirty pieces under consideration, eleven dispense with pulse altogether, the rhythm consisting of a gentle ebb and flow of instrumental colors. (Listen, for instance, to "Inland Sea," "Lizard Point," or "The Lost Day.") Nine have a steady, slow overall rhythm in which the pulse is more or less coordinated among the various parts ("Always Returning," "Roman Twilight"). Seven employ an indefinite, fluctuating pulse which typically results from the striking of a bass note or chord at an approximately designated point in time ("Climate Study"). Two have a steady pulse in the bass only, with free rhythms in the other parts ("A Measured Room," "Two Rapid Formations"). Finally, one piece ("Patrolling Wire Borders") manifests two distinct, uncoordinated planes of pulse.

Eno's most common type of harmonic ploy is a repeating chord progression; nine pieces share this trait. Such progressions may be simply alternations of two chords (minor i and minor ii in a Dorian mode in "A Measured Room"; major I and major VII in a Mixolydian mode in "M386"; I7 and IV in a major mode in "Strange Light"); or they may be somewhat more involved (‖: I | V | ♭VII | IV:‖ in "Patrolling Wire Borders," or ‖: i | iv | i | iv | i | v | VII | VII :‖ in "Sparrowfall"). Non-repeating, weak, and tonally ambiguous progressions in which the chords are taken from within the range of two keys distinguish one or two pieces (like "Slow Water"). In another piece, two major chords a whole step apart alternate at a very indefinite, langorous pace ("Events in Dense Fog"). The remaining compositions use static or ambiguous harmonies, sometimes suggestive of chords but just as often consisting of nothing but a drone with seemingly stray pitches drawn from a diatonic pitch set appearing and disappearing overhead. Seven of these pieces (for instance, "Aragon" and "Inland Sea") can be classed as being in the minor mode, though "mode" here emphatically denotes a pitch set only, not a point of arrival or a set of melodic formulas. Three pieces are based on a complex major chord with added notes ("From the Same Hill," for example). Two are diatonic yet use neither drone nor tertian harmony ("Sparrowfall [2]"). The rest represent individual tonal orientations: a rotating set of pitches alternately suggestive of an F-minor seventh chord and a D♭-major seventh chord ("Unfamiliar Wind [Leeks Hills]"); a static Mixolydian pitch set ("Two Rapid Formations"); a spare use of pitches suggestive of the Phrygian mode ("Task Force"); a chromatic, unclassifiable pitch collection over a constant drone ("Alternative 3"); a predominantly Mixolydian pitch set, with, however, variable third, sixth, and seventh scale degrees ("Tal Coat"); and a shifting harmonic entity involving a minor seventh chord with a prominent fourth above the tonic and thus open to a quartal interpretation ("Lantern March": F-A♭-C-E♭ + B♭ = C-F-B♭-E♭-A♭?).

Although specific tone-color combinations remain as elusive as ever to capture in words, two principles of texture can be formulated that apply to many of Eno's shorter ambient pieces: the principle of layering and the principle of timbral heterogeneity. Each piece tends to use a different combination of tone colors or sound types, striving for a unique timbral identity. The types of sound themselves can perhaps be visualized as falling along a continuum between pure sine tones and pure white noise. But describing this distinction in terms of such visualization may be deceptive in the sense that many of Eno's tones and noises move and change; they are not static shades of color like those of a paint catalog, but have an inner life of their own. Take a single note: Eno will run it through his treatments, adding or subtracting harmonics (filtering or equalization), enhancing its spatiality (delay, reverb, echo), altering its attack-decay envelope, adding subtle or wide vibrato (or asymmetrical frequency modulation effects), subjecting it to amplitude modulation—the list of procedures goes on and on. When Eno is finished, the "single note" may be a very complex and active entity. Some of the sound types Eno uses are recognizably produced by acoustic or electric instruments, though he often treats them to give them a strange, otherworldly quality; bass guitar, acoustic piano, and electric guitar are probably the most common traditional instrumental sound sources in Eno's ambient music.

"Synthesizer" means nothing as a sound type in itself. Among the classes of sound Eno is fond of producing with synthesizers and tape machines are the following, descriptively indicated: tinkling, glass-like; swooshing, ocean or wind-like; complex, irregular, bell-like harmonics; clanking, metallic; water-drop-like; gurgling; jet-plane-like (involving a systematic development or continuous variation of the harmonic structure of the sound); brass-like, string-like, organ-like, and piano-like tones; an array of "beeps and boops"—rapid successions of sounds with quickly changing pitch-profiles and ADSR envelopes[40] associated, for instance, with both the Columbia-Princeton RCA Mark II Synthesizer in the early 1960s, and the synthesized "voice" of robot R2D2 in the *Star Wars* movies of the late 1970s and 1980s; paper-shuffling-like; low-volume, high-density, complex, saturated, aggregative; machine-like, mechanical; "backwards" (sounds with a very slow attack and very fast decay); and animal- or insect-like—elephants, frogs, birds, mosquitoes, crickets. Another class of sounds is that produced by treated or untreated drum machine, but such sounds are present in only a few of the pieces under consideration.

Any given Eno piece is liable to consist of several—approximately three to seven—distinct, heterogeneous timbral layers. There are notable exceptions to this rule—for instance, the relatively homogeneous blend of organ-like sounds in "An Ending" (*Apollo*), a hymn-like piece, or the women's voices of "2/1". But, by and large, Eno is at pains to select sound types that will not obscure each other, that will be different enough to stand out from the others and yet preserve the transparency of the total sound. A typical ambient texture might consist of the following heterogeneous sound types: a very low frequency drone with a rich and active set of upper harmonics; intermittent animal-like noises; a few long, sustained, motivically related melodic phrases of flute-like tones, with pitch material selected from a certain mode, each note being surrounded by a halo of reverberation; and a recurring yet aperiodic water-dropping sound. Nothing here can be confused with anything else; every element will always be clearly audible. It may have been Eno's desire for a separation of each type of sound which led to his creation of a number of pieces in which extremely distinct, timbrally unique events occur just once over a more or less constant ambient background. The norm, however, is a continuum of regularly or irregularly spaced repetitions of events or at least of classes of events.

Several further points may be noted regarding such layered, heterogeneous textures. First, the atmosphere of each piece tends to be subtly yet decisively colored by a particular kind of drone and/or soft background noise layer. The drone is likely to be in the low register, though tenor and alto range drones are also present; and it is usually on the tonic note, although frequently enough it occurs on the fifth above the tonic, creating a continuous tension, a "six-four" type of effect. The background noise layer is likely to consist of some sort of gentle, pervasive, barely audible swooshing or gurgling type of sound, or some variety of active, treated white or pink noise (white noise sounds like a continuous hiss, with all audible frequencies present; pink noise is white noise with some of the highest frequencies filtered out). The background noise layer usually sets up the impression of immense, oceanic spaciousness—the feeling that the music is located in a large cathedral, the outdoors, or even outer space. We hear examples of both swooshing and gurgling noise layers in "Slow Water."

Second, aside from the drone or noise layer, which gives a pervading tint to the overall atmosphere, the density of events tends to be low, further enhancing the impression of the existence of plenty of black space around individual sounds. For all their constant, subtle activity, Eno's short ambient pieces sound remarkably uncluttered, clean, and geometrical. Such a texture of sparse melodic events over a floating harmonic background characterizes "From the Same Hill."

Third, and again augmenting the listener's sense of spaciousness, Eno's use of echo effects tends to be pronounced. He has taken full advantage of the development of digital delay equipment, which typically allows independent adjustment of delay time (the time between the moment the signal is input and the moment the delayed signal is sent out), the delay depth (the strength of the delayed signal), and the repeat level (the number of times the delayed signal will be heard). Long delay times, full delay depths, and high repeat levels, particularly when used in conjunction with sounds or pitches that have long attack and decay characteristics, can result in the creation of vast fictitious acoustical spaces. Echo, reverb, and white noise effects are at work in a piece like "Inland Sea."

Fourth, in many of the shorter ambient pieces, one hears numerous events that are just barely audible. Eno has planted all manner of little quirky sounds in these records: so many, in fact, that the attentive listener often finds himself not quite sure whether a noise came out of the speakers, from somewhere else in the house, or from outside the windows. The music of the pieces seems to blend by imperceptible degrees with the sounds of the environment—which is, of course, precisely what Eno intended. Listen to "The Lost Day" at low volume for a subtle study of events at the threshold level of perception.

The final trait of the ambient style which should be mentioned is the very low degree of "liveness" of sound that characterizes many of Eno's pieces. We have little if any sense that what we hear on these albums is a performance that has been captured through sound recording. Rather, Eno presents us with an entirely fictitious aural tableau. It makes no sense to imagine a group of performers playing this music together in real time—and that is certainly not how the music was made. Our sense of hearing and previous experience with musical instruments tells us that this sound was made with an electric bass guitar, that one with a piano. As to the origins of many other sounds, however, we are not quite sure. Is that a tape of bird song, airplane, organ, human voice? Or have these sounds been synthesized *ex nihilo?* The answers are not really relevant; for the total sound is profoundly "artificial," in the sense that it has been created by artifice, by the systematic application of human intelligence to a set of sounding materials. The natural habitat of this type of music indeed seems to be not the concert hall but the art gallery (where the original actions of the artist/performer are hidden from view, divorced from the present by time and space), the public space (where the observer/listener is not constrained to make an effort to actively engage his aesthetic faculties), or the home (where privacy provides perhaps the ideal situation in which to move in and out of the music according to the psychic metabolism of the moment).

A signal of Eno's impact on and growing stature in the modern art world was the publication of a full-length interview in the prestigious *Artforum International* in 1986.[41] The magazine's cover featured a striking glossy color photograph of a detail of one of his video sculptures, *Living Room:* in its geometrical purity the image of gently shaded rectangles of color on a pitch-black background showed the influence of one of the composer's early heroes, the painter Mondrian. For students of Eno's music, however, the real bonus of the *Artform* issue was a new recording, pressed between the pages on a transparent tear-out floppy 33-⅓ RPM disc.

The new composition, *Glint (East of Woodbridge),* is, as of this writing, Eno's most recently released recording. Although it shares many of the basic traits of the ambient style, it is tempting to interpret it as heralding a new direction in Eno's music, hazardous as such interpretation may be at such close range. *Glint* appears to be composed not so much of cycles of recurring events as of a continuous unfolding of unique events. It also differs from most of the previous ambient music in its greater relative density of events, the higher level of activity. This activity reaches a subdued climax near the middle and then tapers off in a gentle descent—unlike the many ambient pieces whose density and texture remain more or less constant from beginning to end. Unusual too are the concentration of pitch material in the middle and low registers, and the dark, Phrygian modality. At eight and a half minutes, *Glint* explores a medium range of duration; most of Eno's previous pieces are less than five or more than ten minutes long.

It is possible here only to mention in passing some of the other collaborative experiments in the ambient style that Eno has undertaken during the last decade. Among these are two albums with the German synthesizer rock group Cluster, recorded in 1977–78; on these records we can hear Eno trying out his timbral ideas, largely in the framework of music with a steady beat. The Cluster collaborations also provide a direct historical link between Eno and the whole German synthesizer-rock tradition of Kraftwerk, whom he much admired, and Tangerine Dream, whom he has declined to discuss in interviews. Between 1980 and 1985 Eno put out two ambient-style albums with Harold Budd (*Ambient 2: The Plateaux of Mirror* and *The Pearl*), one with John Hassell (*Fourth World Vol. 1: Possible Musics*), one with Michael Brook and Daniel Lanois (*Hybrid*), and one with Roger Eno and Daniel Lanois (*Voices*). Taken together, these records explore territory that Eno first mapped out in his solo records of the previous decade. Although these collaborations do much to flesh out our picture of Eno's complex musical personality, and although each deserves careful listening, in each it is virtually impossible to separate Eno's contributions from those of his fellow musicians. This is why, in describing the ambient sound, I have used mostly compositions attributable to Eno alone.

It is of course impossible to predict the shape of the new musical styles we may yet hope to hear from the forty-year-old Brian Eno. At times he has hinted that an album of a new kind of song may be forthcoming in the next couple of years, although he is evasive on this point, not wishing to raise any hopes in his audience of the early 1970s for a return to his progressive rock style. In fact, he is clearly irked by fans who clamor for more "idiot energy" songs. At an Eno lecture at the Exploratorium in San Francisco in early 1988, a member of the audience innocently asked, "Are you still interested in song forms with lyrics, and can we expect any more songs from you in the near future?" The usually loquacious Eno curtly answered, "Yes—and no," and moved on to the next question.

As *Glint* shows, the ambient style is capable of seemingly perpetual variation and extension: beyond the Phrygian mode of *Glint* the still gloomier tones of the Locrian mode are waiting, not to mention the array of symmetrical scales, such as whole-tone and octatonic, which seem to be particularly suited to the ambient style because of their static, repeating properties, their exotic, non-tonal flavorings, and their limited transposability. Even an atonal ambient style does not seem beyond the realm of the possible, although it would be interesting to see whether Eno could manage to retain the warmth, spaciousness, and accessibility of his music in an atonal framework.

11 Collaborations

Beginning with his work with Roxy Music, Eno has enjoyed working with a host of rock luminaries. Roxy Music's statement was as much visual and conceptual as it was musical, Bryan Ferry tantalizing his audience with his air of jaded elegance and with the endless procession of surreal, anguishing anima/lover figures in his lyrics. On the two albums Eno recorded with Roxy Music, it is difficult to pinpoint Eno's musical contribution, except for a few inspired synthesizer solos of the "funny sounds" variety. Although Eno's solo albums show a decisive turn away from rock after *Before and After Science* (1977), he has continued to collaborate with other musicians in the making of rock albums, and has been much in demand as a producer and session musician. Robert Fripp has called Eno a "catalytic creature" whose thoughtful, interested presence at a recording session was bound to increase the endeavor's chances of artistic success.[1] Of the many records that Eno had a hand in making, those with Fripp, David Bowie, and David Byrne and Talking Heads deserve special mention for the unusual nature of their contents and for their influence on the direction of rock.

WITH ROBERT FRIPP

(No Pussyfooting), the first of the two major Eno/Fripp collaborations, grew out of Eno's early experiments with tape recorders, out of Fripp's ability to supply the appropriate kind of musical input from an electric guitar, and out of the musical chemistry between the two musicians. By the time Eno invited Fripp to come over and play in his London home studio in September 1972,[2] Eno had worked out a system of producing music by using two tape recorders set up so that when a single sound was played, it was heard several seconds later at a slightly lower volume level, then again several seconds later at a still lower volume level, and so on. The length of time between an event and its repetition depended on the speed of the tape and the distance between the two tape recorders. Example 13, which is based on the diagram Eno made for

the back cover of *Discreet Music*, shows the physical setup in simplified form. Only two reels are used, the feeding reel of tape recorder 1 and the take-up reel of tape recorder 2, with the ribbon of tape stretching between the two recorders.

Example 13
ENO AND FRIPP'S SIGNAL-DELAY SYSTEM
USED FOR *(No Pussyfooting)*

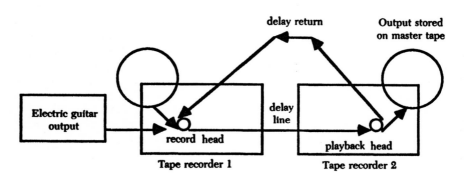

New sounds could thus be introduced and layered on top of the old ones without erasing them. The repeating, looped signal—typically about five seconds long—could be allowed to repeat and decay indefinitely (in such a case, owing to the very slight deterioration of tonal definition each time the signal passed through the loop, the tone color would change almost imperceptibly with time, growing very gradually more noise-like, and shifting toward the bass end of the frequency spectrum), with or without an independent "solo" line being played over the top. The looped signal could be interrupted at will, to create empty acoustical space for new events; or, perhaps most characteristically, it could be made to decay at a slow but steady rate, while new input was being added at a similarly slow but steady rate, so that the total effect was one of a complex, slowly changing, kaleidoscopic musical texture composed of simple motives, each only a few seconds in length, which were most prominent when initially introduced, and which inexorably marched into the aural background.

It takes many words indeed to describe a musical process that, once one hears it, is immediately and intuitively grasped. Side One of *No Pussyfooting* is a twenty-one-minute piece called "The Heavenly Music Corporation" made in one take, using the process described above, with Fripp providing the motivic input, and with Eno "playing" the tape recorders: determining the rate of the layered motives' march into oblivion, creating new acoustical room when necessary or desirable, and adjusting the density or saturation of the timbral space. Contrary to what one might hear during a superficial or inattentive listening, there is nothing mechanical about this process. Fripp and Eno needed to be in creative sync with one another in order to build, tinker with, and dismantle, in real time, the musical structures we perceive.

"The Heavenly Music Corporation" begins with a single sustained note on electric guitar that is looped back on itself to form a continuous drone. After a time, upper harmonics, notably the fifth and minor seventh, begin to emerge. Listening to this drone, the mind's interpretive mechanisms are apt to undergo changes. For a period, we are bound to hear "just a long note," and impatiently wonder what, if anything, is going to "happen." But after a certain point, given the lack of obvious musical activity, we become aware that the single note is an incredibly complex entity in itself: that it is not staying the same at all; that there is rhythm, melody, harmony, and timbre wrapped up inside it; that, in short, it is vibrantly alive, and does not need anything else added or changed to be enjoyed, to be experienced musically.

After several minutes, more conventionally musical things do start to happen. A slow, concentrated, intense guitar melody emerges, phrase by phrase, consisting of isolated notes, short motives, glissandi, or longer linear improvisations. Some of these phrases are allowed to enter into the signal loop, becoming "accompaniment" on their recurrences; at other times, the melody becomes a "solo," detached from the loop, just riding a crest on top of the palpitating mass of sound. The only consistent pulse in "The Heavenly Music Corporation" is of the length of the signal loop, and at about three seconds, this is rather too slow to perceive as a pulse or beat in the traditional sense: it is more akin to the experience of breathing than to the heartbeat.

The harmony of the piece is not functional, nor is it particularly triadic; it is based, rather, on the totality of tones that are prominent in the waves of sound at any given moment. The closest term for this kind of harmony in traditional music theory would be "pandiatonicism." As in Terry Riley's *In C*, however, the tonal center and modal type shift over periods of time, here from F♯ Dorian to A major, finally settling into D major toward the end. Within this general tonal framework, Fripp feels free to borrow notes from outside the prevailing modes: scale degrees three, six, and seven in particular may be played in their natural or flatted (minor) forms. Given the retention, in the loop, of many previously heard tones, maneuvering the overall modal impression takes considerable skill: it is a bit like steering a battleship.

Although the tonal architecture of "The Heavenly Music Corporation" must be credited to Fripp, who supplied the pitch material, Eno himself used pandiatonicism and the drone extensively in subsequent works. If there is a major conceptual difference between this piece and Eno's later extended works, it has to do with teleology. This piece develops, however slowly: it has a definite beginning (the drone), middle (characterized by rhapsodic guitar solos), and end (a long cadential section marked by a repeated and varied slow glissando to the tonic). Eno's later extended works, to the contrary, tend to be non-developmental or cyclic.

In a number of other important general ways, though, "The Heavenly Music Corporation," as a *system*, anticipates Eno's own ambient style. First of all, the piece *is* a system, or process: it represents a way of making music, a concept of music-making, as much as it represents a composition in the traditional sense. The process allowed Eno to operate in his favored gently guiding, rather than authoritarian, role. Making the piece required thought and attention; Eno had to contemplate and inspect the sound as it rolled by, making changes and adjustments. The process, meanwhile, yielded maximal output (a lengthy, complex piece of music) from minimal input (selection of pitches and switches). Finally, the signal-loop procedure itself, with its gradually decaying tone quality, exemplified one of Eno's cherished axioms: "Repetition is a form of change."

Eno has explained the title of "Swastika Girls," the long piece that comprises Side Two of *(No Pussyfooting)*:

> I was walking to the studio one day and there was a piece of magazine someone had ripped out from some porno film magazine, I guess, and it showed a picture of a naked girl with a swastika on her arm giving a "Sieg Heil" salute. . . . I stuck it on the console and we were just kind of vaguely looking at this and talking about this as we were recording that piece, and so that became the title.[3]

"Swastika Girls" was recorded in two days at Command Studios in London, about a year after Eno and Fripp made "The Heavenly Music Corporation" in Eno's home. If it is less successful than the earlier piece, it is because of the much greater overall saturation of the acoustical space: continuous fast guitar-picking on a single chord (E major with added sixth and ninth) and an incessantly busy synthesizer sequence present the backdrop for Fripp's metallic E-Lydian melodic guitar lines. There seems to be a perceptual rule that possibilities for appreciation of timbral subtleties decrease in proportion to the rate of actual notes being played. The frenetic quality of the accompaniment on "Swastika Girls" shows that Eno and Fripp had not yet understood the full weight of this principle; it would be nearly a decade before Eno was able to formulate it simply and elegantly: "Every note obscures another."

Evening Star, released in 1975, was the second and last of the major Fripp/Eno collaborations. The first three tracks on the first side are further experiments in signal looping and guitar and synthesizer layering, ones which for the most part display qualities typical of the emerging ambient style: static harmony based on a major chord with or without added notes, sometimes with Lydian inflections in the melodic parts; a non-developmental unfolding of events, with a distinct timbral character for each piece; and a variety of ostinati. "Wind on Wind," the last cut on Side One, is by Eno alone and was recorded at his home studio. Here the ambient style, at least in one of its aspects, is in full bloom.

Round, soft-attacked, flute-like tones are spatially enhanced through the use of a reverb/delay unit, and short melodic fragments are looped, repeated, and faded. "Wind on Wind," in fact, sounds very much like a short sketch for "Discreet Music." The main difference is that, in "Discreet Music," the musical solution will be diluted, allowing for closer inspection, more leisurely and thorough contemplation, of its elements: the delay time will be lengthened, the melodies simplified or deactivated, and the resulting harmonic density rarefied.

The second side of *Evening Star* consists of a very long Fripp/Eno composition, "An Index of Metals," recorded at Eno's studio with much the same straightforward tape signal-loop apparatus as "The Heavenly Music Corporation," but with Eno providing input from a synthesizer in addition to Fripp's electric guitar input. Considered in the context of Eno's ambient music as a whole, "An Index of Metals" is remarkable for two factors: its high dissonance level and its developmental nature. Insofar as it consists of tones (as opposed to noises or unpitched percussive sounds), Eno's ambient music tends to be very consonant, providing a restful ambiance—even if the latter is sometimes tinged with an undercurrent of tension or melancholy. In "An Index of Metals," the sense of a sinister, intense ambiguity characteristic of many of Eno's strange progressive rock songs comes to the forefront. It is as dark and foreboding as "The Heavenly Music Corporation" is contemplative and rhapsodic, and it achieves this effect largely through heavy, close dissonances.

Some of the highlights in the piece's strategy of continuous development or continuous variation may be sketched out here. It opens with a high, metallic-sounding, ringing E♭-G diad, possibly strummed quickly on guitar strings. Like the drone that opens "The Heavenly Music Corporation," this ringing sound is timbrally complex, with a great deal of inner motion. After about three and a half minutes, some dissonant, complex guitar-produced noise—resembling mosquitoes or metallic butterflies—suddenly enters, and is looped. The tonal situation becomes very uncertain, and the timbral balance shifts from tone to noise. About six minutes into the piece, a characteristic sustained, fuzz-tone Fripp guitar melody enters, playing individual notes that become part of the loop. Around the middle of the eighth minute, an F-B tritone predominates the harmonic proceedings, then develops into a dissonant F-B-C chord; a couple of minutes later, E and E♭ enter, increasing the dissonance even more. The maneuvering of the atonal battleship continues in this general manner, with emphasis on minor seconds and tritones, until during the twentieth minute of the piece a fade-down takes place, the existing signal loop being allowed to run its course with no new inupt. Eventually, the ringing sound from the beginning comes in again in a more complex form—so complex that it is difficult to make out individual pitches—and becomes the most prominent feature of the texture. From about the twenty-sixth minute to the end some three minutes later, little or no new input is added, but Eno adjusts and manipulates the long fade-out of the looped signal, which, owing to the analog nature of the process, becomes ever more noise-like, gradually losing high frequencies and general tonal definition.

In all, "An Index of Metals" is bound to strike the listener not so much as a musical development as an almost tangibly sculptural process, Eno and Fripp using electronic tools to give shape to the invisible black marble of silence. During the 1970s, they occasionally gave live performances together of music that sounded much like what we hear on *(No Pussyfooting)* and *Evening Star*. The rock press paid less attention to their collaborations in this vein than to Fripp's work with King Crimson or Eno's solo rock albums. One critic wrote a sympathetic review of a Fripp/Eno performance at the London Palladium in June 1975 that included the comment:

> There was such variety in the textures created that, depending upon the degree of individual concentration, one could focus on one of any of the levels of sound patterns. One therefore became a participant in the creative process, creating through individual selection individual compositions for oneself, rather than blindly accepting an already well-defined and regulated musical formula.[4]

Fripp was to undertake a global tour during 1979, performing alone in small venues and record stores with his guitar and two tape recorders set up as Eno had taught him; he would repeatedly stress the importance of the audience's creative listening contribution to these performances.[5]

In 1973, Fripp's reputation and standing in the rock press and among a large following in Great Britain and the United States was, if controversial, already firmly established through a string of diverse and original King Crimson albums. For Eno's budding career, the release in the same year of the contemplative *(No Pussyfooting)* and the frenetic *Here Come the Warm Jets* was a risky move, but one that set him on the eclectic course he was to follow. As he explained,

> The difference between those two albums created a kind of confusion about my image, which my managers bewailed. But it proved to be the best move I could have made—and it was quite by accident. It put me in a position where I don't have to be consistent. I can start each record anew, without having a trademark.[6]

WITH DAVID BOWIE

David Bowie, like Eno and David Byrne, had a background in the visual arts; his public career has been as much a matter of shrewd manipulation of his ever-changing, chameleon-like image as it has been a musical evolution. His transformations from space-age androgyne to Ziggy Stardust (a "doomed messianic rock icon"),[7] to the White Duke (purveyor of funk and disco music to the white masses), to reclusive British expatriate living in Berlin, to straight-ahead dance rocker during the 1980s, have been well chronicled elsewhere.[8]

In all of his manifestations, Bowie has garnered the kind of mass popularity that has eluded Eno; one reason for this is that in his music he has remained closer than has Eno to a basic hard rock style. But in their collaboration on three albums between 1977 and 1979, Eno was able to nudge Bowie beyond the limits of rock.

According to Eno, Bowie was interested in working with him because he had found that his own creative ideas were running out. Bowie had heard Eno's *Another Green World* and "saw in that an approach he liked."[9] Eno, for his part, had admired Bowie's 1976 album *Station to Station*. The two got together at Conny Plank's studio in Cologne and set about making *Low*, which was released in 1977. *Low* contains eleven tracks; Eno is listed as co-composer with Bowie of only one of them, "Warszawa," but he was apparently an active contributor throughout.

Low may be viewed as Bowie's *Another Green World*, except that instead of interspersing experimental instrumentals with rock songs, Bowie segregated the two types on the album's two sides; furthermore, the pieces are all either strictly rock or non-rock, with no stylistic exploration in between. Side B is the non-rock, experimental, mostly instrumental side. Eno's musical personality is evident throughout, in an array of metallic and grating sounds, in rhythm-box backings, in the guitar treatments, in the sweeping, string-section-like synthesizer lines. But, in general, the music seems much more Bowie than Eno. Bowie's style incorporates a penchant for strange harmonic twists of a kind Eno tends to avoid. Moreover, Bowie's compositions are considerably more "active" in traditional terms, if not a great deal more linear in a teleological sense, than Eno's tend to be: they contain more simultaneous active melodic lines, more counterpoint, more harmonic activity, a greater density of events, resulting in a generally thicker sound texture. There are also such prominent Bowieisms in *Low* as saxophone and octave-doubled melodies.

Eno made the instrumental tracks for "Warszawa" by himself in the studio during a period when Bowie was away for two days. Upon returning, Bowie added the vocals.[10] "Warszawa" is a slow, severe, frightening composition based on piano drones and organ-like synthesizer and flute/mellotron tones that set up successions of harmonies quite uncharacteristic of Eno's solo work. After several minutes, Bowie's voice enters, singing indecipherable words or vocalizations to simple melodies. The whole is very carefully composed, with a great deal of harmonic and structural preplanning, and shows the influence on Eno of Bowie's more active compositional style.

The whole matter of authorship is complicated in collaborations of this sort. Often, a range of duties seems to be shared by a number of musicians: when there is no neat division of roles (composer, arranger, instrumentalist, producer), but several people are active in all of these spheres at once, then whose piece it is may boil down to who is paying for the studio time, as Eno has suggested.[11] Complex authorial situations arise in many tracks on this disc. "Art

Decade," with whose composition Bowie is credited, is a piece that Eno has said he was responsible for saving from the out-take pile:

> That started off as a little tune that he [Bowie] played on the piano. Actually we both played it because it was for four hands, and when we'd finished it he didn't like it very much and sort of forgot about it. But as it happened, during the two days he was gone I . . . dug that out to see if I could do anything with it. I put all those instruments on top of what we had, and then he liked it and realized there was hope for it, and he worked on top of that adding more instruments. [12]

On Bowie's "Heroes" album of 1977, Eno is listed as responsible for synthesizers, keyboards, and guitar treatments, and as coauthor of four pieces. One is the title track (lyrics by Bowie; music by Bowie/Eno), a rock-anthem type of song whose desperate theme ("We can be heroes . . . just for one day") recalls both Andy Warhol's pop proverb that "Everyone will be famous for fifteen minutes" and the transsexual character in Lou Reed's "Walk on the Wild Side" who "thought she was James Dean for a day." The song's unique sonic character owes much to Robert Fripp's remarkable sustained three-note guitar obbligato, and to Eno's background synthesizer noises which sound something like the chugging of an interstellar freight train.

Side A of "Heroes" is again all rock, having a sort of futuristic party-dance atmosphere that Eno's own albums do not. Side B opens and closes with rock numbers, but between them are three instrumental collaborations, leading directly into one another without breaks, on which Eno's influence is very strong. "Sense of Doubt" is a horrific, minimalistic soundscape with a deep, slow C-B-B♭-A piano motive that keeps returning, under filtered white-noise swooshings and isolated synthesizer chords in A minor, punctuated occasionally by an evil grating sound that can only be described as the yawn of the dead.

Bowie and Eno used the deck of *Oblique Strategies* extensively in the making of "Heroes" and "both worked on all the pieces all the time—almost taking turns."[13] When they began work on "Sense of Doubt," each pulled out a card and kept it a secret:

> It was like a game. We took turns working on it; he'd do one overdub and I'd do the next. The idea was that each was to observe his Oblique Strategy as closely as he could. And as it turned out they were entirely opposed to one another. Effectively mine said, "Try to make everything as similar as possible," . . . and his said, "Emphasize differences."[14]

"Sense of Doubt" leads into "Moss Garden," a piece in Eno's ambient style, featuring continuous synthesizer chords, a high jet-plane sound that repeatedly careens across the field of hearing, and a koto or other stringed instrument providing plucked "melody." "Moss Garden" revolves around two chords, F♯ major and G♯ major, implying a tonic of C♯. Finally, "Neuköln" is something like a German expressionist version of the ambient style: dissonant diminished chords evoking a movie-organ atmosphere; saxophone melodies evoking gang-ster life; and somewhat harsh water-like sounds. Again, Eno alone would not, or perhaps could not, have come up with a chord progression like this.

Lodger (1979), the final Bowie/Eno collaboration, shows Bowie drawing back to more familiar musical territory, and from a musical point of view the album is considerably less interesting than the first two. The overall effect of *Lodger* is rock until you drop, without so much as a soft ballad to break up the pace. Long stretches sound unedited, as if Bowie did not know when to stop, what to subtract. Of the ten songs, Eno coauthored six, and is listed as providing "ambient drone," "prepared piano and cricket menace," synthesizers and guitar treatments, "horse trumpets, Eroica horn," and piano. *Lodger* is overproduced: in the continuous assault of the rock frenetics, Eno's treatments get buried in the busy mix. As he later said, a whole world can be extracted from a single sound; but such effects are easily lost if the input and surroundings are too complicated. Eno and Bowie "argued quite a lot about what was going to happen" on particular tracks, and Eno thought that the resolutions were com-promises in many cases: "It started off extremely promising and quite revo-lutionary and it didn't seem to quite end that way."[15]

WITH TALKING HEADS AND DAVID BYRNE

In 1978, the year following his first collaboration with Bowie, the peripatetic Eno moved to a loft in Soho, Manhattan, and immersed himself in the downtown music-art-performance scene. Though his own commitment to rock was weak-ening, he found some of the new New York punk/new wave groups exciting enough to produce: he helped to catapult Devo to popularity with their album *Q: Are We Not Men? A: We Are Devo!*, and contributed to the growing genre of punk anthology records by producing *No New York*, featuring music by the Contortions, Teenage Jesus and the Jerks, Mars, and DNA. He worked with his old colleague Robert Fripp, also temporarily stationed in New York, on Fripp's first solo album, the experimental, collage-like *Exposure*.

Of greatest consequence, however, was Eno's work with the art rock band Talking Heads, for whom he produced three albums between 1978 and 1980, and with the head Head, David Byrne, with whom he made *My Life in the Bush of Ghosts*, released in 1981. Talking Heads was a band with the right idea in the right place at the right time. The concept was to use a primitivist rock attack with a heavy African accent as a vehicle for a statement about rock and its relationship to the media and other social institutions. The context was the burgeoning performance art and mixed-media scene of downtown New York during the late 1970s, a scene that John Rockwell has described as "a cohesive artistic community"—a community that had sustained the experi-mental efforts of musicians like Philip Glass, Steve Reich, and Glenn Branca, as well as artists simultaneously involved in a number of fields, such as Laurie Anderson, Meredith Monk, and Robert Wilson.[16] The scene fostered an exuberant disregard for traditional distinctions between artistic categories, not to mention the distinction between "high" and "low" art, or classical and popular music. Eno was in his element.

What attracted Eno to Talking Heads was the experimental attitude he had discerned on their first album:

> I found it very, very attractive material, full of potential, and certainly manifesting an intelligence that stood behind the music. And it struck me that the music was all the product of some very active brains that were constructing music in a kind of conceptual way.[17]

Eno and the Heads worked together on three albums. *More Songs about Buildings and Food* (1978) and *Fear of Music* (1979) were coproduced by Eno and Talking Heads. *Remain in Light* (1980) was produced by Eno, and he is also credited with various vocal and instrumental duties as well as with sharing in the songwriting itself. By this time, he had become in effect a ghost member of the band, somewhat in the manner of the Beatles' producer, George Martin, during the late 1960s. Under Eno's guiding hand, the Talking Heads sound became ever more dependent on electronic processing. Following a working method established in his own progressive rock work and used in his collaboration with Bowie, he kept a few "spare" tracks for himself on the reels of twenty-four-track tape as the band laid down the instrumentals and vocals. On the spare tracks, Eno would feed in this or that instrument and treat it electronically. Playing the whole thing back in various rough mixes would lead to further refinement and manipulation of the sound. On the song "Animals," from *Fear of Music*, for instance, Eno took the bass drum signal, fed it through a synthesizer, added a repeat echo, and then filtered out the low-frequency distortion.[18] Rhythmic complications were often introduced by sending a snare drum or other instrument keeping a steady pulse through a delay unit set at some fraction or multiple of the basic beat.[19] Since 1980 such sophisticated studio drum treatments have become commonplace in pop recordings of many varieties; rap music provides some of the most obvious, audible examples. Now, too, of course, electronic drums have become widespread: manufacturers make special drum-shaped, mounted pads which feed a MIDI signal directly into synthesizers, eliminating the need for an acoustic impulse altogether. But many of the types of sounds for which drummers and producers use these can be found on the Eno/Heads collaborative albums.

Particularly striking aspects of the development of Talking Heads' musical style during the Eno years were the simplification of harmonic materials and the increasingly pointillistic nature of the rhythms. In many of the songs on *Remain in Light*, one or two chords provide the harmonic underpinning for an ever-shifting array of percussive and melodic events. In such songs, Eno's graph-paper approach to composition is clearly in evidence: the pulse and its subdivisions, along with a few repetitive melodic or bass fragments, form a background matrix over which dabs or points of color or light are placed. Although the density of rhythmic events in a song like the Dorian-mode-based "Crosseyed and Painless" is high, and although the texture is highly layered (bass, drums, two electric guitars, and a number of cowbells or similar instruments), each layer sounds clean and distinct in the counterpoint of rhythms. Even though many of Eno's ambient pieces lack a steady pulse, their coloristic, spatial approach to composition is much the same.

Eno's increasing involvement with Talking Heads' music-making process was apparently favored by David Byrne, but it was ultimately resented by other members of the group. Eno later told an interviewer of the frustrations of his position:

> I really thought that if, at a certain point, I had had those tracks [from *Remain in Light*] and had carte blanche to write whatever I wanted, song-wise, over the top . . . I think that I could have explored this intricate song form that I was getting into more thoroughly. But I didn't feel comfortable about usurping the compositional role any more than I had done already.[20]

Eno had more of a "carte blanche" to explore this direction in his collaboration with David Byrne on *My Life in the Bush of Ghosts*, recorded in 1979 just prior to the sessions for *Remain in Light*. The title is borrowed from a metaphorical book by Nigerian novelist Amos Tutuola about a young man who ventures beyond the confines and traditions of his native village into the mysterious, unknown bush country. Both Eno and Byrne had, for a number of years, been interested in non-Western musical styles, particularly those of sub-Saharan Africa and of the Arabic cultural sphere; in the Talking Heads/Eno records, such influences function implicitly, but on *My Life in the Bush of Ghosts* they become explicit. Eno's ambitions were high: he wanted to make "fourth world music," which he defined as

> music that is done in sympathy with and with consciousness of music of the rest of the world, rather than just with Western music or just with rock music. It's almost collage music, like grafting a piece of one culture onto a piece of another onto a piece of another and trying to make them work as a coherent musical idea, and also trying to make something you can dance to.[21]

Over rhythmic and harmonic backing tracks played by Eno, Byrne, and eleven other musicians, Eno and Byrne superimposed taped voices from a variety of sources; for example: on "America is Waiting," an "unidentified indignant radio host, San Francisco, April 1980"; on "Mea Culpa," the voice of Dunya Yusin, a Lebanese mountain singer from a recording called *The Human Voice in the World of Islam*;[22] on "Help Me Somebody," fragments of a sermon broadcast by the Reverend Paul Morton in New Orleans in June

1980; and on "Moonlight in Glory," the voice of Egyptian popular singer Samira Tewfik, taken from an EMI recording, *Les Plus Grandes Artistes du Monde Arabe*.

Some critics found the musical borrowings offensive. Jon Pareles wrote that "like most 'found' art, [*My Life in the Bush of Ghosts*] raises stubborn questions about context, manipulation and cultural imperialism."[23] Although the sources of the voices on the album are duly acknowledged on the sleeve, are there ethical or legal limits to the uses an artist can make of another's material? The issue is complex, and is bound to be examined more closely as the media net—not to mention the web of ethnomusicological scholarship—extends its domain and efficiency with each passing year. The idea of fair use, which has always been open to various interpretations, is complicated by the undeniable fact that Westerners are possessed of greater means to reach (and exploit) the cultural products of less developed nations than the other way round.[24] In the middle and late 1980s, the advent of sampling synthesizers, which enable users to take a digital snapshot of a sound from someone else's music and then incorporate that sound into their own, has only made the fair use debate more heated than ever.

My Life in the Bush of Ghosts is an album of pieces that succeed in eerily evoking the image of a pluralistic, worldwide contemporary culture-of-cultures knit tenuously together by modern sound recording and telecommunications. Many, since Marshall McLuhan first worked out the idea, have written about the transformation of human reality in the twentieth-century "global village"; Eno and Byrne's album gives this concept musical form. High-tech studio electronics mix with the sounds of airwave exorcisms, traditional Qu'ran chanting, and a battery of percussion ranging from congas and agaong-gong to found objects such as ashtrays, wastebaskets, and tin cans.

What, if anything, distinguishes *My Life in the Bush of Ghosts*—in the long history of Western art concerned with other arts and cultures—from the grafting of folk melodies into nationalist symphonies, the exoticism of Matisse's paintings of harems or the transfigurative realism of Picasso's cubist collages, the pentatonic orientalism of Debussy's "Pagodes," the antiquarianism of Bach's *stile antico* ricercars, the classicization of jazz in Stravinsky's *Ebony Concerto*, Mozart's "Turkish" music, or the Beatles' popularization of the sitar in "Within You Without You"? The main difference lies in *Ghosts*'s location in a cultural context much broader than most previous artists were capable of envisioning. The context grows ever larger owing to the increasingly accelerated nature of communication and cultural interchange in the contemporary world. During the 1950s, an Elvis Presley could listen to country music and R&B on the radio and make a kind of music that in a straightforward sort of way owed something to both. During the 1980s, American and British pop and rock, having thoroughly assimilated African influences, is broadcast and sent on vinyl and cassette to locations worldwide, including Africa, where it is reprocessed into styles like highlife and Juju, which in turn quickly have an impact on the development of Western pop. At some point this process becomes a closed circuit, a perpetual feedback loop, a two-way or multi-way cultural mirror. The possibilities that remain to be seen in and through such mirrors are endless. Eno and Byrne's *My Life in the Bush of Ghosts,* in its playful celebration of technology, world singing styles, and folk religion, is such a mirror.

"What is music?" is a question that leads in many directions, and certainly I shall make no attempt here to follow all of them. I shall perhaps raise more questions than I answer. If earlier generations of Western music theorists and philosophers have found the question hard to tackle, it is no less refractory today, in an age when ethnomusicologists have discovered that "each culture seems to have its own configuration of concepts" revolving around "music," and that although all cultures appear to have "music," some have no word that corresponds terribly closely to what we in the West understand by that term.[1]

If one of the thrusts of Cage's thought on the subject was that "Everything we do is music" (implying that, at the least, music is a form of human activity), the development of recording and playback technology has produced an opposing idea: today, it seems, we do not have to do anything to participate in music, other than put on a record and take in the sound passively—and such passive listening is certainly one level of activity for which Eno's music is intended.

What is the ontological status of what may seem increasingly to be non-human forms of music—music that is neither performed nor heard actively in any conventional sense? At what level is the human element operative? In much of Eno's music, deeply ingrained notions of competence, practice, and virtuosity (or "athleticism," to use Nettl's term) do not apply—or do they? Eno may have been eager to admit his instrumental incompetence; but in the studio, he sits at the center of a sophisticated body of music-making machinery, just as the traditional composer does when he is writing for an orchestra, and in each case what the mind is able to conceive and the ear to hear is the result of training and discipline as well as imagination.

Recording technology has made all musics seem equal: you put your LP, cassette, or CD onto the stereo, and there it is. But is that all there is to it? What went into the making of this or that music? And with the results coming out of the loudspeakers, does it matter? If for some people it does not matter, there are certainly many for whom it does. Bryan Ferry, the leader of Roxy Music, with whom Eno had collaborated between 1971 and 1973, said years later ("with a polite sniff," according to the chronicler),

> You see, Eno is a very clever fellow, but he's not really a musician. He doesn't know how to play anything. All he can do is manipulate those machines of his. What he does, he does very well, but it's necessarily limited music, I think.[2]

If Eno's non-musicianship was a stumbling block to Ferry, others may have qualms about whether sound that is made totally in the studio and is often impossible to reproduce live should be called music at all. Eno himself has his doubts on this point, as we have seen. To use a current manner of speaking, if music is a real-time activity among cooperating humans producing real-time results, then much of what Eno has done with sound is indeed not music, but some new, different form of art. On the other hand, a good deal of time must be spent by any contemporary keyboardist or electric guitarist simply assessing and mastering technological possibilities; articles and advertisements in current musicians' magazines emphasize equipment—analog and digital synthesizers, MIDI (Musical Instrument Digital Interface), computers, tape recorders, effects devices—to the extent that an advertisement which announces, "The major in Music Synthesis at Berklee emphasizes 'real-time' performance skills" can seem something of an anomaly.[3]

Eno has been involved in a broad range of music-making activities of many different types. At one end of the spectrum are his live performances with other musicians—Roxy Music, Robert Fripp, the Winkies, 801, and others. In the middle are his studio collaborations on rock and ambient music albums. At the other end are his solo ambient records, particularly the title track of *Discreet Music*—a piece that was made almost accidentally, automatically, while Eno was running around the house devoting his attention to other things. Taken as a whole, Eno's work prescribes no single answer to the question of what music is at the level of its making.

A slightly different angle on the ontological question can be drawn by asking where a particular kind of music exists along the line between composed and improvised forms. Different cultures and subcultures invest composition and improvisation with various kinds of value. For the most part, improvisation is currently held in low esteem by traditional art music composers and audiences—it may be a nice idea to think about, but few actually do it; on the other hand, for jazz musicians, and for rock musicians to a lesser extent, it is a way of life.[4] We may think we know the difference between improvisation and composition, but in fact the two concepts are by no means mutually exclusive. Composition in the traditional sense can be seen as a kind of improvisation in ultra-slow motion; conversely, even when improvising "freely," musicians are usually operating within more or less fixed stylistic, formal, textural, "compositional" limits, and in this sense improvising is composing in real time.

Eno has made music that in various ways walks the line between composition and improvisation. The structure of a piece like "2/1" from *Music for Airports* is compositionally predetermined down to the last detail, once the tape loops have been made and set in motion. In many other pieces, Eno used raw materials generated in quasi-improvisational settings and then shaped them in the studio according to his empirical methods of timbral treatment, textural experimentation, and editing. Still other pieces, like some of the instrumental tracks on *Another Green World*, seem to be relatively untreated recordings of free collective improvisations within certain prescribed limits. And in some of his collaborations with Fripp, such as "The Heavenly Music Corporation," once the tape recorders were turned on, both musicians simply played with the variables, whether this meant spontaneously producing certain kinds of melody within a given tonal framework or making alterations along the signal-delay path. Improvised music is ever open to the criticism—and to the very real threat—that the musicians are "just noodling around," simply running on automatic. But in most of Eno's works involving one or another forms of improvisation, we can perceive the active involvement of discerning intelligence in a real-time process.

Insofar as the question of music's essence can be posed at the level of the social context in which music functions, Eno's work again provides a range of answers. Live performance in front of concert audiences has been a part of his career, if a fairly small one. His audiovisual installations take on the character of art exhibits when set up in galleries, and of background ambiance in airports. Finally, his progressive rock and ambient music albums find their primary social context on the home stereo system, where they can function as decorative or fine art, depending on the inclination of the user. Eno does not flinch when asked to comment on the criticism that some of his works seem to be "merely decorative":

> I find it revealing that Kandinsky acquired the license for what he was doing in 1912–15 through having had a background in the decorative arts—his fairy-tales, illustrations, Jugendstil, mythologies, and so on. In those contexts you're allowed to be fanciful and brightly coloured without having to defend it. In a way it *was* decorative art, and decorative art has an enviable freedom in some respects.[5]

It may be a bit facile to say that music is what people think it is, yet thinking about it—theoretically, ontologically, historically, aesthetically—is undeniably part and parcel of the musical experience.[6] Eno, in a steady stream of liner notes, interviews, and articles, has provided a continuous flow of theorizing about his own music, and some knowledge of this theorizing can indeed add to the listener's appreciation of the music itself. In a fundamental way, however, the music is able to, and does, speak for itself. Theorists have always made a supplemental exegetical exercise out of translating musical symbols, whether heard or written, into non-musical concepts, typically involving some combination of verbal language and mathematics. Music theory as a sort of exalted numbers game has a long history, stretching back to Pythagoras' calculation of interval ratios, running through Renaissance enthusiasm for niceties of diatonic, chromatic, and enharmonic genera, through Enlightenment reduction of harmonic phenomena to functional root progressions, to Schenkerian voice-leading graphs and set-complex theory during the present century. Eno has been more inclined to theorize about music-making processes than about musical materials *per se*, but when he plans compositions around the idea of layers of synchronized or non-synchronized cycles of events—and speaks to the press about it—he is contributing to the ongoing Western music theory tradition, however marginally aware he may be of that tradition.

Yet the theoretical tradition has had little direct impact on the way most people perceive music. Although theory and analysis certainly represent a continuous conversation—and probably an indispensable one—in worldwide musical discourse, I doubt whether a precise measurement of the tape-loop lengths of Eno's "2/1" is likely to hold any greater sway over most listeners' reaction to the sounding surface than is an explanation of the operation of tone-row forms in Webern's Symphony, Opus 21. A suggestion that recurring cycles underlie the piece's structure is enough, and Eno knows it.

THE MUSIC'S HISTORY

If we ignore for the moment all the discussion and debate concerning popular music and art music, originality and epigonism, we may be struck by the fact that most Western music of all kinds since 1950 has indeed found something to rally around, something that is deeply symbolic and symptomatic of our culture and its values. I am referring to electronic technology, the sound recording, and the attendant transformation of the listening experience. Though value is granted to "live" music, and to the vitality of direct participation—whether as performers or as audience—in musical events, the rise of electronic technology has affected the meaning of music in ways still only dimly guessed at. Even when electronic amplification is not used during the concert itself (and it must be, if more than about 3,000 people are going to hear what is going on), one almost inevitably sees the dangling microphones with wires leading to hidden tape recorders that are engaged in preserving the music— if only for the contemporary composer, who may never otherwise hear his piece again. It is as though the event is not real unless it is frozen on tape.

In one form or another, the image of technology is a central icon in contemporary culture, and that image has profoundly affected the ways in which music is perceived, used, and considered.[7] Brian Eno can be singled out as a musician who has taken serious stock of technology's position in the world, and of his position vis-à-vis technology. With his eclectic background in conceptual art, progressive rock, and tape manipulation, he has been particularly qualified to do so, and has been able to approach technological resources in fresh new ways, lending his own musical tastes and sensibilities to the process.

Where exactly does Eno stand in the history of electronically produced and distributed music? In Chapter 1, I brought up some of the conceptual issues involved in attempts to distinguish popular from art music, and concluded that there was little point in trying to assign Eno's music to either category. Here I would sum up the contribution of Eno's music to both mega-genres, and suggest that he is among the musicians who have done much to obscure or erase the distinction between them.

After the invention of magnetic recording tape, early experiments in electronic music in France and Germany during the 1940s and 1950s took on an aura of rarefied research. Composers were entranced with the possibilities of making new sounds and manipulating them on tape; new aesthetic realms seemed to open up, and the last thing these composers wanted to do was to produce music that sounded in any way conventional. For several years approaches to the new tools were split along national lines—those of the Germans, with their purely electronically generated music; or of the French, with their *musique concrète*, consisting of manipulated found sounds. An American— John Cage—was taking a different approach, with his strange, irreverent performance pieces in which radios were tuned randomly. Another American, Milton Babbitt, was less interested in the newly revealed timbral universe than in the fact that working with oscillators, filters, and tape enabled him to create precisely planned, complex rhythmic and pitch structures beyond the abilities of mere human musicians to play.

Thus, from its very beginnings, electronic music, though often considered as a single category, never implied a single aesthetic, a single kind of sounding surface, or a particular philosophy of music making. Electronic music is not something in itself; it is something different people use for different purposes. Echoes of many of the early approaches can be heard in Eno's work. Karlheinz Stockhausen's *Gesang der Junglinge* (1956), with its treated voices that bleed imperceptibly into electronically produced sounds, has parallels in Eno's continual search for a blend of the recognizable and the otherworldly.[8] Edgar Varèse's *Poème electronique*, a spatial installation in Le Corbusier's Philips Pavilion at the Brussels World's Fair in 1958, used four hundred loudspeakers and was combined, in a non-synchronized way, with visual projections of photographs, paintings, montages, and printed and written phrases—a total environment, in short, very reminiscent of Eno's later audiovisual installations. I have already discussed at length Cage's influence on Eno, and here stress only the element of playful conceptual experimentation so evident in both composers' work with electronics. Babbitt's electronic serialism constitutes a "system" whose intellectual properties Eno might well admire: Eno, too, has

made pieces that almost seem to write themselves once certain structural parameters are laid down. But, aesthetically, Eno and Babbit are poles apart.

During the 1960s, approaches to electronic music technology proliferated,
and again Eno's work can be seen as an extension of trends set in motion during
that period. One important development was the realization of composers that,
by and large, audiences would not abide performerless concerts of electronic
music. Watching spinning reels of tape on the stage was simply not engaging;
there had to be at least the suggestion of some sort of visible human activity.
A range of new performance practices sprang up, typically involving either
real-time human/machine interaction or mixed-media conglomerations of events
in which the taped electronic music was not the sole or even primary focus of
attention. Eno's albums (and concerts) with Robert Fripp are of the "interaction"
type, and his audiovisual installations are of the mixed-media type.

A milestone in the public acceptance of electronic music technology was
Walter Carlos's *Switched-On Bach* of 1968. During the previous decades, composers had attempted to integrate electronic intruments—such as the Ther-
emin, Ondes Martenot, Ondioline, and Univox—into a more or less traditional
musical setting, but for the most part electronics had been used to create
strange, metallic, mechanical-sounding noises that many people simply could
not accept as music. It took a new, compact, portable instrument—the Moog
synthesizer—and a virtuoso electronic reading of a set of unquestionably can-
onic art-music masterpieces to convince audiences (and undoubtedly many
composers and musicians as well) that the new technology could produce
something more than disembodied beeps and boops. *Switched-On Bach* was
simultaneously conservative and radical: if it left little doubt that what one
heard was actually music, the process involved in its making gave one pause.
The commercial success of Eno's ambient music may well rest on a similar
dialectic: in its resolutely consonant tonal idiom, and in its relaxed, gentle,
smooth emotional ambience, it does not demand that the listener cope with a
violently expressive modernist musical idiom in addition to coping with unfa-
miliar timbral realms and conceptual subtleties. Its aesthetic surface is warmly
inviting, altogether lacking in the machine-music connotations that have plagued
electronic music from its beginnings.

The history of electronic technology in rock reads rather differently from its
history in the art-music world. In the beginning was the amplifier—a device
that quickly outgrew its original purpose of making things louder. In the hands
of musicians like Chuck Berry and Muddy Waters, who plugged in their guitars,
the amplifier became an instrument capable of producing a wide variety of new
tone colors, while elevating its user to the status of a technological shaman—
unlike the art-music electronic composer, whose image was more that of a
research technician in a white lab coat. From its beginnings, electronics in rock
have emphasized the human/technology performance interface.[9]

Among the electronic landmarks in rock up to the time of Eno's arrival on the scene, one would have to include the experiments in studio multi-tracking techniques and electronic and *concrète* sound sources by the Beatles (*Sergeant Pepper's Lonely Hearts Club Band*, 1967) and the Beach Boys (*Pet Sounds*, 1966); Jimi Hendrix's dazzling late-1960s integration of technology and showmanship, noise and music, composition and improvisation; Pete Townshend's use of the synthesizer in a non-keyboard manner in songs like "Baba O'Reilly" (*Who's Next*, 1971); the layered electronic textures and glorification of the synthesizer as an organ-like keyboard instrument in albums by classical/progressive rock groups like Emerson, Lake & Palmer and Yes; and Stevie Wonder's funkification of electronics during the early and middle 1970s. Pink Floyd's 1973 album *Dark Side of the Moon* deserves mention here because of its tight synthesis of electronic and traditional instrumental textures, and because, a decade and a half after its release, it is still on the album charts, continuing to influence younger musicians. Like Walter Carlos with *Switched-On Bach*, all of these musicians extended the timbral range of more or less preexistent musical styles with the help of the new technology, and in the process were able to carry a large audience on toward an appreciation of the musical possibilities.

The German synthesizer rock movement helps throw Eno's work into perspective. The two leading groups, Kraftwerk and Tangerine Dream, have been interpreted as representing two poles in an ongoing struggle between classical and romantic aesthetic ideals. Kraftwerk, Eno, the Doors, Thomas Dolby, and others sought streamlined, economical textures and refrained from excessive rhetorical display; Tangerine Dream, Emerson, Lake & Palmer, Gary Wright and other "romantics" built up lavish, quasi-orchestral textures and went after passionate emotional statements. Bob Doerschuk puts it in the following way:

> In their adherence to the traditional elements of rock, these ["classical"] keyboardists parallelled Stravinsky's return to Mozartean classical form in symphonic music some fifty years earlier. Long after the words "punk" and "new wave" had lost their shock value, this idea persisted and continued to grow in rock. It is accurate to describe the proliferation of keyboard-oriented dance bands as a classical reaction to the new romanticism, and to recognize the musicians in these groups as the new classicists. [10]

Doerschuk goes on to assess Eno's influence on rock. His lack of keyboard technique meant that his work "was unencumbered by the traditional perceptions that piano training often imposed on other performing synthesists." Other rock keyboardists found little in Eno's music to imitate in terms of a specific playing style, but his many types of songs, his ambient music, his conceptual approach to avant-garde and classical sources, and his work as a producer did stimulate "countless young artists to liberate themselves from the musical conventions in which they had been raised, and to follow no dogma—including Kraftwerk's techno-rock gospel—blindly." [11]

In Chapter 2 I discussed the important impact early minimalist music had on Eno during the late 1960s; he was fond of Terry Riley's *In C*, was positively enamored of Steve Reich's *It's Gonna Rain*, and had performed LaMonte Young's *X for Harry Flynt*. Here I would point out that the minimalism/rock connection, as a whole, is not so much one of overlapping styles—though in both genres many have noted the marked emphasis on rhythmic subtlety and repetition—as it is one of overlapping audiences, involving a generation brought up on phonograph records and increasingly uninhibited by or unconcerned with the philosophical and ideological distinctions between high and low art. From a social point of view, the decisive event in the connection between rock and minimalist genres is not to be found among examples of stylistic fusion, as in, for instance, Terry Riley's *A Rainbow in Curved Air* (1969), Mike Oldfield's *Tubular Bells* (1973), or King Crimson's *Discipline* (1981); rather, it is to be found in the signing of a multi-record contract—a symbol of success in the rock world, and decidedly an anomaly in the art music world—with CBS by Philip Glass. Glass cut his teeth in downtown New York rock clubs and went on to write operas performed at the Met, while still remaining in touch with his earlier constituency by collaborating with popular music luminaries like David Byrne, Paul Simon, and Linda Ronstadt on his 1986 album *Songs from Liquid Days*.

While Eno has written no operas, he stands very much at the center of this fluid historical situation in which genres and audiences mix and blend, causing confusion not only among those who would persist in categorizing music as art *or* popular at the abstract level, but also among those whom the ever-changing demographics of music consumption force to invent new marketing strategies: the record industry and retailers. If one goes into a record shop in a town like Berkeley, California, one finds Eno's ambient music in bins whose labels have been created only within the last few years: in Tower Records the label reads "Space/Meditation," and in Leopold's, next door, it reads "New Age." The 1980s have seen a proliferation of recorded music linked stylistically to Eno's first ambient experiments of over a decade ago and to the minimalist music that has been in the air since the 1960s.

New age music, as the music industry seems to be leaning toward calling the genre, has begun to develop its own record labels, distribution networks, radio shows, periodicals, and catalogs.[12] What one finds in the record bins is a variety of music ranging from untreated stereo recordings of ocean surf, forest wind, and whale song to compositions written and executed entirely by computer programs, such as Larry Fast's *Synergy: Computer Experiments, Vol. 1* (1980). Somewhere in the middle is a range of electro-acoustic music by composer/performers such as the American Steve Roach (*Structures from Silence*, 1984) the German Chaitanya Deuter (*Nirvana Road*, 1984), the Greek Vangelis Papathannasiou (*Chariots of Fire*, 1981), and the Japanese Kitaro (*Silk Road I & II*, 1986), as well as solo acoustic piano improvisations, arrangements, and compositions by the genre's commercial heavyweight, the Windham Hill label's George Winston. Solo flute recorded by Paul Horn inside the Taj Mahal, vocal multiphonics recorded by David Hykes in a French cathedral, hammer dulcimer by Laraaji recorded with electronic echo by Eno in a studio: such are the varieties of new age music. Most of it shares a tranquil atmosphere, a nondevelopmental nature, a focus on tone color as a primary element of musical expression, and a high level of unabashed diatonicism and consonance.

Eno's direct contributions to this genre are manifest: his records sit in the bins alongside the rest. His position as one of the founders of the genre is more difficult to claim unequivocally. The minimalists of the 1960s came first; but it may well have been Eno's original, popular ambient records of the late 1970s, as much as any other factor, that got the ambient sound into people's ears, that provided the foundation for and impetus behind a thorough exploration of a new area of musical possibilities.

THE MUSIC'S BEAUTY

Let us return to the paradoxical questions raised at the beginning of this book. Is Eno's music divinely simple or merely simplistic? Is it primal and elemental, or primitive and elementary? Posed in this way, such questions do not invite easy answers, because Eno's music is designed to operate on many different levels. In his progressive rock, there is certainly the level of harmonic primitivism, though not quite the "three-chord primitivism" of which Rockwell wrote in connection with the rock and roll of the 1950s. But what a wealth of other levels in Eno's songs: verbal irony and wordplay; musical nostalgia, contemporaneity, and futurism; experimentation in different kinds of compositional processes; and a number of different song types—assaultive, pop, strange, and hymn-like, none of them used quite conventionally, and taken together adding up to a rich variety of expression.

Eno's ambient music is likewise multi-leveled. It has apparent surface simplicity, unassertiveness, and a high degree of consonance: hence its suitability for use as an ignorable background "tint." But Eno has simultaneously succeeded in packing enough subtle musical information into his ambient pieces to enable them to withstand close, repeated listening.

In Western music, whether popular or classical, originality is a major criterion of aesthetic importance and success. As we have seen, Eno believes that the importance of innovation in the creation of artworks is greatly overrated, accounting for only a small percentage of a piece's real content. Can we point to anything specific, in terms of a style, a technique, a use of musical materials, that constitutes Eno's original musical contribution? He has not really invented any new song types, though his strange songs are still among the strangest in the rock repertory. He has made no breakthroughs in harmonic, formal, melodic, or rhythmic technique. His conceptual approach to art and music is firmly rooted in ideas that had become public domain by the mid-1960s. Even the gentle aesthetic of his ambient music was not particularly revolutionary. Music with a similarly relaxing and repetitive surface has been around for centuries, for instance in certain Baroque keyboard ground basses and Viennese symphonic slow movements; even the idea of music as part of an environmental ambiance had already taken many forms—organ music in church, dinner music for aristocrats, carillons echoing across greens and rooftops, film music, commercial Muzak itself—before Eno seized on it.

Eno should be considered, then, not so much as an innovator as one of those artists who takes a number of existing trends and ideas and forges them into a new synthesis. Again, the comparison of Eno to Stravinsky seems apt—Stravinsky, who wrote Russian ballets, neo-classical orchestral works, jazz-art hybrids, sacred polyphony, and twelve-tone pieces, putting his own individual stamp on everything he touched, and doing it all at the highest level of craft.

Part of Stravinsky's craft involved orchestration, and it is indeed in the realm of timbre and texture that claims for innovation on Eno's part can most convincingly be made. Timbre has conventionally been regarded as a secondary element of musical expression—the colors that enliven and highlight the real musical structure, the skin that covers the music's skeleton and muscle. Lack of attention to nuances of timbre, and relegation of the whole matter to secondary importance in the compositional process, are so deeply entrenched in our cultural inheritance and consequently in our listening practices as to present a real stumbling-block to those who would listen to Eno's ambient music with a horizontal, linear orientation. For this is sculptural, spatial, non-narrative music—music that we are invited to move in and around and through, music that encourages us to listen for the fine-tuning of the harmonic series, the balance between tone and noise, the perpetual play of shifting hues. In Eno's ambient music and, to a lesser extent, in his progressive rock, the traditional balance of and interaction among elements is reversed: motivic work is there, harmony is there, rhythm is there (somewhere), but Eno's use of these elements is often just as conventional as the orchestration of Beethoven's symphonies. If in the classical work the timbre may be said to adorn the structure, then in the ambient work the structure adorns the timbre.

To appreciate the lengths to which Eno has gone to give breath and life to the color of sound itself, one need only listen to a piece like "Discreet Music"—a work which, for Eno, is relatively monochromatic—side by side with a new age piece apparently sharing similar aesthetic ideals and a similar approach to musical materials, such as Steve Roach's "Structures from Silence." The surface effect is much the same in both: the pieces are long (almost exactly half an hour), slow, quiet, diatonic, consonant, repetitive, electronically produced, recorded with very long reverberation times that lend the music a sense of spaciousness. But in Roach's composition, the tone colors themselves are rather formica-like: clean, flat, smooth, constant and unchanging, with just a touch of low-depth chorusing. In "Discreet Music," on the other hand, the tone color is constantly undergoing shifts of equalization, so that the "same" melodies resemble now a whistle, now a flute, now a muted foghorn. The third of Arnold Schoenberg's *Five Pieces for Orchestra*, Op. 16, of 1912 ("The Changing Chord—Summer Morning by a Lake—Colors") is based on a similar idea: a lack of dramatic external motion and obvious rhythmic events in the music is offest by constantly changing, subtle shifts in orchestration. Schoenberg even coined a word for this idea: *Klangfarbenmelodie*, a melody of sound colors. Whether he is aware of it or not, Eno has taken this idea and made it the basis of his musical style. [13]

If the aesthetic impact of Eno's music depends to a large extent on timbre and texture (texture being simply layers or levels of individual timbres), another important—and related—contribution is his "holograph" paradigm of composition, according to which music can be made that seems to stay substantially the same even while continuously shifting in its details. While the idea itself is not original, being derived primarily from his study of minimalist tape-phase pieces, Eno has systematically pursued a set of musical possibilities that the new paradigm illuminates. The paradigm itself necessitates a tonal frame of reference no more than serial methods necessitate an atonal frame of reference, yet most minimalists working along these lines have made their music single-mindedly tonal, and Eno is no exception. Once again, this is a case of an artist who is exploring new territory, yet who feels that the maps he makes must be capable of being read—and enjoyed. Eno has said as much: he wants his music to be seductive. [14]

In the preceding chapters we have seen a number of writers attempt to capture some of the language-defying sense of Eno's music through picturesque and sometimes surreal metaphors. And indeed, as in writing of any kind about music of any kind, there comes a point when language fails. Medieval philosophers saw, heard, and conceived music as an evocation of the myriad overlapping rhythms of the cosmos. Eno's long ambient pieces, consisting of overlaid cycles of sound events, give contemporary life to this ancient image. The duration of the world is vast, an hour on a "Thursday Afternoon" short; yet time during that hour seems to expand, to slow down, invested with the sense of the magical which it has fallen to art to summon up. If we may occasionally yearn for some time-lapse photography to speed things up, that may be because we live in an artificially accelerated age.

Music deals with time and exists in time, and it may be considered a sacred observation of the mystery of time. Whether through classical symphony, Renaissance mass, reggae dance, jam session, or ambient soundscape, time marked by music is set aside, consecrated. Music concentrates time, making us aware of different levels of temporal magnification, from immense historical vistas to momentary transitions. It enhances and focuses our ability to perceive changes, fluctuations, and developments. Music is paradoxical: profoundly unnaturalistic, presenting an abstract temporal tableau, it may nevertheless poignantly evoke not only realms of everyday experience, but images of the grandeur of eternity. Eno's music is capable of thus transforming time, for those who would listen.

EPILOG—1989–1995

Around 1989, when this book had not quite yet been published—it was still in dissertation form, with more technical lingo, methodological baggage, and notated musical examples than the book as it exists now—I met Brian Eno backstage at the Palace of Fine Arts in San Francisco. One of his new audio-visual installations was humming away in a building behind the nearby Exploratorium. He was there to be interviewed in front of an enthusiastic, appreciative packed house by Bay Area composer and new music champion Charles Amirkhanian, who had kindly arranged the meeting between us.

Before the interview show, Eno came into the dressing room and we were introduced by his manager. Amazingly enough, he was just like all the descriptions I'd read: slightly built, with an ingenuous smile, oddly forthright and self-effacing at the same time. He displayed an easy sense of humor, opinionated yet self-deprecating.

Eno had with him a bound copy of my dissertation, which Charles had given him earlier that week, and he had already read portions of it. The problem was, in the taxi on the way over to the Palace of Fine Arts, he had unwittingly sat on a juicy wad of chewing gum, which was now ungraciously affixed to his posterior regions. Consequently, much of our keenly anticipated encounter took place with the great Brian Eno bent over a dressing table while an assistant nimbly applied a razor blade to a delicate area on the seat of his stylish black pants.

With the dissertation open before him on the table, Eno flipped through the pages, reading out loud and commenting on various passages. He said he was sincerely impressed with the effort that had gone into the book, while simultaneously making amusing remarks to the effect that he couldn't believe anyone would actually write an academic thesis about his music. He liked it, though, joking that I'd somehow found all the best things he'd ever said and assembled them together in one place.

As the sure-fingered assistant continued to perform his deft surgical removal of the offending blob, Eno lighted on a passage where I'd described one of his ambient compositions as being in the Dorian mode. He chuckled and said, "I didn't know that piece was in Dorian mode."

This—and it was confirmed in subsequent communications between us—turned out to be the aspect of the book that most fascinated Eno. For as a musician, Eno was self-educated but largely untrained: Well-versed in a variety of philosophical issues surrounding music, its history, and its production, he nevertheless had less knowledge of traditional music theory, harmony, counterpoint, and form than the average American college music student. So to read my learned analyses of his works was an eye-opener.

In his heavily analytical 1973 book *Twilight of the Gods: The Music of the Beatles*, musicologist Wilfrid Mellers mused that "Some people seem to find it inherently risible that pop music should be discussed in technical terms at all; when the senior critic of *The Times* wrote the first musically literate piece about the Beatles it was greeted with hoots of mirth both from the Beatles themselves and from their hostile critics."

Perhaps times have changed; or perhaps Brian Eno is simply unusually literary for a pop figure—and unusually open-minded when it comes to taking in different perspectives that hold the potential to develop and advance his own work. He told me that reading my book made him want to go back and listen to some of his old pieces again, re-evaluate them with this new knowledge, and, possibly, to try composing new music with some of the tools he'd gleaned. As a music theorist and analyst, I felt that this was the most gratifying tribute a musician could have possibly paid my work.

ENO'S MUSIC OF THE 1990S

In the past five years, Eno has continued to issue a steady stream of music, installations, articles, interviews, and lectures; he has lent his gently stimulating touch as a producer, keyboardist, and collaborator to an almost countless number of studio sessions; and he has maintained his position in the forefront of quality rock music, notably through his design of the U2 1992 *Zooropa* world tour stage set, complete with a torrential, visually overwhelming array of video images and effects.

In short, he is a person at the full height of his creative powers.

Eno released four major musical works during this period: *Wrong Way Up* (1990), an album of slightly skewed poppish songs with John Cale; *The Shutov Assembly* (1992), a colorful anthology of varied ambient pieces; *Nerve Net* (1992), an astonishing set of studies in rhythm and near-atonality; and *Neroli* (1993), a rather severe exercise in dark modal minimalism.

WRONG WAY UP

In 1990, Eno gave his public what many of them had long been waiting for—a new album of songs. Unfortunately, in this instance the chemistry and contrast between Eno and Cale is not enough to produce much in the way of tangible musical interest. Most of these songs sound amateurish: silly, over-produced ditties without the acerbic edge that turned some of Eno's songs of the 1970s into something admirably demented.

A number of the songs are campy, in the vein of the Beatles' "Yellow Submarine," borrowing elements from folk music, British music hall, and nursery rhyme. But here the campiness, instead of being jolly and light-hearted, gets bogged down in bulky, ponderous, unconvincing electronic arrangements. There's little light, little transparency here—little in the way of the unique, unreasonable textures that Eno is capable of creating—textures that are capable of turning a ho-hum song into a compelling piece of music.

In a way, *Wrong Way Up* exposes Eno's weaknesses as a songwriter. Songwriters craft melodies and chords, and arrangers and singers create the performance. Eno does not write real vocal melodies—they tend to be static, they don't "go" anywhere—and he doesn't really understand the power of functional harmony to create, support, and propel emotional movement. Eno is not a songwriter, but rather a deft manipulator of sounds, colors, and blocks of music. So when he writes a song and the arrangment isn't up to snuff, there's little left to sustain interest.

THE SHUTOV ASSEMBLY

In this delightfully variegated collection, Eno takes us into his workshop as he plays with the same sorts of musical building blocks that date back to his works of the late 1970s, creating music suitable for establishing a certain background mood, for enhancing creative activities, or for deep contemplation.

As a whole, what sets this collection—recorded between 1985 and 1990—apart from earlier efforts is the de-emphasis of pitch and mode. To put this another way, Eno was experimenting with atonality.

For example, if the pitch set used in the second piece, "ALHONDIGA," corresponds to any known mode or scale, it is not readily apparent to me. My mind strains to find a tonic center of gravity, a point at the middle of the galaxy of pitches around which they all revolve and to which they are all logically related; but such a center does not seem to exist. Other pieces in *The Shutov Assembly*, such as "FRANCISCO," are similar.

The fourth composition, "LANZAROTE," is a reissue of the *Glint* (East of Woodbridge) flexi-disk first released in 1986. In the original edition of this book, I wrote that "As *Glint* shows, the ambient style is capable of seemingly perpetual variation and extension: beyond the Phrygian mode of *Glint*, the still gloomier tones of the Locrian mode are waiting ... Even an atonal ambient style does not seem beyond the realm of the possible."

With *The Shutov Assembly*, Eno sticks his toe into the still largely uncharted universe of atonality, the universe that has no up and down, no central point, no gravity. Schoenberg and Webern, experiencing giddy vertigo as they floated in that vast domain, felt they had to invent, through sheer force of artifice, a viable theoretical construct to impose a semblance of order on it: That construct was the 12-tone system.

The "word square" that shows the titles of the individual pieces on the CD's back cover is eerily reminiscent of the kind of 12-tone pitch matrixes I used to pore over in graduate seminars on Schoenberg, Webern, Stockhausen, Boulez, and the later Stravinsky. I do not know whether, or to what extent, Eno used or adapted actual 12-tone techniques in *The Shutov Assembly*. But in a 1992 interview in *Opal Information,* Eno cited Webern as one of his favorite composers. And Eno has always had a penchant for cyclic systems; as I pointed out in the original edition of this book, the serial organization of "2/1" from *Music for Airports* is reminiscent of Webern pieces like the first movement of his Symphony, Op. 21.

(Note: if some of this sounds cryptic, please refer to the definitions of "Atonality," "Mode," and "Tonality" in the *Glossary* of this book.)

NERVE NET

Eno's most adventurous solo release in the 1990s—and perhaps of all time—has been *Nerve Net* of 1992. If I had to choose a single Eno album to take with me to a desert island for the rest of my life, this would be it, because it's got it all: vintage weird Eno vocals; brash, unusual synthesizer textures up the wazoo; tonality, atonality, and just about everything in between; a number of really sublimely irritating pieces (notably the two long mixes of "Web"); and hey, you can dance to it, too.

Not since 1981's *My Life in the Bush of Ghosts* had Eno used percussive elements so relentlessly and successfully. On *Nerve Net*, the drumming, electronic drumming, and percussion—by Sugarfoot Moffett, Markus Draws, Isaac Osapanin, Winston Ngukwe, Ernest Darling, Cecil Stamper III, Richard Bailey, Benmont Tench, Ian Dench, and Eno himself—stand out for their precision, power, and raw intensity.

Indeed, in *Nerve Net* as a whole, Eno once again excels in coaxing outrageous performances out of all his instrumentalists and vocalists, somehow managing to create, out of the widest, most disparate palette of sounds, something that congeals—and rocks.

NEROLI

Neroli consists of 58 uninterrupted minutes of a single mode (the dark, mysterious Phrygian), a single timbre (a sort of heavily equalized electric piano-type sound), a single dynamic level (*pianissimo*, very soft), and a limited register (most of the fundamental tones are within the baritone/bass range of the human voice). The atmosphere of slow, hesitant foreboding is maintained from beginning to end. In short, it's a highly minimalistic statement, suitable for late-night or Sunday morning meditations.

BERKELEY, CALIFORNIA
MARCH 1995

Eno on the Internet

An Eno site—kind of an electronic fan club—is now maintained on the Internet. If you're interested, you can dial in at http://www.acns.nwu.edu/eno-l. The site's mission statement reads:

"This Eno World Wide Web project was created from materials found archived on the Internet at various sites and from contributions from the subscribers to the Eno mailing list.

"The intent was in part to create a WWW demo project that would show what can be done with musical discographies and FAQs using the WWW and a good multimedia browser such as Mosaic.

"We hope this will inspire other folks to contribute to existing projects like the WNUR Jazz WWW server or the American Resource Server."

Through the Internet, it is now possible to read a variety of articles about Eno, to download bibliographies and discographies, and to communicate with other people about Eno and his work. It's kind of like finding a shelf of Eno materials in a library, and so, if you are truly an Enophile, it's an experience highly to be recommended.

Reproduced below is one of the more interesting items in the Eno World Wide Web project. I quote it in full because it is vintage Eno.

ENO & EMAIL

A reader of the Eno mailing list contacted someone who appears to be Brian Eno and asked him if he'd like to contribute to the mailing list. The reply:

From: Brian One
To: zilch
Subject: Re: eno-l mailing list

Hello Paul. Thanks for getting in touch. You might be surprised to know that I don't want to join your mailing list. Don't misunderstand me—I'm very happy that you're doing it, and pleased that there's enough interest in me and my work to (hopefully) sustain it, but I just don't personally want to be part of it.

You must wonder why this is. I think the reason I feel uncomfortable about such a thing is that it becomes a sort of weight on my shoulders. I start to feel an obligation to live up to something, instead of just following my nose wherever it wants to go at the moment. Of course success has many nice payoffs, but one of the disadvantages is that you start to be made to feel responsible for other people's feelings: What I'm always hearing are variations of "why don't you do more records like—(insert any album title)" or "why don't you do

*more work with—(insert any artist's name)?" I don't know why, these
questions are unanswerable, why is it so bloody important to you,
leave me alone . . . . these are a few of my responses. But the most important reason is "If I'd followed your advice in the first place I'd
never have got anywhere."*

*I'm afraid to say that admirers can be a tremendous force for con-
servatism, for consolidation. Of course it's really wonderful to be acclaimed for things you've done—in fact it's the only serious reward,
because it makes you think, "It worked! I'm not isolated!" or something like that, and it makes you feel gratefully connected to your
own culture. But on the other hand, there's a tremendously strong
pressure to repeat yourself, to do more of that thing we all liked so
much. I can't do that—I don't have the enthusiasm to push through
projects that seem familiar to me (—this isn't so much a question of
artistic nobility or high ideals: I just get too bloody bored), but at the
same time I do feel guilt for "deserting my audience" by not doing
the things they apparently wanted. I'd rather not feel this guilt, actually, so I avoid finding out about situations that could cause it.*

*The problem is that people nearly always prefer what I was doing a
few years earlier—this has always been true. The other problem is
that so, often, do I! Discovering things is clumsy and sporadic, and
the results don't at first compare well with the glossy and lauded
works of the past. You have to keep reminding yourself that they
went through that as well, otherwise they become frighteningly accomplished. That's another problem with being made to think about your
own past—you forget its genesis and start to feel useless awe towards
your earlier self. "How did I do it? Wherever did these ideas come
from?" Now, the workaday everyday now, always looks relatively less
glamorous than the rose-tinted then (except for those magic ·hours
when your finger is right on the pulse, and those times only happen
when you've abandoned the lifeline of your own history).*

*So good luck with it, but I won't be taking part. If you need infor-
mation, contact LIN BARKASS at OPAL INFORMATION BOX 141,
LEIGH ON SEA, ESSEX.*

— — — — — *end forwarded· message* — — — — — — — — — — —

NOTES

CHAPTER 1. ENO'S WORK IN PERSPECTIVE

[1] Eno himself has published a comprehensive, though not exhaustive list of his works, categorized as solo albums, singles, album productions and coproductions, primary collaborations, secondary collaborations, selected commissions to score music, selected uses of *Music for Films* and other compositions, video works, audiovisual installations, and publications. See Brian Eno and Russell Mills, *More Dark Than Shark*, commentaries by Rick Poynor, designed by Malcolm Garrett, photography by Martin Axon, additional photography by David Buckland (London: Faber and Faber, 1986), 138–9. See also the Discography in this book.

[2] Brian Eno and Peter Schmidt, *Oblique Strategies: Over One Hundred Worthwhile Dilemmas*, boxed set of cards, limited edition of 500 copies, London, 1975; revised and reissued, London, 1978, 1979.

[3] Bruno Nettl, *The Western Impact on World Music: Change, Adaptation, and Survival* (New York: Schirmer, 1985), 85.

[4] Brian Eno, liner notes to *Discreet Music*, Editions EG EGS 303, 1975.

[5] Carl Dahlhaus, *Analysis and Value Judgement* (New York: Pendragon Press, 1983), 6.

[6] Bruno Nettl, *The Study of Ethnomusicology: Twenty-nine Issues and Concepts* (Urbana, Chicago, and London: University of Illinois Press, 1983), 305.

[7] Philip Tagg, "Analysing Popular Music," *Popular Music 2: Theory and Method* (Cambridge: Cambridge University Press, 1982), 42.

[8] Paul Taylor, *Popular Music Since 1955: A Critical Guide to the Literature* (Boston: G. K. Hall & Co., 1985).

[9] Janell Duxbury, *Rockin' the Classics and Classicizin' the Rock: A Selectively Annotated Discography*, Discographies, Number 14 (Westport, Ct. and London: Greenwood Press, 1985), 117. This extraordinary source provides a useful overview of this field of music. Interestingly, and perhaps inevitably, though, the discography's method, like Tagg's axiomatic triangle, proves unable to catch Eno's unique blend of musical popularism and classicism in its net: he is represented by only two entries, both of them of marginal significance in terms of a total understanding of his work: Eno is cited as rockin' the Pachelbel Canon on *Discreet Music* (though this is not so much a rock arrangement—the only instruments are strings—as a compositional "derangement" of the melody) and as having recorded with the Portsmouth Sinfonia (which really had nothing to do with rock music at all).

[10] Jon Pareles and Patricia Romanowski, eds., *The Rolling Stone Encyclopedia of Rock & Roll* (New York: Rolling Stone Press/Summit Books, 1983), 447.

[11] John Rockwell, "Art Rock," in Jim Miller, ed., *The Rolling Stone Illustrated History of Rock & Roll* (New York: Rolling Stone/Random House, 1976), 322–6.

[12] John Rockwell, *All American Music: Composition in the Late 20th Century*, (New York: Knopf, 1983), table of contents.

[13] Jon Pareles, "Riffs: Eno Uncaged," *Village Voice* 27 (4 May 1982), 77.

[14] Ed Naha, "Review: *Taking Tiger Mountain (By Strategy)*," *Crawdaddy* (May 1975), 76.

[15] Lester Bangs, "Eno," *Musician, Player & Listener* 21 (Nov. 1979), 43.

[16] Stephen Demorest, "The Discreet Charm of Brian Eno," *Horizon* 21 (June 1978), 83.

CHAPTER 2. BACKGROUND AND INFLUENCES

[1] Charles Amirkhanian, interviewer, "Eno at KPFA: 2 Feb. 1980, 13 March 1980, and 2 April 1980," seven 10-inch reels of ¼" tape (private collection of Charles Amirkhanian, Berkeley, Ca.). A typescript was made of the first of these interviews: "Brian Eno interviewed 2/2/80 for KPFA Marathon by C. Amirkhanian, transcribed 10/29/83 [by] S. Stone." In the notes to follow I shall cite the typescript as Amirkhanian, "Eno at KPFA."

[2] Kurt Loder, "Eno," *Synapse* (Jan./Feb. 1979), 26–7.

[3]Mark Howell, "From a Strangers Evening with Brian Eno," *Another Room* (June/July 1981), n. p.

[4]Loder, "Eno," 26.

[5]George Rush, "Brian Eno: Rock's Svengali Pursues Silence," *Esquire* 98 (Dec. 1982), 130.

[6]Jim Aikin, "Brian Eno," *Keyboard* 7 (July 1981), 62. In another interview Eno cited Don and Juan's "Chicken Necks" as another example of what he called "mystery music." Loder, "Eno," 26.

[7]Rob Tannenbaum, "A Meeting of Sound Minds: John Cage and Brian Eno," *Musician* 83 (Sept. 1985), 67.

[8]Tannenbaum, "Cage and Eno," 67. In another interview Eno cited Jack Teagarden as an example of the kind of big-band jazz he heard from his uncle's collection. Loder, "Eno," 27.

[9]Loder, "Eno," 26.

[10]Loder, "Eno," 26.

[11]Larry Kelp, "Brian Eno: Making Fourth World Music in Record Studio," *Oakland Tribune*, 11 Feb. 1980, C–7.

[12]Roman Kozak, "Math Qualities of Music Interest Eno," *Billboard* 90 (13 May 1978), 51.

[13]John Cage, *Silence* (Middletown, Ct.: Wesleyan University Press, 1976; first published 1961).

[14]Cage, *Silence*, 54.

[15]Cage, *Silence*, 76.

[16]Cage, *Silence*, 78.

[17]Cage, *Silence*, 80.

[18]Cage, *Silence*, 79.

[19]Stephen Demorest, "Discreet Charm of Eno," 85.

[20]Richard Williams, "Crimso Meets Enol," *Melody Maker* 47 (4 Nov. 1972), 65.

[21]Frank Rose, "Four Conversations with Brian Eno," *Village Voice* 22 (28 Mar. 1977), 69.

[22]Amirkhanian, "Eno at KPFA," 7.

[23]Aikin, "Eno," 60.

[24]Cage, *Silence*, 59.

[25]Stephen Grant, "Brian Eno Against Interpretation," *Trouser Press* 9 (Aug. 1982), 28.

[26]Tannenbaum, "Cage and Eno," 66.

[27]Tannenbaum, "Cage and Eno," 69–70.

[28]Tannenbaum, "Cage and Eno," 70.

[29]Jan Steele and John Cage, *Voices and Instruments*, Obscure/Editions EG OBS 5, 1976.

[30]Tannenbaum, "Cage and Eno," 68.

[31]See E. H. Gombrich, *Art and Illusion: A Study in the Psychology of Pictorial Representation*, the A. W. Mellon Lectures in the Fine Arts, 1956, National Gallery of Art, Washington (Princeton: Princeton University Press, 1972), 5, 244.

[32]Anthony Korner, "Aurora Musicalis," *Artforum* 24:10 (Summer 1986), 79.

[33]Tannenbaum, "Cage and Eno," 68.

[34]Steve Reich, liner notes to *John Cage: Three Dances; Steve Reich; Four Organs*, Capitol/Angel S36059, 1973.

[35]John Hutchinson, "Brian Eno: Place #13," color brochure (Dublin: Douglas Hyde Gallery, 1986), n.p.

[36]Tannenbaum, "Cage and Eno," 68.

[37]Eric Salzman, *Twentieth-Century Music: An Introduction*, Prentice-Hall History of Music Series, H. Wiley Hitchcock, ed. (Englewood Cliffs, N.J.: Prentice-Hall, 1974), 187.

[38]Aikin, "Eno," 60.

[39]Brian Eno, text for a lecture to Trent Polytechnic, 1974; quoted in Brian Eno and Russell Mills, *More Dark Than Shark*, commentaries by Rick Poynor, designed by Malcolm Garrett, photography by Martin Axon, additional photography by David Buckland (London: Faber and Faber, 1986), 43.

CHAPTER 3. ON OTHER MUSIC: ENO AS CRITIC

[1]Brian Eno, "Works Constructed with Sound and Light: Extracts from a talk given by Brian Eno following the opening of his video installation, Copenhagen, January 1986," color brochure (London: Opal Ltd., 1986), n. p.

[2]Jensen, "The Sound of Silence: A Thursday Afternoon with Brian Eno," *Electronics & Music Maker* (Dec. 1985), 25.

[3]Steven Grant, "Eno Against Interpretation," 28.

[4]Cynthia Dagnal, "Eno and the Jets: Controlled Chaos," *Rolling Stone* 169 (12 Sept. 1974), 16.

[5]Allan Jones, "Eno—Class of '75," *Melody Maker* 50 (29 Nov. 1975), 14.

[6]Bruce Dancis, "Studio Plays Big Role in Music Composition, Says Brian Eno," *Billboard* 92 (22 March 1980), 29.

[7]George Rush, "Eno: Rock's Svengali Pursues Silence," 132.

[8]Mick Brown, "On Record: Brian Eno," *Sunday Times Magazine*, 31 Oct. 1982, 10.

[9]Jensen, "Sound of Silence," 25.

[10]Simon Frith, *Sound Effects: Youth, Leisure, and the Politics of Rock'n'Roll* (New York: Pantheon Books, 1981).

[11]The demographics of record consumption is actually a complex subject, with hard data not always easy to come by or interpret. A 1985 joint market survey by the Recording Industry Association of America and the National Association of Recording Merchandisers found that "the demographic breakdown showed the staying power of the Big Chill generation and its elders—the 35-plus demographic accounted for 26% of prerecorded music purchased, with people age 30–34 buying 11%. Younger listeners, however, held sway, with a total of 63%—the 25–29 group, 14%; 20–24, 15%; 15–19, 25%; and 10–14, 9%." Bill Holland, "Cassettes Take 2–1 Lead Over Vinyl in Survey," *Billboard* 98:50 (13 Dec. 1986), 73.

[12]Lee Moore, "Eno = MC Squared," *Creem* 10 (Nov. 1978), 68.

[13]Rob Tannenbaum, "Cage and Eno," 106.

[14]Amirkhanian, "Eno at KPFA," 13.

[15]Frank Rose, "Eno: Scaramouche of the Synthesizer," *Creem* 7 (July 1975), 70.

[16]Brown, "On Record: Brian Eno," 94. Paul Simon has said that "Bridge Over Troubled Water" "took somewhere around ten days to two weeks to record, and then it had to be mixed." Jon Landau, "Paul Simon: 'Like a Pitcher of Water,' " in Ben Fong-Torres, ed., *The Rolling Stone Interviews*, Vol. 2 (New York: Warner, 1973), 398.

[17]John Rockwell, "The Odyssey of Two British Rockers," *New York Times*, 23 July 1978, II:16. In the same article, Robert Fripp is quoted expressing much the same distaste as Eno with regard to early and mid-1970s British progressive rock: "I don't wish to listen to the philosophical meanderings of some English halfwit who is circumnavigating some inessential point of experience in his life."

[18]Tannenbaum, "Cage and Eno," 68.

[19]Brian Eno, "Pro Session: The Studio as Compositional Tool—Part I," lecture delivered at New Music New York, the first New Music America Festival, sponsored in 1979 by the Kitchen, excerpted by Howard Mandel, *Down Beat* 50 (July 1983), 57. "Part II" of this lecture appeared in the next issue of *Down Beat* (Aug. 1983).

[20]Moore, "Eno = MC Squared," 67.

[21]Michael Zwerin, "Brian Eno: Music Existing in Space," *International Herald Tribune*, 14 Sept. 1983, 7.

[22]Zwerin, "Eno: Music Existing in Space," 7.

[23]Rockwell, "Odyssey of Two British Rockers," 16.

[24]Moore, "Eno = MC Squared," 68.

[25]Amirkhanian, "Eno at KPFA," 8.

[26]Amirkhanian, "Eno at KPFA," 9.

[27]Amirkhanian, "Eno at KPFA," 22.

[28]Amirkhanian, "Eno at KPFA," 23.

[29]Dancis, "Studio Plays Big Role, Says Eno," 29.

[30]Demorest, "Discreet Charm of Eno," 82.

[31]Amirkhanian, "Eno at KPFA," 21.

[32]Amirkhanian, "Eno at KPFA," 22.

[33]Aikin, "Brian Eno," 45.

[34]Aikin, "Brian Eno," 45.

[35]Aikin, "Brian Eno," 45.

[36]Aikin, "Brian Eno," 64.

[37]Loder, "Eno," 26.

[38]Glenn O'Brien, "Eno at the Edge of Rock," *Andy Warhol's Interview* 8 (June 1978), 32.

[39]O'Brien, "Eno at Edge of Rock," 32.

[40]Bill Milkowski, "Brian Eno: Excursions in the Electronic Environment," *Down Beat* 50 (June 1983), 57.

[41]Brian Eno, "Pro Session—Part II," 53.

[42]Rose, "Four Conversations with Eno," 67.

[43]Milkowski, "Brian Eno: Excursions," 57.

[44]Hutchinson, "Eno: Place #13," n. p.

[45]Hutchinson, "Eno: Place #13," n. p.

[46]Tom Johnson, "New Music, New York, New Institution," *Village Voice* 24 (2 July 1979), 89.

[47]Amirkhanian, "Eno at KPFA," 19.

[48]Geoff Brown, "Eno's Where It's At," *Melody Maker* 48 (10 Nov. 1973), 41.

[49]Korner, "Aurora Musicalis," 78.

[50]Aikin, "Brian Eno," 57.

[51]Amirkhanian, "Eno at KPFA," 14.

[52]Amirkhanian, "Eno at KPFA," 24.

[53]Tannenbaum, "Cage and Eno," 69.

[54]Joseph Kerman, *Contemplating Music: Challenges to Musicology* (Cambridge, Mass.: Harvard University Press, 1985), 54.

[55]Kurt Loder, "Squawking Heads: Byrne and Eno in the Bush of Ghosts," *Rolling Stone* 338 (5 March 1981), 46.

CHAPTER 4. THE EAR OF THE NON-MUSICIAN

[1]Eno, Trent Polytechnic lecture, *More Dark Than Shark*, 40.

[2]Zwerin, "Eno: Music Existing in Space," 7.

[3]Arthur Lubow, "Brian Eno: At the Outer Limits of Popular Music, the Ex-glitter Rocker Experiments with a Quiet New Sound," *People Weekly* (11 Oct. 1982), 94.

[4]Brown, "Eno's Where It's At," 41.

[5]Demorest, "Discreet Charm of Eno," 83.

[6]Lester Bangs, "Eno Sings with the Fishes," *Village Voice* 23 (3 Apr. 1978), 49.

[7]Robert Palmer, "Brian Eno, New Guru of Rock, Going Solo," *New York Times*, 13 March 1981, III:17.

[8]Grant, "Eno Against Interpretation," 29.

[9]Hutchinson, "Eno: Place #13," n. p.

[10]Eno, "Pro Session—Part I," 56.

[11]Korner, "Aurora Musicalis," 77.

[12]Quoted in David H. Cope, *New Directions in Music*, 2nd ed. (Dubuque, Iowa: Wm. C. Brown, 1980), 211.

[13]Jensen, "Sound of Silence," 23.

[14]Jensen, "Sound of Silence," 24.

[15]Jensen, "Sound of Silence," 24.

[16]Hutchinson, "Eno: Place #13," n. p.

[17]Jensen, "Sound of Silence," 23.

[18]Bangs, "Eno," 40.

[19]Aikin, "Brian Eno," 52.

[20]See, for instance, Walter Piston, *Harmony*, 3rd ed. (New York: W.W. Norton, 1962), 18, where the author offers a "Table of Usual Root Progressions": "I is followed by IV or V, sometimes VI, less often II or III.

II is followed by V, sometimes VI, less often I, III, or IV.

III is followed by . . ."

[21]Jann Wenner, *Lennon Remembers: The Rolling Stone Interviews* (San Francisco: Straight Arrow Books, 1971), 48.

[22]Nettl, *The Study of Ethnomusicology*," 33.

[23]Brown, "Eno's Where It's At," 40.

[24]S. Davy, "Eno: Non-Musician on Non-Art," *Beetle* (Jan. 1975), n. p.

[25]Cope, *New Directions in Music*, 196–222. The "Antimusic" chapter contains a useful bibliography of books and articles, recordings and publishers, and films.

[26]Aikin, "Brian Eno," 66.

[27]O'Brien, "Eno at Edge of Rock," 31.

[28]Aikin, "Brian Eno," 55.

[29]Milkowski, "Brian Eno: Excursions," 57.

[30]Tom Mulhern, "Robert Fripp on the Discipline of Craft & Art," *Guitar Player* 20 (Jan. 1986), 91.

[31]Moore, "Eno = MC Squared," 68.

[32]Moore, "Eno = MC Squared," 68. A similar anecdote is related in Bangs, "Eno," 40.

[33]Richard Cromelin, "Records: The Inmates Have Taken Over: Kevin Ayers, John Cale, Nico, Eno & the Soporifics, *June 1, 1974*," *Creem* 6 (Dec. 1974), 65.

[34]Milkowski, "Brian Eno: Excursions," 57.

[35]Mark Howell, "Strangers Evening with Eno," n. p.

[36]Aikin, "Brian Eno," 45.

[37]Aikin, "Brian Eno," 57.

[38]Aikin, "Brian Eno," 56–7.

CHAPTER 5. LISTENERS AND AIMS

[1]Rush, "Eno: Rock's Svengali," 132. Eno remarked in 1982 that his records "don't sell terribly well—around 100,000, I suppose, which is enough to make some money from. My music is used in quite a lot of films, TV things, other uses. That's strictly bonus income, because they use stuff that already exists." Grant, "Eno Against Interpretation," 29.

[2]Rush, "Eno: Rock's Svengali," 132.

[3]Jim Aikin, "Brian Eno," *Keyboard* 7 (July 1981), 64.

[4]Rockwell, "Odyssey of Two British Rockers," II:16.

[5]Milton Babbitt, "Who Cares If You Listen?," *High Fidelity* 8 (Feb. 1958), 38.

[6]Quoted in Tom Hull, "Eno Races Toward the New World," *Village Voice* 21 (12 Apr. 1976), 88.

[7]Milkowski, "Eno: Excursions," 16.

[8]Millkowski, "Eno: Excursions," 16.

[9]Grant, "Eno Against Interpretation," 29.

[10]Milkowski, "Eno: Excursions," 17.

[11]Eno, "Pro Session—Part I," 56.

[12]Grant, "Eno Against Interpretation," 30.

[13]Korner, "Aurora Musicalis," 78.

[14]See W. K. Wimsatt and M. C. Beardsley, "The Intentional Fallacy," *The Sewanee Review* 54 (1946). In the words of musicologist Philip Gossett, Wimsatt and Beardsley "attack as irrelevant to criticism questions, such as 'What was the poet's intention in writing this poem?' or 'What did he mean by this allusion?,' whose answers must be statements divorced from a reading of the poem itself and usually expressed in language not derived from it." Gossett, "Beethoven's Sixth Symphony: Sketches for the First Movement," *Journal of the American Musicological Society* 28 (Summer 1974), 260.

[15]Tannenbaum, "Cage and Eno," 70.

[16]Dagnal, "Eno and the Jets," 16.

[17]Brown, "Eno's Where It's At," 40.

[18]Brown, "Eno's Where It's At," 40.

[19]Allan Jones, "Eno: On Top of Tiger Mountain," *Melody Maker* 49 (26 Oct. 1974), 39.

[20]Tannenbaum, "Cage and Eno," 72.

[21]Jensen, "Sound of Silence," 22.

[22]Lee Moore, "Eno = MC Squared," 67.

[23]Bangs, "Eno," 42.

[24]Aikin, "Brian Eno," 62.

[25]Kristine McKenna, "Eno," *Wet* 25 (July/Aug. 1980), 45.

[26]Judy Nylon, "Eno's Other Green Worlds," *Circus* (27 Apr. 1976), 23.

[27]Brian Eno, "Generating and Organizing Variety in the Arts," *Studio International* 984 (Nov./ Dec. 1976), 279–83. The article was reprinted in Gregory Battock, ed., *Breaking the Sound Barrier: A Critical Anthology of the New Music* (New York: Dutton, 1981).

[28]Eno, "Generating and Organizing Variety," 279.

[29]Eno, "Generating and Organizing Variety," 283.

[30]Stafford Beer, *Brain of the Firm: The Managerial Cybernetics of Organization* (London: Allen Lane, 1972), 69. Quoted in Eno, "Generating and Organizing Variety," 283.

[31]Eno, "Generating and Organizing Variety," 283.

[32]Eno was involved with four performances of the piece, one of which was recorded. Cornelius Cardew, *The Great Learning*, DGG 2538216.

[33]Eno, "Generating and Organizing Variety," 281. The Beer quotation is from *Brain of the Firm*, 69.

[34]Michael Nyman, *Decay Music*, Obscure/Editions EG OBS 6, 1976.

[35]Eno, "Generating and Organizing Variety," 281–2.

[36]Eno, "Generating and Organizing Variety," 282.

[37]Eno, "Generating and Organizing Variety," 282.

[38]Eno, "Generating and Organizing Variety," 282.

CHAPTER 6. THE COMPOSITIONAL PROCESS

[1]Eno, "Pro Session—Part I," 57.

[2]Eno, "Pro Session—Part I," 56.

[3]Eno, "Pro Session—Part I," 56. The idea that *recording* is solely responsible for the spatialization of music is debatable. A recent pointed scholarly exchange in the pages of the journal *19th Century Music* revolved around the issue of whether or not it is valid to view the tonal structure of Verdi's operas as existing on an ideal, "spatial" plane outside the temporal plane of actual performance and perceived, heard, local modulations. Whatever side one favors in that debate, it is probably true that the debate itself could not arise with reference to music that has not been notated: in the case of the Verdi operas, it is the *score* that takes music out of the time dimension and puts it into the space dimension, or at least makes it much more susceptible to "spatial perception" and structural tonal analysis. Music notation has perhaps always had this sort of spatializing effect, but it is interesting that the linear versus spatial debate has intensified

since the advent of sound recording. See Sigmund Levarie, "Key Relations in Verdi's *Un Ballo in Maschera*," *19th Century Music* 2 (1978), 143–7; Joseph Kerman, "Viewpoint," *19th Century Music* 2 (1978), 186–91; and Levarie's reply to Kerman, *19th Century Music* 3 (1979), 88–9.

[4]Eno, "Pro Session—Part I," 57.

[5]Eno, "Pro Session—Part I," 57.

[6]Eno, "Pro Session—Part II," 50.

[7]Loder, "Eno," 24.

[8]McKenna, "Eno," 42.

[9]Aikin, "Brian Eno," 59.

[10]Aikin, "Brian Eno," 59.

[11]Aikin, "Brian Eno," 59.

[12]Aikin, "Brian Eno," 59.

[13]Robert Fripp produced an album by the guitar and vocal group the Roches in what he called *audio verité*. The effect is that of a sparkling, well-balanced live performance. The Roches, *The Roches*, Warner Brothers BSK 3298, 1979.

[14]Eno, "Pro Session—Part II," 50.

[15]Eno, "Pro Session—Part II," 53.

[16]Eno, "Pro Session—Part II," 50.

[17]Eno, "Pro Session—Part II," 50.

[18]Bangs, "Eno," 42.

[19]Zwerin, "Eno: Music Existing in Space," 7.

[20]Bangs, "Eno," 42.

[21]Brown, "Eno's Where It's At," 41.

[22]Bangs, "Eno," 42. For information on synthesizers—what they are and what they can do—see the articles "Synthesizer" and "Electro-acoustic music" in Don Randel, *The New Harvard Dictionary of Music* (Cambridge, Mass. and London: Belknap/Harvard University Press, 1986). The latter article includes a bibliography. Also useful and informative are Greg Armbruster, ed., *The Art of Electronic Music* (New York: Quill/Keyboard, 1985), and Bob Doerschuk, *Rock Keyboard* (New York: Quill/Keyboard, 1985).

[23]Milkowski, "Eno: Excursions," 15.

[24]Eno has used the Arp 2600 only once in his recorded music, in making *Music for Airports*. The Minimoog is "a very old one—one of the first ones they made, I suspect." Aikin, "Brian Eno," 45.

[25]Milkowski, "Eno: Excursions," 15.

[26]Jensen, "Sound of Silence," 24.

[27]O'Brien, "Eno at Edge of Rock," 32. Handbooks and owners manuals do indeed often steer the electronic musician toward certain limited options sanctioned by the well-intentioned manufacturers. For instance, the operating guide that comes with a Peavey KB-300 keyboard amplifier says with regard to the mid-range equalization control: "CAUTION MUST BE EXERCISED IN ORDER TO AVOID OVERBOOSTING OR OVERCUTTING THE MID-RANGE. Experience has proven that, for most applications, a very slight mid-range cut tends to produce a 'tight' and well-defined sound. Generally, large amounts of mid-range boost are extremely unpleasant and probably will never be used except for special effects."

[28]Aikin, "Brian Eno," 48.

[29]Aikin, "Brian Eno," 50.

[30]Aikin, "Brian Eno," 50.

[31]Aikin, "Brian Eno," 48.

[32]Aikin, "Brian Eno," 50.

[33]Arthur Lubow, "Eno, Before and After Roxy," *New Times* 10 (6 March 1978), 73.

[34]Bangs, "Eno," 40. Eno also mentions that the top string always used to cut his finger—a fact that probably indicates that he never played enough guitar to build up calluses.

[35]Milkowski, "Eno: Excursions," 17.

[36]Aikin, "Brian Eno," 50.

[37]Aikin, "Brian Eno," 50. Some of Eno's specific equipment: Lexicon Prime Time, Lexicon 224 digital reverb, Lexicon EMT 250 digital reverb, Roland 501 echo unit, Project WEM fuzz box. See list of "Brian Eno's Equipment," Milkowski, "Eno: Excursions," 17.

[38]Aikin, "Brian Eno," 55.

[39]Bangs, "Eno," 42.

[40]Grant, "Eno Against Interpretation," 29.

[41]Aikin, "Brian Eno," 58.

[42]Aikin, "Brian Eno," 58.

[43]Tannenbaum, "Cage and Eno," 106.

[44]Grant, "Eno Against Interpretation," 30.

[45]McKenna, "Eno," 42.

[46]Grant, "Eno Against Interpretation," 30.

[47]McKenna, "Eno," 44.

[48]Loder, "Eno," 24.

[49]Bangs, "Eno," 43.

[50]O'Brien, "Eno at Edge of Rock," 31.

[51]Jensen, "Sound of Silence," 23.

[52]O'Brien, "Eno at Edge of Rock," 31.

[53]Eno and Schmidt, Oblique Strategies.

[54]Cage, of course, had used the I Ching extensively in his own compositional strategies. See Charles Hamm, "John Cage," The New Grove Dictionary of Music and Musicians (1980). The I Ching itself exists in many versions; see, for example, The I Ching or Book of Changes: The Richard Wilhelm Translation Rendered into English by Cary F. Baynes, Bollingen Series 19 (Princeton: Princeton University Press, 1967).

[55]O'Brien, "Eno at Edge of Rock," 31.

[56]O'Brien, "Eno at Edge of Rock," 31.

[57]Brian Eno and Peter Schmidt, "Peter Schmidt and Brian Eno," Arts Review 29 (9 Dec. 1977), 737.

[58]Moore, "Eno = MC Squared," 67.

[59]Zwerin, "Eno: Music Existing in Space," 7.

[60]See Betsy Bowden, Performed Literature: Words and Music by Bob Dylan (Bloomington: Indiana University Press, 1982).

[61]Jann Wenner, ed., Lennon Remembers: The Rolling Stone Interviews (San Francisco: Straight Arrow/Rolling Stone, 1971), 188.

[62]See Richard Goldstein, The Poetry of Rock (New York: Bantam Books, 1969), David R. Pichaske, The Poetry of Rock: The Golden Years (Peoria, Ill.: The Ellis Press, 1981), and Bruce Pollock, In Their Own Words: Lyrics and Lyricists 1955–1974 (New York and London: Macmillan, 1975).

[63]Amirkhanian, "Eno at KPFA," 3.

[64]Tannenbaum, "Cage and Eno," 70.

[65]Amirkhanian, "Eno at KPFA," 2–3.

[66]Bangs, "Eno," 42.

[67]Rose, "Eno: Scaramouche of the Synthesizer," 70.

[68]Aikin, "Brian Eno," 64.

CHAPTER 7. THE MUSICIAN AS PHILOSOPHER

[1]Eno and Mills, More Dark Than Shark, 73.

[2]Howell, "Strangers Evening with Eno," n. p.

[3]Rose, "Four Conversations with Eno," 70.

[4]Mick Brown, "Life of Brian According to Eno," *Guardian*, 1 May 1982, 10.

[5]O'Brien, "Eno at Edge of Rock," 32.

[6]Amirkhanian, "Eno at KPFA," 5.

[7]Hutchinson, "Eno: Place #13," n. p. "Synchronicity" (*Synchronizität*) is a word coined by Swiss psychologist C. G. Jung and refers to the occurrence or experience of meaningful coincidences that cannot be explained on the basis of known natural laws. Carl Jung, "Synchronicity: An Acausal Connecting Principle," in *The Structure and Dynamics of the Psyche*, 2nd ed., Collected Works of C. G. Jung, Vol. 8, Bollingen Series 20 (Princeton: Princeton University Press, 1969), 417–519.

[8]Hutchinson, "Eno: Place #13," n. p.

[9]Loder, "Eno," 26.

[10]Grant, "Eno Against Interpretation," 30.

[11]Jensen, "Sound of Silence," 25.

[12]Grant, "Eno Against Interpretation," 29.

[13]Aikin, "Brian Eno," 66.

[14]Jensen, "Sound of Silence," 24–5.

[15]Hutchinson, "Eno: Place #13," n. p.

[16]Leonard B. Meyer, *Music, the Arts and Ideas: Patterns and Predictions in Twentieth-Century Culture* (Chicago and London: University of Chicago Press, 1967), 87–232.

[17]Edward Whitmont, *Return of the Goddess* (New York: Crossroad, 1984).

[18]Simon Frith, *Sound Effects: Youth, Leisure, and the Politics of Rock'n'Roll* (New York: Pantheon, 1981).

[19]Barbara Bradby, "Do-Talk and Don't Talk: Conflicting Voices in Sixties Girl-Group Songs," paper delivered at the Third International Conference on Popular Music Studies, Université du Québec à Montréal, 10 July 1985.

[20]Iain Chambers, "Glam Rock," in his *Urban Rhythms: Pop Music and Popular Culture* (New York: St. Martin's, 1985), 128–38.

[21]Lubow, "Eno, Before and After Roxy," 72.

[22]Lubow, "Eno, Before and After Roxy," 72.

[23]Lubow, "Eno, Before and After Roxy," 72.

[24]Howell, "Strangers Evening with Eno," n. p.

[25]Loder, "Eno," 25.

[26]Loder, "Eno," 26. Robert Fripp, Eno's friend and collaborator, has used similar terms to express his apolitical yet radical stance. In one of his several philosophical manifestoes, Fripp put it like this: "My belief is that all political activity directed towards changing the means of working is ineffective without a change in our way of working, and that this is essentially personal. If we change our way of doing things, structural change necessarily follows. If we wish for this personal change we need discipline, and the only effective discipline is self-discipline. External discipline, i.e., control, the normal direction of authoritarian agencies, generates an at least equal reaction." Robert Fripp, liner notes to *Let The Power Fall: An Album of Frippertronics*, Editions EG EGS 110, 1981.

[27]Brown, "Life of Brian According to Eno," 10.

[28]McKenna, "Eno," 44.

[29]Rose, "Four Conversations with Eno," 70.

[30]Eno and Mills, *More Dark Than Shark*.

[31]Grant, "Eno Against Interpretation," 30.

[32]Milkowski, "Eno: Excursions," 15.

[33]Milkowski, "Eno: Excursions," 16–7.

[34]Tannenbaum, "Cage and Eno," 72.

[35]Korner, "Aurora Musicalis," 79.

CHAPTER 8. TAKING ROCK TO THE LIMIT

[1]This selection criterion means that little or no mention will be made in these pages of the roughly three dozen other albums Eno has produced or played on. His contribution to most of these other albums is briefly noted in the "Discography" below.

[2]For full listings of the musicians on this and other albums, see "Discography."

[3]Brown, "Eno's Where It's At," 41.

[4]Dagnal, "Eno and the Jets," 21.

[5]Bangs, "Eno," 42.

[6]Lester Bangs, "Records: *Here Come the Warm Jets*," *Creem* 6 (Oct. 1974), 61.

[7]Robert Christgau, "The Christgau Consumer Guide," *Creem* (April 1975), 11.

[8]Ed Naha, "Record Lovers Guide: Picks of the Month: Brian Eno: *Here Come the Warm Jets*," *Circus* (Dec. 1974), 61.

[9]Dagnal, "Eno and the Jets," 16.

[10]Gordon Fletcher, "Records: *Here Come the Warm Jets*," *Rolling Stone* 172 (24 Oct. 1974), 74.

[11]Dagnal, "Eno and the Jets," 21.

[12]Stephen Demorest, "Eno: the Monkey Wrench of Rock Creates Happy Accidents on *Tiger Mountain*," *Circus* (Apr. 1975), 52.

[13]Robert Christgau, "The Christgau Consumer Guide," *Creem* (June 1975), 13.

[14]Henry Edwards, "Bryan Ferry and Eno: Hot Rockers Rock Apart," *After Dark* 8 (June 1975), 67.

[15]Pete Matthews, "Review: Eno: *Taking Tiger Mountain (By Strategy)*; Nico: *The End*; Sparks: *Propaganda*," *Records and Recording* (Jan. 1975), 60.

[16]"Don't Overlook These Discs," *Circus* (May 1975), 62.

[17]Wayne Robins, "Records: Taking Rock's Future by Artifice: Roxy Music, *Country Life*; Eno, *Taking Tiger Mountain (By Strategy)*," *Creem* 6 (Mar. 1975), 67.

[18]Ed Naha, "Review: *Taking Tiger Mountain (By Strategy)*," *Crawdaddy* (May 1975), 76.

[19]Milkowski, "Eno: Excursions," 15.

[20]Bangs, "Eno," 42.

[21]Interview by Allan Jones, *Melody Maker* (29 Nov. 1975); quoted in Eno and Mills, *More Dark Than Shark*, 98.

[22]Demorest, "Discreet Charm of Eno," 85.

[23]Henry Edwards, "Records: *Another Green World*," *High Fidelity* (June 1976), 101.

[24]Hull, "Eno Races Toward New World," 88.

[25]Charley Walters, "Records: Eno's Electronic Sonic Exotica: *Another Green World*," *Rolling Stone* 212 (6 May 1976), 67–8.

[26]Alexander Austin and Steve Erickson, "On Music: Tell George Orwell the News," *Westways* 72 (Jan. 1980), 70.

[27]Lubow, "Eno, Before and After Roxy," 72.

[28]Demorest, "Discreet Charm of Eno," 84–5.

[29]Mikal Gilmore, "Record Reviews: *Another Green World, Discreet Music, Evening Star*," *Down Beat* 43 (21 Oct. 1976), 26.

[30]Jon Pareles, "Records: *Another Green World*," *Crawdaddy* (June 1976), 78.

[31]Bangs, "Eno Sings with Fishes," 49. Bangs eventually came around to a much more positive view of even Eno's most quiet, non-foreground music; see his "Eno," *Musician, Player & Listener* 21 (Nov. 1979). In fact, Eno became something of an obsession for him; Robert Fripp informed me that Bangs was working on a book about Eno at the time of his death.

[32]Joe Fernbacher, "Records: *Before and After Science*," *Creem* 9 (Apr. 1978), 67.

[33]Mitchell Schneider, "Brave New Eno: *Before and After Science*," *Crawdaddy* 84 (May 1978), 64.

[34]Russell Shaw, "Record Reviews: *Before and After Science*," *Down Beat* 45 (13 July 1978), 36.

CHAPTER 9. ENO'S PROGRESSIVE ROCK: THE MUSIC

[1]Eno and Mills, *More Dark Than Shark*, 16.

[2]The biblical quotation is from Matthew 19:24. The translation of Lao-Tzu is from R. H. Blyth, *Zen in English Literature and Oriental Classics* (New York: Dutton, 1960), 141.

[3]Eno and Mills, *More Dark Than Shark*, 14.

[4]Pareles and Romanowski, eds., *The Rolling Stone Encyclopedia of Rock & Roll*, 437.

[5]O'Brien, "Eno at Edge of Rock," 31.

[6]Dagnal, "Eno and the Jets," 16.

[7]Bangs, "Records: *Here Come the Warm Jets*," 62.

[8]Eno and Mills, *More Dark Than Shark*, 22.

[9]In my harmonic abbreviations, upper-case Roman numerals normally stand for major chords, lower-case for minor. In this case, where the texture at the beginning of the song is highly active and contrapuntal, interpretation of the pillars of the harmonic framework as "major" or "minor" is moot. At the beginning, an implied minor mode appears to be governing the lines; when the text enters, the mode swings to major.

[10]See Peter Winkler, "The Harmonic Language of Rock," abstract of unpublished paper first delivered to the Keele University/Sonneck Society conference on American and British Music, Keele, England, 5 July 1983.

[11]Eno, "Pro Session—Part II," 51.

[12]Quoted in James Mansback Brody, liner notes to *Iannis Xenakis: Electro-Acoustic Music*, Nonesuch H–71246, n. d.

[13]Rose, "Four Conversations with Eno," 72.

[14]Bangs, "Eno," 40.

[15]See Roman Kozak, "Rock'n'Rolling: Flo & Eddie, Eno & Phil, Godley & Creme Visited," *Billboard* 94 (3 Apr. 1982), 72.

[16]Joe Zawinul (b. 1932) is a jazz composer, keyboard player, and band leader.

CHAPTER 10. THE AMBIENT SOUND

[1]*Webster's New Twentieth Century Dictionary of the English Language, Unabridged*, 2nd ed., s. v. "ambient."

[2]*Webster's New Collegiate Dictionary*, s. v. "ambiance." The dictionaries I have checked do indeed spell it this way. In common usage, "Ambience" with an "e" has not only a different pronunciation (*ambience* vs. *ahmbiance*) but somewhat different connotations; read on.

[3]Rod Smith, "What Is Spacemusic!," *FM 91 Public Radio* (Feb. 1987), 6.

[4]*Webster's New Collegiate Dictionary*, s. v. "ambitendency."

[5]Brown, "Eno's Where It's At," 41.

[6]Amirkhanian, "Eno at KPFA," 6.

[7]Eno, liner notes to *Discreet Music*.

[8]Eno, liner notes to *Discreet Music*.

[9]O'Brien, "Eno at Edge of Rock," 31.

[10]O'Brien, "Eno at Edge of Rock," 31.

[11]Eno, liner notes to *Discreet Music*.

[12]For an account of the La Guardia audiovisual installation, see Gregory Miller, "The Arts: Video," *Omni* 3 (Nov. 1980), 28–9.

[13]Brian Eno, liner notes to *Ambient 1: Music for Airports*, Editions EG EGS 201, 1978.

[14]Tannenbaum, "Cage and Eno," 68.

[15]For detailed comments by Eno on the genesis of *Music for Airports* in a Cologne airport waiting room, see Korner, "Aurora Musicalis," 77. For an account of how Eno organized the 22 tape loops used in "1/2," see O'Brien, "Eno at Edge of Rock," 31. For details on the making of

"1/1," a piece co-composed with Robert Wyatt and Rhett Davies, and more improvisational than serial in nature, see Brian Eno, "Pro Session: The Studio as Compositional Tool—Part II," 53.

[16]Hutchinson, "Eno: Place #13," n. p. This probably contains Eno's most complete statement on the development and aims of his video works.

[17]Eno, "Works Constructed with Sound and Light," n. p.

[18]Eno, "Works Constructed with Sound and Light," n. p.

[19]Hutchinson, "Eno: Place #13," n. p.

[20]Tannenbaum, "Cage and Eno," 69.

[21]Anthea Norman-Taylor and Lin Barkass, "Brian Eno," *Opal Information* 3 (Dec. 1986), 11.

[22]For critical accounts of audiovideo installations by Eno, see: Craig Bromberg, "Brian Eno at Concord," *Art in America* 71:8 (Sept. 1983), 173–4; Kevin Concannon, "Michael Chandler and Brian Eno, Institute of Contemporary Art," *Artforum* 22 (Apr. 1984), 85–6; Ursula Frohne, "Review: Brian Eno: Tegel Airport, Institut Unzeit, Berlin," *Flash Art* (Apr./May 1984) 42–3; C. Furlong, "AFI Frames the Field: The National Video Festival," *Afterimage* 9:5 (Oct. 1981), 4–5; Kim Levin, "The Waiting Room," *Arts Magazine* 55 (Nov. 1980), 5; Dorine Mignot, " 'The Luminous Image': 22 Video-Installationen im Stedelijk Museum Amsterdam," *Kunstforum International* 9/10 (Jan./Feb. 1985), 59–83; David Ross, "Brian Eno," *Matrix/Berkeley* 44 (June/ July 1981), n. p.; and Pier Luigi Tazzi, "Milan: Brian Eno, Chiesa di S. Carpoforo," *Artforum* 23 (Feb. 1985), 97–8.

[23]Jensen, "Sound of Silence," 21.

[24]Mikal Gilmore, "Record Reviews: *Another Green World, Discreet Music, Evening Star*," 26.

[25]James Wolcott, "Records: Nearer My Eno to Thee: *Another Green World, Discreet Music*," *Creem* 7 (Apr. 1976), 60.

[26]Michael Bloom, "Records: *Ambient 1: Music for Airports*," *Rolling Stone* 296 (26 July 1979), 60–1.

[27]Ken Emerson, "Brian Eno Slips into 'Trance Music,' " *New York Times* (12 Aug. 1979), D:22.

[28]Tom Johnson, "Music: The New Tonality," *Village Voice* 23 (16 Oct. 1978), 115–6.

[29]Johnson, "New Music, New York, New Institution," 88–9.

[30]Hull, "Eno Races Toward New World," 87.

[31]Liner notes to *Music for Films*, boxed set version, Editions EG EGBS2, 1983. It is on this version that I base my comments.

[32]Liner notes to *Music for Films*.

[33]Michael Davis, "Records: *Music for Films*," *Creem* 10 (Apr. 1979), 61.

[34]Pareles, "Riffs: Eno Uncaged," 77–8.

[35]Mark Peel, "Disc and Tape Reviews: *Ambient #4—On Land*," *Stereo Review* 47 (Nov. 1982), 105.

[36]George Rush, "Brian Eno: Rock's Svengali," 132.

[37]Robert Payes, "Review: *On Land*," *Trouser Press* 9 (Aug. 1982), 41; Glen O'Brien, "Glenn O'Brien's Beat: My Mother the Ear," *Andy Warhol's Interview* 12 (Sept. 1982), 107–8.

[38]Liner notes to *Apollo: Atmospheres & Soundtracks*, Editions EG Eno 5, 1983.

[39]Liner notes to *Music for Films, Vol. II*, Editions EG EGSP-2, 1983.

[40]ADSR stands for attack-decay-sustain-release. Taken together, these characteristics of a given note or sound describe its "envelope," or amplitude profile in time. It is generally thought that a sound's envelope has just as great an impact on the perception of its character as its harmonic spectrum. Envelope and harmonic spectrum are the two primary determinants of timbre.

[41]Korner, "Aurora Musicalis," 76–9.

Chapter 11. Collaborations

[1]Interview broadcast from KFOG San Francisco, 12 Nov. 1986.

[2]September 9 is given as the date of recording of Side One on the album cover. Elsewhere, Fripp

has said that the recording session took place in July of the same year: see inner liner notes to Robert Fripp, *God Save the Queen*, Polydor MPF 1298, 1980.

[3]Amirkhanian, "Eno at KPFA," 16.

[4]Allan Jones, "Caught in the Act: Fripp and Eno: Formal Beauty," *Melody Maker* 50 (14 June 1975), 49.

[5]The "Frippertronics" style that grew out of this tour represented a streamlining of the Eno/Fripp approach to the signal-loop situation. The primary published recording representing this style is *Let the Power Fall: An Album of Frippertronics*, Editions EG EGS 110, 1981.

[6]Demorest, "Discreet Charm of Eno," 83–4.

[7]Pareles and Romanowski, *Rolling Stone Encyclopedia of Rock & Roll*, 61.

[8]The significance of Bowie's impact on Britain in the early 1970s is especially well treated in Iain Chambers' discussion of "glam rock," in his *Urban Rhythms: Pop Music and Popular Culture* (New York: St. Martin's, 1985), 128–38. See also Kevin Cann, *David Bowie: A Chronology* (London: Vermillion, 1983).

[9]Loder, "Eno," 26.

[10]O'Brien, "Eno at Edge of Rock," 32.

[11]Amirkhanian, "Eno at KPFA," 27.

[12]O'Brien, "Eno at Edge of Rock," 32.

[13]O'Brien, "Eno at Edge of Rock," 32.

[14]O'Brien, "Eno at Edge of Rock," 32.

[15]Amirkhanian, "Eno at KPFA," 27–8.

[16]John Rockwell, *All American Music*, 244.

[17]Loder, "Eno," 24.

[18]Amirkhanian, "Eno at KPFA," 11.

[19]Milkowski, "Eno: Excursions," 57.

[20]Loder, "Squawking Heads," 46.

[21]Amirkhanian, "Eno at KPFA," 12.

[22]Tangent Records TGS 131.

[23]Jon Pareles, "Records: Does this Global Village Have Two-Way Traffic? *My Life in the Bush of Ghosts*, David Byrne and Brian Eno," *Rolling Stone* 340 (2 April 1981), 60.

[24]As far as I know, Eno and Byrne have suffered no legal repercussions related to the borrowings on the version of *Ghosts* that was eventually released. The estate of Kathryn Kuhlman, the faith healer and radio evangelist, did refuse them permission to use excerpts from a Kuhlman address taped off the air in Los Angeles. Kurt Loder, "Squawking Heads: Byrne and Eno in the Bush of Ghosts," *Rolling Stone* 338 (5 March 1981), 45. For a brief summary of a scholarly conference at which a number of sessions and papers addressed the issue of the appropriation of music, see Ruth Stone, "From the Editors: Hijacking Music," *Society for Ethnomusicology Newsletter* 21 (Jan. 1987), 2.

CHAPTER 12. ESSENCE, HISTORY, AND BEAUTY

[1]Nettl, *The Study of Ethnomusicology*, 21. "The Art of Combining Tones," the chapter from which this quotation is taken, is a masterful and exhilarating treatment of the semantic and ontological question of music's essence; Nettl, a senior scholar with a lifetime of study of the musics of the world behind him, has as close to a global point of view as may be possible for any individual at the present time.

[2]Ed Ward, Geoffrey Stokes, and Ken Tucker, *Rock of Ages: The Rolling Stone History of Rock & Roll* (New York: Rolling Stone/Summit, 1986), 490.

[3]Advertisement for Berklee College of Music, *College Musician* 1 (Fall 1986), 37.

[4]For an overview of "Improvisation, extemporization" in Western and non-Western cultures, see the article by Bruno Nettl in Don Randel, ed., *The New Harvard Dictionary of Music* (Cambridge, Mass. and London: Belknap Press/Harvard University Press, 1986), 392–4.

[5]Hutchinson, "Eno: Place #13," n. p.

[6]There is a creative element in the musical perceptions, attitudes and thoughts of all audiences, not simply in those of composers and performers. People do not take in music passively, no matter how rigid the current Western division of labor into musicians and non-musicians may appear. John Blacking, "Music in the Making: Problems in the Analysis of Musical Thought," Bloch Lectures, University of California, Berkeley, 1986.

[7]The cultural symbolism or mythology behind this state of affairs is so involved that I can do no more here than point the reader in its general direction. Among the works that have helped to guide my own thinking on this vast topic are Jacques Ellul, *The Technological Society* (New York: Vintage, 1964), a classic statement of the pervasiveness of efficiency-engendering yet creativity-strangling "technique" in every aspect of modern life; Carl Sagan, *The Dragons of Eden: Speculations on the Rise of Human Intelligence* (New York: Random House, 1977), which includes a discussion of "information" as a biological, genetic phenomenon that spilled over first into the brains of the higher mammals and is now filling up libraries and computer tape at an exponentially growing rate; John Shepherd, Phil Virden, Graham Vulliamy, and Trevor Wishart, *Whose Music? A Sociology of Musical Languages* (London: Latimer, 1977), a multi-pronged set of Marxist arguments concerning, among other things, the relationships between media, social process, and music, culture-specific oral and visual orientational modes, tonality's encoding of the industrial world sense, and the social stratification of twentieth-century music; Carl Jung, *Civilization in Transition*, 2nd ed., Collected Works of C. G. Jung, Vol. 10, Bollingen Series 20 (Princeton: Princeton University Press, 1970), a probing series of essays in which the author applies to a wide range of modern issues and problems his insights and theories having to do with the functioning of the personal and collective unconscious; and E. F. Schumacher, *Small is Beautiful: Economics as if People Mattered* (New York: Harper & Row, 1975), a plea for social, political, economic, and cultural decentralization in an age of dangerously powerful, technologically based modes of organization.

[8]Conceptual pieces by Stockhausen from the 1960s, like *Aus den Sieben Tagen*, certainly belong to the whole process-art movement that so influenced Eno, yet so far as I know Eno has never mentioned Stockhausen in interviews or published works. The link between Stockhausen and Eno was Cornelius Cardew, yet the conceptual relationship between the three musicians is complicated—Cardew having gone through a violent break with Stockhausen, and Eno having rejected Cardew's political stance. See Cardew, *Stockhausen Serves Imperialism, and Other Articles* (London: Latimer New Dimensions, 1974).

[9]Greg Armbruster, ed., *The Art of Electronic Music: The Instruments, Designers, and Musicians Behind the Artistic and Popular Explosion of Electronic Music*, compiled by Tom Darter (New York: Quill/Keyboard, 1984).

[10]Bob Doerschuk, ed., *Rock Keyboard* (New York: Quill/Keyboard, 1985), 157. Much of Doerschuk's book, which consists of *Keyboard* magazine interviews with over two dozen musicians strung together by perceptive commentary, is organized around the classical/romantic idea, with chapter subtitles like "The Rock Organ Romantics," "Advent of the New Romantics," and "Electronics and the Classical Ethic." Linear interpretations of the history of rock using concepts borrowed from art music have proven tempting to more than one writer. Compare Eric Salzman, *Twentieth-Century Music*, 189, 191: "Rock rather quickly passed through its own classical period, the end of which was symbolized by the breakup of the Beatles. . . . The pop movement . . . is passing quickly through a cycle of classicism, romanticism, experimentalism, neo-classicism, and revival—the same cycle which jazz took a few decades and traditional music a couple of centuries to pass through"; and John Rockwell, "Art Rock," in Jim Miller, ed., *The Rolling Stone Illustrated History of Rock & Roll*, 322: "There is a morphology to artistic movements. They begin with a rude and innocent vigor, pass into a healthy adulthood and finally decline into an overwrought, feeble old age. Something of this process can be observed in the passage of rock and roll from the three-chord primitivism of the Fifties through the

burgeoning vitality and experimentation of the Sixties to the hollow emptiness of the so-called progressive or 'art' rock of the Seventies."

[11]Doerschuk, *Rock Keyboard*, 149.

[12]*Billboard* does not yet have an official chart for this kind of music, but has been running articles on its commercial development (e.g., Steven Dupler, "New Age Labels Seek New Angles," in which record companies are said to be facing a "glutted" market; one label executive is quoted as saying that among the tasks of the year is to "separate the crap from the real music"), and an anonymous agent has been running an advertisement called the "Monthly British New Age Chart." See *Billboard* 99 (31 Jan. 1986), 1, 68. A nationally syndicated weekly public radio program, "Music from the Hearts of Space," emanates from San Francisco, under the direction of Anna Turner and Stephen Hill; Eno has reportedly written a fan letter to the show, which reads in part, "If I'd been offered the chance to design a late night radio show, I don't think I would have come up with anything closer to my own taste." See Rod Smith, "What is Spacemusic!," *FM 91 Public Radio* (California State University, Sacramento, Feb. 1987), 5. Anna Turner and Stephen Hill also publish the catalog *Spacemusic: Music by Mail, 1986,* a 97-page annotated listing of hundreds of LPs, CDs, and cassettes. The first issue of John Patrick Lamkin, ed., *Music of the Spheres: A New Age Music & Art Quarterly* (Taos, N.M., 1986), came out in early 1987.

[13]A recent historical and theoretical discussion of Schoenberg's famous movement is found in Wayne Slawson, *Sound Color* (Berkeley, Los Angeles, and London: University of California Press, 1985).

[14]The concept of scientific research as a process conditioned by and heavily dependent on the invention of paradigms was advanced systematically by Thomas Kuhn, *The Structure of Scientific Revolutions* (Chicago: University of Chicago Press, 1962). An analogous process can be seen to operate in music history.

GLOSSARY

This glossary defines many of the musical terms used in this book; it is not intended as a comprehensive list of musical vocabulary. A fine reference work such as Don Michael Randel's *The New Harvard Dictionary of Music* (Cambridge, Mass.: Belknap Press of Harvard University Press, 1986) makes a valuable addition to any musician's or music lover's library.

Cross-references are indicated by **bold type.**

AEOLIAN MODE. See Mode.

ALEATORY MUSIC. A trend in avant-garde composition since the 1950s. The French composer Pierre Boulez and others wrote scores that gave performers unprecedented degrees of freedom, allowing them to choose notes, interpret graphic notation, rearrange a piece's sections, and so on. Aleatory music is somewhere between composed and improvised music.

ATONALITY. The absence of any feeling of tonality or key. Atonal music was pioneered by the composers Arnold Schoenberg (Austria), Charles Ives (United States), and Alexander Scriabin (Russia) in the early years of the twentieth century. Atonal music characteristically makes free use of all twelve notes of the chromatic scale. Many later composers have experimented with atonality, and it remains a viable force in the musical world today, though largely ignored by the vast majority of active popular musicians.

CADENCE. A sense of psychological pause between phrases or at the end of a piece of music. The harmonic (chord) progressions used to articulate such breaks or endings are also called cadences.

CHORD. Any combination of three or more notes. Chords are the building blocks of harmony. In tonal music (see **Tonality**), the most common types of chords are **triads** and **seventh chords.**

CHORD SYMBOLS. Letters or numbers used to indicate chords. The standard Roman numeral system is used in this book. In the key of C major:

C	Dm	Em	F	G	Am
I	ii	iii	IV	V	vi.

In the key of C minor:

Cm	E♭	Fm	Gm	A♭	B♭
i	III	iv	v	VI	VII.

The Roman numeral system has the advantage that it is "global"—that is, the numerals can be applied to the chords of any key. Using Roman numeral chord symbols is like thinking on the plane of one universal, abstract key.

CHROMATIC ALTERATION. Raising or lowering a note by a half-step.

CHROMATIC SCALE. The set of 12 pitches within an octave: A-A♯-B-C-C♯-D-D♯-E-F-F♯-G-G♯.

COMMON PRACTICE PERIOD of music history. Roughly 1600–1900. During this time span, Western art music composers created and spoke in what was felt to be a common, international, even universal musical language. Music from the common practice period constitutes the bread and butter of symphonies, chamber groups, opera companies, choral ensembles, and solo recitals.

CONSONANCE AND DISSONANCE. Perceived psychological qualities of intervals and chords. In general, intervals and chords that sound restful, euphonious, stable, or smooth are considered consonant; ones that sound tense, harsh, unstable, or scratchy are considered dissonant. From the Middle Ages to the present day Western theorists have debated and categorized the relative consonance and dissonance of the array of intervals and chords; such categorizing is a hazardous enterprise since aural judgements are to some degree subjective, and depend on the tunings used as well as the musical context. Generalized consonance and dissonance levels can, however, be assessed in actual pieces of music, or even in whole musical styles. Haydn's style is consonant compared to Schoenberg's, with Bach's somewhere in between. Most styles utilize both dissonance and consonance, and indeed the constant battle between the two plays a primary role in the psychological meaning of the music.

COUNTERPOINT. The art or craft of combining two or more simultaneous melodies to produce a satisfying and logical flux of consonance and dissonance.

DIATONIC SCALE. The white notes on the piano keyboard. Using a pattern of whole-steps and half-steps (whole, whole, half, whole, whole, whole, half) results in a scale with seven notes to the octave. Diatonicism is thus basically "white-note music," although the diatonic scale can be transposed to incorporate the black keys as well.

DISSONANCE. See Consonance and dissonance.

DORIAN MODE. See Mode.

DRONE. A long, unchanging pitch or pitches, sometimes sustained for the entire length of a musical piece, typically in the medium-to-low registers. Some types of music, for instance certain kinds of classical Indian music, use players whose sole function is to play a drone instrument.

DYNAMICS. The dimension of loud and soft in music.

ENVELOPE of a sound. One of the primary determinants of timbre. An isolated tone or noise can be described in terms of how fast the sound arises from silence, how fast the initial attack decays, how long the sound is sustained, and how long it takes for it to fall back to silence. The total profile of attack-decay-sustain-release is known as the (ADSR) envelope. Percussive instruments like drums and cymbals typically have sharp attacks; wind instruments have relatively longer attacks. A note struck on a piano will slowly decay to silence, whereas other sounds can be sustained indefinitely.

EQUAL TEMPERAMENT. The system of tuning pianos and other keyboard instruments that rose to prominence in the middle of the eighteenth century, displacing a variety of other tuning systems such as mean-tone temperament and just intonation. In equal temperament, all half-steps are exactly the same distance apart, and all keys contain the same intervallic relationships. This makes modulation to all keys possible, but, according to some critics, results in the loss of important values of absolute consonance, since in equal temperament the only acoustically pure interval is the octave.

ETHNOMUSICOLOGY. The study of the musics of the world, especially those of non-Western cultures. Ethnomusicology as a discipline has been strongly influenced by anthropological concepts and methods.

FORM. The shape, in time, of a piece of music. All forms are governed by the principles of *repetition* and *contrast* in varying degrees. Repetition gives unity and coherence to a piece; contrast lends variety and interest.

FUNCTIONAL HARMONY. The system of chords and chord progressions (movements from one chord to another) developed by Western composers after 1600 and still widely used in both popular and art music. Functional harmony works with principles of tension and resolution, one chord leading to the next in ways that listeners have come to feel are logical and satisfying. A course in functional harmony is a staple of every college music curriculum. Since 1900, many composers have abandoned functional harmony, searching for new systems of harmonic organization, while many popular songwriters, unaware of the tradition of functional harmony as such, have empirically created chord progressions that accomodate their own musical needs.

FUNDAMENTAL. See **Harmonic series.**

GROUND BASS. A repeated bass melody used as the foundation of a musical composition or improvisation.

HALF-STEP. The smallest interval in the Western musical system.

HARMONIC. See **Harmonic series.**

HARMONIC SERIES and related terms. Rapidly vibrating objects like the strings in a piano vibrate not only along their entire length but along fractions of their length. The vibration along the entire length produces the **fundamental** tone heard, which is normally the loudest. The various fractional vibrations produce the various **overtones**, which are softer than the fundamental. The relative strength of the overtones plays a large role in determining the timbre of the instrument. "Harmonic series" (or "harmonic spectrum") is the name for the array of overtones plus the fundamental. **Harmonic** (used as a noun) is more or less synonymous with "overtone." The only difference between **partial** and **overtone** is that the fundamental is considered a partial, though not an overtone.

HARMONY. In the broad sense, the vertical dimension of music: the interaction of simultaneous pitches to produce chords. The study of harmony also includes chord progressions, or movements from one harmonic entity to another. In the narrow sense, "harmony" can mean simply "chord." Harmony in the musical sense implies no aesthetic judgement; it can be **consonant** or **dissonant.**

INDETERMINATE MUSIC. Type of music pioneered by American composer and philosopher John Cage and others in the 1950s in which certain elements are determined not by conscious choice, but by chance operations such as the tossing of dice.

INTERVAL. The vertical distance between any two pitches. The smallest interval in common use in Western music is the half-step, also known as the minor second and the semitone. All other intervals are whole-number multiples of the half-step. The commonly used intervals are named as follows:

Half-steps	Interval name
1	minor second
2	major second
3	minor third

4	major third
5	perfect fourth
6	augmented fourth or diminished fifth
7	perfect fifth
8	minor sixth
9	major sixth
10	minor seventh
11	major seventh
12	octave

KEY. 1.) The physical black and white controls of the piano keyboard—the things your fingers touch—are called keys. 2.) Key in the theoretical sense means a **scale** with a specific **tonic** note, such as the key of C major. See **Tonality.**

LOCRIAN MODE. See **Mode.**

LYDIAN MODE. See **Mode.**

MELODY. Any coherent succession of pitches can be called a melody. A melody is usually a continuous line of music that stays within a one- or two-octave range. Melodies may be phrased to a greater or lesser extent. **Motives** are often used as the building blocks of longer melodies.

METER (noun); METRICAL (adj.). A meter is a pattern of accented and non-accented beats. Most pieces of popular and classical music are strongly metrical—that is, involve a consistent pattern of accenting from beginning to end. Many kinds of music, however, use shifting patterns of accents, and still other kinds use no "beat" or sense of pulse at all.

MIDDLE C. The C nearest the middle of the piano. Middle C is also approximately the pitch at the middle of the total human vocal range.

MINIMALISM. Musical style developed in the 1960s by Terry Riley, Steve Reich, and others. Minimalism was a reaction against the intellectual complexities and harsh dissonance of **atonal** and serial music of the preceeding decades. Minimalist music is usually highly **tonal** (sometimes using drones and static harmonies) and highly rhythmic (often using percussive and/or keyboard instruments); such music tends to be highly repetitive at some levels, though constantly changing at others. Much minimalist music seems to call for a "vertical" mode of hearing, as opposed to the "horizontal" mode of traditional music: the music presents itself as a spatial object to be contemplated like a sculpture, rather than as a linear argument to be followed like a plot. (See **Vertical listening.**) Some of the "new age" music of the late 1970s and 1980s can be seen as an outgrowth of the minimalist aesthetic.

MIXOLYDIAN MODE. See **Mode.**

MODE. 1.) In general terms, a mode is simply a **scale.** Any set of pitches arranged in a consistent pattern and used as the basis of a piece of music can be considered a mode. 2.) In the specific sense of the word, a mode is one of the "Church modes" recognized by music theorists as early as the eleventh century. These modes are still in use, particularly the two that are equivalent to our modern major and minor scales. The Church modes were originally associated with specific **tonics** (D for Dorian, E for Phrygian, etc.); today they are freely transposed. In psychological terms, the modes can be rated on a "brightness/darkness index," as in the following chart, where 1 stands for the brightest mode and 7 stands for the darkest:

Ionian mode (major scale): C D E F G A B / Bright: 2
Dorian mode: D E F G A B C / Somewhat dark: 4
Phrygian mode: E F G A B C D / Very dark: 6
Lydian mode: F G A B C D E / Very bright: 1
Mixolydian mode: G A B C D E F / Fairly bright: 3
Aeolian mode (minor scale): A B C D E F G / Dark: 5
Locrian mode: B C D E F G A / Extremely dark: 7

MOTIVE. Motives are short melodic or rhythmic fragments used as the building blocks of longer melodies or of entire musical pieces. Motives can be repeated literally, or can be elaborated or varied in any number of ways. The motivic procedure is found in many kinds of music ranging from classical sonata to jazz improvistion.

MUSICOLOGY. Literally, the science of music. In an ideal world, musicology might mean the study of all forms of music—their history, social and spiritual functions, aesthetics, and technical aspects (acoustics, theory, instruments, etc.). In the real academic world, musicology has largely consisted of the study and criticism of the history of Western art music. Other related academic disciplines include ethnomusicology, music theory, and composition.

NOTE. 1.) Any single pitch produced by a musical instrument: the sound itself. 2.) A symbol used in musical notation for such pitches: whole note, quarter note, etc.

OBBLIGATO. A significant, yet secondary and largely ornamental melodic line.

OCTAVE. The fundamental interval of all music. Pitches an octave apart "sound the same"—it's just that one is higher and the other is lower. Pitches an octave apart sound so similar that they are given the same name, making the labeling of musical pitches a cycle of recurring letters (A–G) rather than a linearly extended series. The acoustical explanation of the psychological phenomenon of the octave hinges on the fact that frequencies of notes an octave apart always stand in the archetypal number relationship 1:2. Middle C, for instance, represents a vibration of 256 cycles per second; the C an octave above it represents a vibration of 512 cycles per second.

OSTINATO. A short, repeated, "obstinate" melody forming the background structure of a piece of music. (Think of the Beatles' "Day Tripper.") Ostinatos are widely used in composed as well as improvised music.

OVERTONE. See Harmonic series.

PANDIATONICISM. A type of harmony in which notes of the diatonic scale are freely combined. Neither so smooth as functional harmony nor so harsh as atonality, pandiatonic chords have been used by composers as a sort of middle ground since the early years of the twentieth century.

PARTIAL. See Harmonic series.

PHRYGIAN MODE. See Mode.

PITCH. The realm of pitch is the realm of high, medium, and low sounds. In the specific sense, pitch means roughly the same thing as "note"—that is, a discrete level in the overall vertical sound-spectrum. Tone has a related meaning, but refers specifically to the sound produced, whereas note can also refer to the notated symbol for the sound, and pitch can refer to the abstract idea of the sound. Tone also carries the connotations of a "musical" tone—that is, a sound produced by regular, periodic fluctuations in air pressure. In this sense, the concept of tone is used to distinguish "musical" sounds from noise, which arises from irregular, aperiodic vibrations, and can be high- or low-pitched.

REGISTER. A rather loose term referring to the pitch spectrum: low pitches are in the low register, medium pitches are in the middle register, and high pitches are in the high register. Human voices, as well as many other instruments, can be classed according to register: bass (low), tenor (medium low), alto (medium high), and soprano (high).

REPEAT SIGNS. The sign :‖ tells the performer to go back and repeat everything before the sign, or as far back as the sign ‖:.

ROMAN NUMERAL NOTATION. See chord symbols.

ROOT (of a triad or other chord built in thirds). The defining member of a chord—the note by which the chord is named. No matter what the voicing or spacing used for a chord may be, and no matter what the actual bass (lowest) note is, the root remains the same: it is the lowest note of the chord when the chord is arranged so that its member notes stack up neatly in thirds. The root of the chords A-C-E and C-E-A is the same: A.

SCALE. 1.) Broadly, the total pitch material available for making music in any given culture or style. 2.) Specifically, any of a large number of pitch-sets, traditionally arranged in ascending order. In this sense "scale" is almost indistinguishable from "mode" in the large sense.

SERIALISM, SERIALLY ORGANIZED MUSIC. Serialism is a method of organizing musical materials such as pitch (but also, sometimes, rhythm, dynamics, and timbre) in specific, repeating ways. The serial method grew out of Arnold Schoenberg's twelve-tone system, and provided many mid-twentieth-century composers with an alternative to tonality. In serially organized music, various quasi-mathematical operations are performed on pre-determined pitch sets to provide the melodic and harmonic materials for the composition.

SEVENTH CHORD. Four-note chord built in thirds. The most commonly used types are shown here:

B	B♭	B♭
G	G	G
E	E	E♭
C	C	C
Major 7th	Dominant 7th	Minor 7th

SUBDOMINANT. In Roman numeral notation (see Chord symbols), the subdominant is IV—that is, the triad based on the fourth scale step.

SYNCOPATION. Displacement of accents from their normal place in the measure. Traditionally, 4/4 meter had accents on beats 1 and 3; in much jazz and rock, 4/4 has accents on beats 2 and 4, giving jazz and rock a syncopated feel. Accenting beats 2 and 4 has become such a convention in itself, however, that perhaps it should not be called syncopation any more. For syncopation to exist, there must be a metrical norm such that displacement of accents will be felt as a temporary violation thereof.

TEMPO. The speed of the basic pulse or beat in a piece of music. Music with no pulse or beat has no tempo as such.

TEXTURE. The blend of the various instruments, voices, melodic lines, and chords in a piece of music. Three basic types of texture are: *monophonic* texture (one melodic line with no accompaniment); *homophonic* texture (a melodic line with some kind of susidiary accompaniment); and *polyphonic* texture (two or more simultaneous, interacting melodic lines)—see **Counterpoint.** Between pure homophony (for instance a singer accompanying himself with chords on guitar) and pure polyphony (for instance a fugue by Bach) there is a range of mixed textures in which several distinct layers of sound vie for attention.

THEME. Loose term signifying the basic topic or idea of a piece of music. Depending on the form of the piece, a theme can be short or long, a melody or a chord progression, or even a small motive or hook.

THEME AND VARIATIONS. Musical form that can be diagrammed A A¹ A² A³ . . . Aⁿ. A theme is stated at the beginning of the piece and is then subsequently repeated in any number of varied ways.

THEORY (OF MUSIC), MUSIC THEORY. The body of interpretive, analytical, and acoustical knowledge that has grown up around the practice and performance of music. In the Western theoretical tradition, harmony, counterpoint, and form have received the most attention.

TIMBRE; TONE COLOR. A violin, piano, human voice, and guitar sound different, even when they all play the same note. The quality of sound that distinguishes one instrument from another is called timbre. Timbre has always been an important part of the musical experience; when one hears an electronic version of a piece by Bach, or an orchestral version of a rock song, one realizes how important timbral values are in determining one's response to music. Composers have always used the distinctive timbres of various instruments to color their music. However, in the past few decades, musicians have begun to compose *with* timbre, making the color of sound itself the primary focus of interest. The development of synthesizer technology, with its limitless timbral options, has significantly affected the way modern musicians think about music; a whole new universe of sound color has opened up. In technical terms, the two primary determinants of timbre are: the relative strength of the various overtones in a given note (see **Harmonic series**); and the note's amplitude profile or envelope (the sharpness of attack, the level of sustain, and the length of time it takes for the note to stop sounding when released). The sounds of traditional acoustic instruments often have extremely complex envelopes and overtone spectra, and it has taken time and effort for synthesizer designers and users to develop equally complex and interesting sounds through electronic means.

TONALITY; TONAL MUSIC; TONAL SYSTEM. 1) In the broadest sense, tonal music is music using a specific **scale** or **mode** and showing a tendency to give one note in that scale more structural weight than the others. The majority of all musical types from all times and places is tonal in this broad sense. 2) In a narrower sense, tonality is a harmonic system that dominated Western music for several centuries. (See **Common practice period.**) Tonal music in this sense is composed in a specific **key**—that is, it uses a particular major or minor scale and emphasizes the key-note or **tonic** as a point of departure and return. Tonal music is based on a harmonic system having the **triad** as its fundamental unit; chords progress from one to another according to accepted principles of **functional harmony** and **voice-leading.** The "tonal system" is the total complex of twenty-four major and minor keys and their interrelationships. 3) "Tonality" is also used in a more limited sense, as a synonym for "key": "the tonality of C major." 4) In recent years, popular music publications and electronic equipment owner's manuals have used the word "tonality" to mean "timbre." The different voices (sounds, patches) on a synthesizer, for instance, are said to represent different "tonalities." This usage is incorrect—another hopeless mix-up in the convoluted history of musical terminology.

TONE. 1.) Synonym for pitch. 2.) The overall sound-quality a player or singer is capable of producing: "She sings with good tone." In this sense, tone means something similar to tone color and timbre.

TONE COLOR. See **Timbre.**

TONE-ROW. A set of pitches in a fixed order used as the basis of a composition employing the serial method.

TONIC. 1) The psychologically central pitch in a piece of tonal music; the key-note. See **Tonality.** 2) The central chord in a piece of tonal music. In the key of C major, the C-major triad is the tonic chord.

TONIC-DOMINANT RELATIONSHIP. In tonal music of the common practice period, one chord progression has a special significance: the progression from dominant to tonic, or from V to I in Roman numeral notation. (See **Chord symbols.**) Through perpetual usage, the movement from dominant to tonic chords (for instance, G to C in the key of C major) has come to acquire a feeling of tension followed by resolution, and is typically used at the end of musical phrases and at the end of a composition.

TRANSPOSE. To take music out of one key and play it or write it in another.

TRIAD. Three-note chord built in thirds. Triads are the harmonic building blocks of functional tonality, and hence of most contemporary popular music and Western art music composed before 1900. The four basic types of triad are illustrated here:

G	G	G♭	G♯
E	E♭	E♭	E
C	C	C	C
Major	Minor	Diminished	Augmented

VERTICAL LISTENING. Most traditional and popular music unfolds horizontally with time, and the listener hears the music as if listening to a verbal statement, thesis, or argument. In recent years, many composers have become interested in creating a type of music to be heard vertically or spatially: the listener finds himself or herself at the center of a universe of sound whose details can be inspected at leisure. Such music tends to rely on subtle gradations of timbre rather than on the traditional elements of melodic and harmonic development and progression. See also **Minimalism.**

VOICE-LEADING. In traditional counterpoint, a fixed number of melodic lines interact with each other to produce the texture and harmony of the music. Voice-leading refers to the movement of the individual melodic lines, and to principles of how each line is to be "led" in order to avoid harsh and illogical dissonances.

WHOLE TONE. Interval containing two semitones or half-steps.

WHOLE-TONE SCALE. Scale consisting solely of whole tones, such as C-D-E-F♯-G♯-A♯-C.

BIBLIOGRAPHY

This bibliography contains materials by and about Eno, other articles and books used in my research, and other works cited in this book. As an aid to the curious browser, annotations are provided for some of the sources. Unsigned articles (mostly record reviews) are listed after a "?" and are placed alphabetically according to the name of the journal or magazine.

AIKIN, Jim. "Records: *The Plateaux of Mirrors* and *Fourth World, Vol. 1: Possible Musics*," *Contemporary Keyboard* 6 (Sept. 1980), 71.
———. "Brian Eno," *Keyboard* 7 (July 1981), 42 ff.
AMIRKHANIAN, Charles. "Eno at KPFA: 2 Feb. 1980, 13 March 1980, 2 April 1980," seven 10-inch reels of ¼" tape. Berkeley, California: collection of Charles Amirkhanian. Some six hours of taped Eno interviews conducted on three separate occasions in 1980. The first—by far the longest and most substantive—has been transcribed (see next listing).
———. "Brian Eno Interviewed 2/2/80 for KPFA Marathon," unpublished typescript from taped interview of Eno by Charles Amirkhanian, transcribed by S. Stone, 29 Oct. 1983. Berkeley, California: collection of Charles Amirkhanian. 31 pp.
ARMBRUSTER, Greg, ed. *The Art of Electronic Music: The Instruments, Designers, and Musicians Behind the Artistic and Popular Explosion of Electronic Music.* Compiled by Tom Darter. New York: Quill/Keyboard, 1984. 315 pp. Valuable and detailed summary of the field, refreshing for its refusal to rigidly separate developments in rock, art music, film music, and new age music; contains a sixty-four-page "History of Electronic Musical Instruments" and interview/profiles of nearly thirty leading designers and musicians.
AUSTIN, Alexander, and Steve Erickson. "On Music: Tell George Orwell the News," *Westways* 72 (Jan. 1980), 70–2. Includes appraisal of Eno.
BANGS, Lester. "Records: *Here Come the Warm Jets*," *Creem* 6 (Oct. 1974), 61–2.
———. "Records: 'The Lion Sleeps Tonight (Wimoweh)/I'll Come Running (To Tie Your Shoes),' " *Creem* (Oct. 1975), 71.
———. "Eno Sings with the Fishes," *Village Voice* 23 (3 Apr. 1978), 1, 49.
———. "Eno," *Musician, Player & Listener* 21 (Nov. 1979), 38–44.
BARNETT, Homer. *Innovation: The Basis of Cultural Change.* New York: McGraw-Hill, 1953. 462 pp.
BARRELL, Tony. "Eno Interview." Australian Broadcasting Commission, Radio Station JJJ, 21 Jan. 1978. Quoted in Eno and Mills, *More Dark Than Shark* (see entry below).
BATESON, Gregory. *Steps to an Ecology of Mind.* New York: Ballantine, 1972. 541 pp.
BECKER, Howard S. *Art Worlds.* Los Angeles: University of California Press, 1982. 408 pp. Interesting insights on the popular culture/high culture dialectic.
BECKETT, Alan. "Popular Music," *New Left Review* 39 (1966), 87–90.
———. "Stones," *New Left Review* 47 (1968), 24–9.
———. "Mapping Pop," *New Left Review* 54 (1969), 82–4.
?. "Review: *Here Come the Warm Jets*," *Beetle* (May 1974), n. p.
BECKETT, Samuel. *Company.* New York: Grove, 1980. 63 pp.
BEER, Stafford. *Brain of the Firm: The Managerial Cybernetics of Organization.* London: Allen Lane, 1972. 319 pp.
BELL, Craig. "Records: '7 Deadly Finns,' " *Creem* (June 1975), 70.
BELL, Daniel. "Sensibility in the Sixties," *Commentary* 51 (1971), 63–73. Somewhat reactionary account of some of the ideological currents in the popular and high arts: the "dissolution of art," the "democratization of genius," "the Dionysian Pack," etc.
Berklee College of Music, advertisement. *College Musician* 1 (Fall 1986), 37.
BLACKING, John. "Music in the Making: Problems in the Analysis of Musical Thought." Bloch Lectures, University of California, Berkeley, 1986.
BLOOM, Michael. "Brian Eno: Theory and Practice," *Boston Phoenix* (10 Oct. 1978), Music Supplement.

————. "Records: *Ambient 1: Music for Airports,*" *Rolling Stone* 296 (26 July 1979), 60–1.

BLYTH, R. H. *Zen in English Literature and Oriental Classics.* New York: E.P. Dutton, 1960. 446 pp.

BOWDEN, Elizabeth Ann. *Performed Literature: Words and Music by Bob Dylan.* Bloomington, Indiana: Indiana U. Press, 1982. 239 pp. The result of an English Ph.D. dissertation at the University of California, Berkeley.

BRADBY, Barbara. "Do-Talk and Don't Talk: Conflicting Voices in Sixties Girl-Group Songs." Paper delivered at the Third International Conference on Popular Music Studies, Université de Québec à Montréal, 10 July 1985. Argues, through exhausitive analysis of pronoun usage in a number of songs, that the girl groups had their own identities, and were not merely passive actresses in a drama of male pop aspirations and marketing strategies.

BROMBERG, Craig. "Brian Eno at Concord," *Art in America* 71:8 (Sept. 1983), 173–4. Review of a showing of Eno's video piece *Mistaken Memories of the Medieval City.*

BROWN, Charles T. *The Art of Rock'n'Roll.* Englewood Cliffs: Prentice-Hall, 1983. 202 pp.

BROWN, Geoff. "Eno's Where It's At," *Melody Maker* 48 (10 Nov. 1973), 40–1.

————. "Here Come the (Luke) Warm Jets," *Melody Maker* 49 (23 Feb. 1974), 18.

————. "Review: *Here Come the Warms Jets,*" *Melody Maker* (16 March 1974), 31.

BROWN, Mick. "Life of Brian According to Eno," *Guardian* (1 May 1982), 10.

————. "On Record: Brian Eno," *Sunday Times Magazine* (31 Oct. 1982), 94.

BROWN, Roger. "The Creative Process in the Popular Arts," *International Social Science Journal* 20 (1968), 613–24.

BURKHOLDER, J. Peter. "Museum Pieces: The Historicist Mainstream in Music of the Last Hundred Years," *Journal of Musicology* 2 (1983), 115–34. Treats, among other things, the strange exclusion of jazz and popular music from many musicologists' concept of "new music" (which can be as much as 75 years old). To be fair, it should be pointed out here that there are signs of change in the musicological establishment. The discipline's most prestigious American organ, the *Journal of the American Musicological Society,* under the editorship of Anthony Newcomb, has in recent years been publishing articles on jazz, such as Scott DeVeaux's "Bebop and the Recording Industry: The 1942 Recording Ban Reconsidered," 41 (Spring 1988), 126–65.

CAGE, John. *Silence: Lectures and Writings by John Cage.* Middletown, Ct.: Wesleyan University Press, 1976. 276 pp.

CARDEW, Cornelius. *Stockhausen Serves Imperialism, and Other Articles.* London: Latimer New Dimensions, 1974. 126 pp.

CARRIER, David. "Interpreting Musical Performances," *Monist: An International Quarterly Journal of General Philosophical Inquiry* 66:2 (1983), 202–12. Carrier's goal is to develop a theory of musical performance, according to the thesis that "musical performance involves moral obligation." The serious, theoretical discussion ranges over thoughts of E. H. Gombrich, Charles Rosen, Nelson Goodman, and others. Eno's provocative liner notes to *Discreet Music* are brought into the discussion as an example of "the abolition of [the] conception of performance in much [contemporary] non-directional music."

CARROLL, Noel. "Reviews: Choreographers Showcase 1," *Dance Magazine* 56 (Apr. 1982), 104. Brief notice on a program by young choreographers, one of whom used music from Byrne and Eno's *My Life in the Bush of Ghosts.*

CARSON, Tom. "Records: *Before and After Science,*" *Rolling Stone* 265 (18 May 1978), 82–3.

?. "Review: *Another Green World,*" *Cassettes and Cartridges* (Feb. 1976), 443.

?. "Review: *Here Come the Warm Jets,*" *Cassettes and Cartridges* (June 1974), 113.

CHAMBERS, Iain. *Urban Rhythms: Pop Music and Popular Culture.* New York: St. Martin's, 1985. 272 pp.

CHESTER, Andrew. "For a Rock Aesthetic," *New Left Review* 59 (1970), 83–7.

————. "Second Thoughts on a Rock Aesthetic: The Band," *New Left Review* 62 (1970), 75–82.

CHRISTGAU, Robert. "The Christgau Consumer Guide: *Here Come the Warm Jets,*" *Creem* (Apr. 1975), 11.

————. "The Christgau Consumer Guide: *Taking Tiger Mountain (By Strategy),*" *Creem* (June 1975), 11.

P. "Record Lovers Guide: Don't Overlook These Discs: *Taking Tiger Mountain by Strategy,*" *Circus* (May 1975), 62.

P. "Review: *Another Green World,*" *Circus* (8 Apr. 1976), 16.

COCKRELL, Dale. "Sergeant Pepper's Lonely Hearts Club Band and Abbey Road, Side Two: Unification within the Rock Recording." Master's thesis, University of Illinois at Urbana, 1973. A quasi-Schenkerian approach to two large-scale song structures of the Beatles' most ambitious phase; has been criticized on the grounds of the putative inappropriateness of the analytical method.

COGAN, Robert, and Pozzi Escot. *Sonic Design: The Nature of Sound and Music.* Englewood Cliffs, N.J., Prentice-Hall, 1980. 191 pp.

COHEN, Mitchell. "Records: *My Life in the Bush of Ghosts,*" *High Fidelity* 31 (May 1981), 77.

CONCANNON, Kevin. "Michael Chandler and Brian Eno, Institute of Contemporary Art," *Artforum* 22 (Apr. 1984), 85–6.

COPE, David. *New Directions in Music.* 2nd ed. Dubuque, Iowa: Wm. C. Brown, 1976. 271 pp. Excellent survey.

CROMELIN, Richard. "Records: The Inmates Have Taken Over: Kevin Ayers, John Cale, Nico, Eno & the Soporifics, *June 1, 1974,*" *Creem* 6 (Dec., 1974), 64–5.

DAGNAL, Cynthia. "Eno and the Jets: Controlled Chaos," *Rolling Stone* 169 (12 Sept. 1974), 16–7.

————. "Eno & Co: ACNE," *Rolling Stone* 169 (12 Sept. 1974), 17. "ACNE" is an acronym for [Kevin] Ayers, [John] Cale, Nico and Eno; this brief article recounts their short-lived live collaborations of 1974.

DAHLHAUS, Carl. *Analysis and Value Judgement.* Translated from the German by Sigmund Levarie. New York: Pendragon Press, 1983. 87 pp.

DANCIS, Bruce. "Studio Plays Big Role in Music Composition, Says Brian Eno," *Billboard* 92 (22 March 1980), 29.

DAVIS, Michael. "Records: *Music for Films,*" *Creem* 10 (Apr. 1979), 61.

DAVY, S. "Eno: Non-Musician on Non-Art," *Beetle* (Jan. 1975), n. p.

DAWBARN, B. "When Does Pop Become Art?," *Melody Maker* 42 (June 10, 1967), 8.

DEMOREST, Stephen. "Eno: the Monkey Wrench of Rock Creates Happy Accidents on *Tiger Mountain,*" *Circus* (Apr. 1975), 50–3.

————. "The Discreet Charm of Brian Eno: An English Pop Theorist Seeks to Redefine Music," *Horizon* 21 (June 1978), 82–5.

DENNIS, Brian. "Repetitive and Systemic Music," *Musical Times* 65 (1974), 1036–8. The paragraph-long *New Grove Dictionary of Music and Musicians* article on "minimalism" does little but refer the reader to a two-item bibliography. This is one of those items. Written before Eno's development of the ambient sound, it does not take him into account, but provides a bit of historical background and analysis of a few pieces.

DILIBERTO, John. "Ultravox," *Down Beat* 50 (May 1983), 18. Extensive interview of the band whose first album Eno produced.

DOCKSTADER, T. "Inside-out: Electronic Rock," *Electronic Music Review* 5 (1968), 15–20. Survey of uses of electronics by groups like the Beatles, the Rolling Stones, the Jefferson Airplane, the Doors, Big Brother and the Holding Company, the Blues Project, the Beach Boys, and Jimi Hendrix. Dockstader concludes: "Most of the electronic rock I've heard so far recalls the *musique concrète* of the fifties . . . there is, as yet, little evidence of sophisticated generation or control of sound."

DOERSCHUK, Bob. *Rock Keyboard.* New York: Quill/Keyboard, 1985. 187 pp.

DUPLER, Steven. "New Age Labels Seek New Angles," *Billboard* 99 (31 Jan. 1986), 1.

DURGNAT, Raymond. "Rock, Rhythm and Dance," *British Journal of Aesthetics* 11 (1971), 28–47. Brilliant approach to the aesthetics of rock via its rhythm, which is seen to awaken a particular sense of time that has been lost to modern man.

————. "Symbolism and the Underground," *Hudson Review* 22 (Autumn 1969), 457–68. An art historian, Durgnat is fascinated by the parallels between these movements of the nineteenth and twentieth centuries; the "Underground," never quite defined, refers to the whole complex of counter-culture/psychedelia/Eastern-religion/rock music of the late 1960s.

DUXBURY Janell, *Rockin' the Classics and Classicizin' the Rock: A Selectively Annotated Discography*. Discographies, Number 14. Westport, Ct. and London: Greenwood Press, 1985. 188 pp.

EDWARDS, Henry. "Bryan Ferry and Eno: Hot Rockers Rock Apart," *After Dark* 8 (June 1975), 66–7.

————. "Records: *Another Green World*," *High Fidelity* (June 1976), 101.

ELLUL, Jacques. *The Technological Society*. Translated from the French by John Wilkinson. New York: Vintage, 1964. 449 pp. Somewhat dated but still chilling indictment of contemporary values.

EMERSON, Ken. "Brian Eno Slips into 'Trance Music,' " *New York Times* (12 Aug. 1979), D:22.

EMMERSON, Simon. "Seven Obscure Releases," *Music and Musicians* 25 (Jan. 1977), 20–2. Documents, discusses, and critiques the development of British experimental music through discussion of recordings on the Obscure label cofounded by Eno.

ENO, Brian. "Music for Non-Musicians," private publishing of 25 copies, ca. 1970, none of which is known to exist today, according to Eno's management, Opal Ltd., London. This intriguing little essay is, however, discussed in Eno and Mills, *More Dark Than Shark*.

————. "Text for a lecture to Trent Polytechnic," 1974. This essay is quoted in Eno and Mills, *More Dark Than Shark*.

————. "Shedding Light on Obscure Records," *Street Life* (15–28 Nov. 1975).

————. "Generating and Organizing Variety in the Arts," *Studio International* 984 (Nov./Dec. 1976), 279–83. Reprinted in Battcock, Gregroy, ed., *Breaking the Sound Barrier: A Critical Anthology of the New Music* (New York: Dutton, 1981), 129–141. In Battcock's anthology, Eno's thoughts find a place side by side with those of Benjamin Boretz, Earle Brown, Elaine Barkin, Josef Rufer, and a host of other contemporary composers, critics, and thinkers. See Terence O'Grady review below.

————. "Self-Regulation and Autopoiesis in Contemporary Music," unpublished paper, 1978. Slated for appearance in an anthology that never materialized, this essay is quoted in Eno and Mills, *More Dark Than Shark*.

————. "Video-installatie Mistaken Memories of Medieval New York, 1981." Amsterdam: Stedelijk Museum, 1982. 2 pp.

————. (excerpted by Howard Mandel). "Pro Session: The Studio as Compositional Tool," in two parts, *Down Beat* 50 (July 1983), 56–7, and *Down Beat* (Aug. 1983), 50–2.

————. "Works Constructed with Sound and Light: Extracts from a talk given by Brian Eno following the opening of his video installation, Copenhagen, January 1986." Color brochure. London: Opal Ltd., 1986.

————. "Brian Eno: Place #13, The Douglas Hyde Gallery, Dublin." Color brochure. Dublin: Douglas Hyde Gallery, 1986. 15 (unnumbered) pp. See also Hutchinson in this bibliography.

ENO, Brian, and Russell Mills. *More Dark Than Shark*. "Commentaries by Rick Poynor, designed by Malcolm Garrett, photography by Martin Axon, additional photography by David Buckland." London: Faber and Faber, 1986. 144 pp. Mills illustrates the lyrics (never before published in written form) to Eno's songs written between 1973 and 1977. Each song receives a distinct artistic treatment, with notes by Mills explaining the development of his painterly response to the words of the text. Eno provides notes on the genesis of some of the songs, as well as some discussion of the musical and studio processes involved; interspersed throughout are reproductions of pages from Eno's notebooks—diagrams, drawings, wordplay, aphorisms, plans for projects, and "amateur mathematics." Also included is a useful classified Eno work list for the period 1972–1986.

ENO, Brian, and Peter Schmidt. "Peter Schmidt and Brian Eno," *Arts Review* 29 (9 Dec. 1977), 737–8.

ENO, Brian, and Peter Schmidt. *Oblique Strategies.* Limited edition of 500 copies, London: 1975; revised and reissued, London: 1978, 1979.

Enovations. Journal of the official Eno fan club.

ERICKSON, Robert. *Sound Structure in Music.* Berkeley: University of California Press, 1975. 205 pp.

FERNBACHER, Joe. "Records: *Before and After Science,*" *Creem* 9 (Apr. 1978), 67.

FLETCHER, Gordon. "Records: *Here Come the Warm Jets,*" *Rolling Stone* 172 (24 Oct. 1974), 74.

FLETCHER, Peter. *Roll Over Rock.* London: Stainer & Bell, 1981. 175 pp. Assesses the split between "classical" and "pop," in a textbook-like format suitable for a course introducing the general student to the history of Western music in all its forms.

FRIPP, Robert. "Speaking of Jimi," *Guitar Player* 9 (Sept. 1975), 7.

FRITH, Simon. *Sound Effects: Youth, Leisure, and the Politics of Rock'n'Roll.* New York: Pantheon, 1981. 294 pp. Revised version of *The Sociology of Rock.* Frith treats rock under three headings: ideology (its history and relation to mass culture), production (musicians and the music industry), and consumption (involving youth, leisure, and sexuality). His insistence on focusing on the merely commercial aspects of rock can be maddening to the musician; yet there's nothing quite like this book for the overview it gives of the rock industry and its functions.

FROHNE, Ursula. "Review: Brian Eno: Tegel Airport, Institut Unzeit, Berlin," *Flash Art* (Apr./May 1984), 42–3.

FURLONG, C. "AFI Frames the Field: The National Video Festival," *Afterimage* 9:5 (Oct. 1981), 4. Interesting insights into the commercial and artistic uses of the new medium. A 53-minute, 4-monitor installation by Eno gets a brief notice.

GABREE, John. "Serious Rock: Current Revolution in Pop Music," *Nation* 206 (June 24, 1968), 836–8. Early journalistic attempt to document the advent of progressive rock. Gabree writes: "What is new is that pop music is reaching an audience that previously has been interested only in classical music or jazz."

GAERTNER, James. "Art as the Function of an Audience," *Daedelus* 86 (1955), 80–93.

GILMORE, Mikal. "Record Reviews: *Another Green World, Discreet Music, Evening Star,*" *Down Beat* 43 (21 Oct. 1976), 24–5.

———. "Record Reviews: *801 Live,*" *Down Beat* 44 (20 Oct. 1977), 26–7.

GOLDSTEIN, Richard. *The Poetry of Rock.* New York: Bantam Books, 1969. 147 pp. David Horn summarizes: "Some 70 rock music lyrics from Chuck Berry to the Doors . . . comments on individual artists and writers." Paul Taylor adds: "When it was published, the question of popular lyrics aspiring to be poetry was in issue of some importance. It now seems largely irrelevant."

GOLDWASSER, Noë. "Flowers Si, Cars, No . . . the Real Sorrow and the Fake Piety . . . Eno Already: Mad Tapemonger to Highbrow It," *Village Voice* 21 (26 Jan. 1979), 16–7.

GOMBRICH, E. H. *Art and Illusion: A Study in the Psychology of Pictorial Representation* The A. W. Mellon Lectures in the Fine Arts, 1956, National Gallery of Art, Washington. Princeton: Princeton University Press, 1972. 466 pp.

GOSSETT, Philip. "Beethoven's Sixth Symphony: Sketches for the First Movement," *Journal of the American Musicological Society* 28 (Summer 1974), 248–84.

GRABEL, Richard. Eno interview, *New Musical Express* (24 April 1982).

GRANT, Steven. "Brian Eno Against Interpretation," *Trouser Press* 9 (Aug. 1982), 27–30.

HAMM, Charles. "John Cage," *The New Grove Dictionary of Music and Musicians* (1980).

HARDY, Phil, and Dave Laing, eds. *The Encyclopedia of Rock.* London: Aquarius, 1976. St Albans: Panther, 1976. 3 vols.

HENSCHEN, Robert. "Contemporary: *Music for Airports,*" *Music Journal* 37 (Sept./Oct. 1979), 62.

HOFFMAN, Alan Neil. "On the Nature of Rock and Roll: An Enquiry into the Aesthetic of a Musical

Vernacular." Ph.D. dissertation (Music), Yale University, 1983. 231 pp. Locates the "aesthetics" of rock within the matrix of three parameters: rock is a *recorded* music, it is a type of *song*, and it is a kind of *dance* music. Hoffman's way of approaching rock music, for all its formalism, does not seem to go beyond the obvious.

HOFFMAN, Frank W. *The Literature of Rock, 1954–1978.* Metuchen, New Jersey: Scarecrow, 1981. 337 pp.

HOGGART, Richard. "Humanistic Studies and Mass Culture," *Daedelus* 99 (1970), 451–72. In an interesting attempt to formulate the proper attitude of academic humanism toward mass culture, Hoggart runs through the familiar dichotomies springing from mass versus fine art: brutal/genteel, low/high, processed/alive, evasive/honest, conventional/challenging, symptomatic/representative, exploitative/disinterested, etc. Although he allows that these dichotomies do not adequately assess the situation, his final stance is "to reassert the power and overriding importance of the high arts for the student of culture."

HOLDEN, Stephen. "Pop Record Producers Attain Stardom," *New York Times* (17 Feb. 1980), II:20.

HOLLAND, Bill. "Cassettes Take 2–1 Lead Over Vinyl in Survey," *Billboard* 98:50 (13 Dec. 1986), 73.

HOUNSOME, Terry, ed. *New Rock Record.* New York: Facts on File, 1983. 719 pp.

HOWELL, Mark. "From a Strangers Evening with Brian Eno," *Another Room* (June/July 1981), n. p.

HULL, Tom. "Eno Races Toward the New World," *Village Voice* 21 (12 Apr. 1976), 87–8.

HUTCHINSON, John. "From Music to Landscape: A Personal Reaction to Brian Eno's Video Installations," in Brian Eno, "Brian Eno: Place #13," color brochure. Dublin: Douglas Hyde Gallery, 1986, n. p.

HYNDE, Chrissie. Eno interview, *New Musical Express* (2 Feb. 1974).

I Ching, or Book of Changes: The Richard Wilhelm Translation Rendered into English by Cary F. Baynes. 3rd ed. Bollingen Series 19. Princeton: Princeton University Press, 1967. 740 pp.

INGHAM, John. "Cracked Musician's Head Is On the Mend," *New Musical Express* (1 March 1975), 8.

ISLER, Scott. "Going, Going, Ghana! David Byrne and Brian Eno Bring Africa to Soho," *Trouser Press* 61 (May 1981), 23–7.

JENSEN, Alan. "The Sound of Silence: A Thursday Afternoon with Brian Eno," *Electronics & Music Maker* (Dec. 1985), 20–5.

JOHNSON, Tom. "Music: The New Tonality," *Village Voice* 23 (16 Oct. 1978), 115–6. Rare attempt, in a popular periodical, to come to grips with the renewed interest, on the part of contemporary composers such as Eno, Reich, Riley, and Rzewski, in writing tonal music.

———. "New Music, New York, New Institution," *Village Voice* 24 (2 July 1979), 88–9. This rambling review of the 10-day festival "New Music, New York" ambitiously attempts to sum up developments in the new music scene of the 1970s, highlighting the growing generational split between the older generation—Cage-inspired, Eastern-philosophy-influenced—and the younger—electric guitars in hand, performance-art-oriented. Eno appeared at the festival, reportedly pleading for inclusion of a sensual element in new music and criticizing what he felt was the over-stressed intellectual element.

JONES, Allan. "Eno: On Top of Tiger Mountain," *Melody Maker* 49 (26 Oct. 1974), 39.

———. "Albums: Eno's Touch of Velvets: Eno, *Taking Tiger Mountain (By Strategy),*" *Melody Maker* 49 (2 Nov. 1974), 69.

———. "Caught in the Act: Fripp and Eno: Formal Beauty," *Melody Maker* 50 (14 June 1975), 49.

———. "Eno—Class of '75," *Melody Maker* 50 (29 Nov. 1975), 14.

JUNG, Carl. *Civilization in Transition.* 2nd ed. Collected Works of C. G. Jung, Vol. 10, Bollingen Series 20. Princeton: Princeton University Press, 1970. 609 pp.

———. "Synchronicity: An Acausal Connecting Principle," in his *The Structure and Dynamics of the Psyche.* 2nd ed. Collected Works of C. G. Jung, Vol. 8, Bollingen Series 20. Princeton: Princeton University Press, 1969, pp. 417–519.

KAPLAN, Abraham. "The Aesthetics of the Popular Arts," in James Hall and Barry Ulanov, eds., *Modern Culture and the Arts.* New York: McGraw-Hill, 1967, pp. 62–78. Originally in *Journal of Aesthetics* (Spring 1966).

KARPELES, Maud. "The Distinction Between Folk and Popular Music," *Journal of the International Folk Music Council* 20 (1968), 9–12.

KELP, Larry. "Brian Eno: Making Fourth World Music in Record Studio," *Oakland Tribune* (11 Feb. 1980), C:6–7.

KENT, Nick. "The Freewheelin' Brian Eno," *New Musical Express* (18 May, 1974), 15.

KERMAN, Joseph. *Contemplating Music: Challenges to Musicology.* Cambridge, Mass.: Harvard University Press, 1985. 255 pp. Thoughtful contemporary critique of the changing goals, methods, and subject matter of Kerman's own discipline.

———. "Viewpoint," *19th Century Music,* 2 (1978), 186–91.

KORNER, Anthony. "Aurora Musicalis," *Artforum* 24:10 (Summer 1986), 76–9. Includes a tear-out phonodisc of a new Eno composition, *Glint: East of Woodbridge.*

KOZAK, Roman. "Math Qualities of Music Interest Eno," *Billboard* 90 (13 May 1978), 51.

———. "Rock'n'Rolling: Flo & Eddie, Eno & Phil, Godley & Creme Visited," *Billboard* 94 (3 Apr. 1982), 12, 72.

KUHN, Thomas. *The Structure of Scientific Revolutions.* Chicago: University of Chicago Press, 1962. 172 pp.

LA BARBARA, Joan. " 'RadioVisions'—NPR's Exploration of the World of Sound," *High Fidelity* 31 (Dec. 1981), MA–13. Review of NPR's "adventurous new series opening broadcasting vistas," in which Eno found himself in the company of the likes of Henry Cowell, Virgil Thomson, Lou Harrison, Charles Ives, Leonard Bernstein, Aaron Copland, Lukas Foss, Daniel Lentz, John Cage, and Gunther Schuller.

LAKE, Greg, and others. "British Rock: Are We Facing Disaster?," *Melody Maker* 49 (21 Sept. 1974), 8–9.

LAMKIN, John, ed., *Music of the Spheres: A New Age Music & Art Quarterly.* Taos, N.M.: 1987.

LANDAU, Jon. "Paul Simon: 'Like a Pitcher of Water,' " in Ben Fong-Torres, ed., *The Rolling Stone Interviews, Vol. 2.* New York: Warner, 1973, 389–430.

LEVARIE, Sigmund. "Key Relations in Verdi's *Un Ballo in Maschera,*" *19th Century Music* 2 (1978), 143–7. See also Levarie's reply to Joseph Kerman's criticisms (Kerman 1978, above), in *19th Century Music* 3 (1979), 88–9.

LEVIN, Kim. "The Waiting Room," *Arts Magazine* 55 (Nov. 1980), 5. Review of a multi-artist installation that was set up for a day in Grand Central Station, New York City. Eno's videos, it is reported peevishly, "didn't grab the attention." (Were they supposed to?)

LIMBACHER, James. *The Song List: A Guide to Contemporary Music from Classical Sources.* Ann Arbor: Pierian, 1973. 229 pp.

LODER, Kurt. "Eno," *Synapse* (Jan./Feb. 1979), 24–7.

———. "Squawking Heads: Byrne and Eno in the Bush of Ghosts," *Rolling Stone* 338 (5 March 1981), 45–6.

LOGAN, Nick and Bob Woffinden. *The New Musical Express Book of Rock.* London: Star, 1977. 553 pp. See also the revised editions of 1978 and 1979; originally *The Illustrated Encyclopedia of Rock.* New York: Harmony, 1977. 256 pp.

LOUD, Lance. "Eno & Rupert: No Excess Genius," *Circus Raves* (Sept. 1975), 16–17.

LUBOW, Arthur. "Eno, Before and After Roxy," *New Times* 10 (6 March 1978), 72–3.

———. "Brian Eno: At the Outer Limits of Popular Music, the Ex-glitter Rocker Experiments with a Quiet New Sound," *People Weekly* (11 Oct. 1982), 91, 93–5.

MACDONALD, Ian. Eno interview, *New Musical Express* (26 Nov. 1977).

MACKINNON, Angus. Eno interview, *New Musical Express* (12 July 1975).

MARSH, Dave and John Swenson. *The New Rolling Stone Record Guide*. New York: Random House/Rolling Stone, 1983. 648 pp.

MARSHALL, Tony. "The Life of Brian," *Observer Magazine* (23 Oct. 1983), 28–9.

MASTRIANI, Tony. "Records: *Taking Tiger Mountain (By Strategy)*," *Creem* (May 1975), 69.

MATTHEWS, Pete. "Review: Eno: *Taking Tiger Mountain (By Strategy)*; Nico: *The End*; Sparks: *Propaganda*," *Records and Recording* (Jan. 1975), 60.

McKENNA, Kristine. "Eno," *Wet* 25 (July/Aug. 1980), 41–5.

?. "The Roxy Music File," *Melody Maker* 47 (14 Oct. 1972), 16.

MELLY, George. *Revolt into Style: The Pop Arts*. London: Allen Lane, 1970. 245 pp.

MELTZER, Richard. *The Aesthetics of Rock*. New York: Something Else Press, 1970. 346 pp. Stream-of-consciousness response to the phenomenon of rock music. Laborious reading.

MERTON, Richard. "Comment," *New Left Review* 47 (1968), 29–31. Cf. the articles by Chester and Beckett.

————. "Comment," *New Left Review* 59 (1970), 88–96.

MEYER, Leonard. *Music, the Arts and Ideas: Patterns and Predictions in Twentieth-Century Culture*. Chicago and London: University of Chicago Press, 1967. 342 pp.

MIGNOT, Dorine. " 'The Luminous Image': 22 Video-Installationen im Stedelijk Museum Amsterdam," *Kunstforum International* 9/10 (Jan./Feb. 1985), 59–83.

MILES, ?. Eno interview, *New Musical Express* (27 Nov. 1976).

MILKOWSKI, Bill. "Brian Eno: Excursions in the Electronic Environment," *Down Beat* 50 (June 1983), 14 ff.

MILLER, Kathy. "Eno: Naked and Neurotic," *Creem* 6 (Dec. 1974), 18.

MILLER, Gregory. "Brian Eno: On Video," *Soho News* (2 July 1980).

————. "The Arts: Video," *Omni* 3 (Nov. 1980), 28–9. Description/review of the video/music installation by Eno that was set up in the Marine Terminal of New York's La Guardia Airport.

MILLER, Jim, ed. *The Rolling Stone Illustrated History of Rock & Roll*. New York: Rolling Stone/Random House, 1976. 382 pp.

MOORE, Lee. "Eno = MC Squared," *Creem* 10 (Nov. 1978), 26, 67–8.

MULHERN, Tom. "Robert Fripp on the Discipline of Craft & Art," *Guitar Player* 20 (Jan. 1986), 88–103.

?. "Review: *Another Green World*," *Music Journal* (June, 1976), 44.

?. "Review: *Evening Star, Taking Tiger Mountain by Strategy*," *Music Journal* 37 (Sept./Oct. 1979), 26.

NAHA, Ed. "Record Lovers Guide: Picks of the Month: Brian Eno: *Here Come the Warm Jets*," *Circus* (Dec. 1974), 61.

NAHA, Ed. "Review: *Taking Tiger Mountain (By Strategy)*," *Crawdaddy* (May 1975), 76.

NASSOUR, Ellis and Richard Broderick. *Rock Opera*. New York: Hawthorn, c. 1973. 248 pp.

NELSO, Paul, ed. "The Year in Records: Vindication on Vinyl in 1981 . . . *My Life in the Bush of Ghosts*, David Byrne and Brian Eno," *Rolling Stone* (24 Dec. 1981), 101.

NETTL, Bruno. *The Study of Ethnomusicology: Twenty-nine Issues and Concepts*. Urbana: University of Illinois Press, 1983. 410 pp. A landmark study. Nettl's chapter "I've Never Heard a Horse Sing" (pp. 303–14) includes a brief history of how ethnomusicologists have used the categories of folk, art, popular, and primitive music.

————. *The Western Impact on World Music: Change, Adaptation, and Survival*. New York: Schirmer; London: Collier Macmillan, 1985. 190 pp. Many chapters in Nettl's book discuss the uses of technology in, and impact of technology on, non-Western musics; the (incredibly short) chapter on "Pop" (pp. 84–6) focuses on the dissemination of Western popular styles. Nettl characteristically dwells on exactly what people in the West (and those in other parts of the world) mean by "popular music."

?. "The Creation of the Universe," *New York* 18 (25 Nov. 1985), 83. Glowing review of the PBS scientific documentary, for which Eno wrote the evidently cosmically evocative music: "It

haunts and splashes and insinuates and confounds. It seems in its eerie modulations to be
agreeing with Sandage—'There is no center to the beginning'—and to be asking Sandage's
big-bang question: 'Why is there something instead of nothing?' "

?. "Review: *Taking Tiger Mountain by Strategy*," *New Musical Express* (9 Nov. 1974).

?. "Records: *Another Green World*," *New Musical Express* (22 Nov. 1975), 20–1.

NORMAN-TAYLOR, Anthea, and Lin Barkass, compilers. *Opal Information* (1986–). This is a newsletter put out by Opal Ltd., Eno's management company. It features articles by and about the
musicians and artists represented by Opal.

NYLON, Judy. "Eno's Other Green Worlds," *Circus* (27 Apr. 1976), 23.

O'BRIEN, Glenn. "Eno at the Edge of Rock," *Andy Warhol's Interview* 8 (June 1978), 31–3.

———. "Bop Art," *Artforum* 20 (Feb. 1982), 47–8. Substantial, if tongue-in-cheek critical account
of the links between pop art and pop music: "So here was a zeitgeist you could shake your
booty to." Eno's achievements are discussed and summed up: "He has probably traveled more
in both worlds than any of his contemporaries."

———. "Glenn O'Brien's Beat: My Mother the Ear," *Andy Warhol's Interview* 12 (Sept. 1982),
107–8.

O'GRADY, Terence. "Reviews of Books: *Breaking the Sound Barrier: A Critical Anthology of the
New Music*, Edited by Gregory Battcock," *Musical Quarterly* 69 (Winter 1983), 138–44. Eno's
essay "Generating and Organizing Variety in the Arts" was reprinted in the anthology under
review here. O'Grady wrote his dissertation on the music of the Beatles.

PADGETT, Stephen. "New Age: Definitions," *Grammy Pulse: Official Publication of the National
Academy of Recording Arts & Sciences* 4 (Sept. 1986), 8–9.

PALMER, Robert. "Brian Eno, New Guru of Rock, Going Solo," *New York Times* (13 March 1981),
III:17.

PARAKILAS, James. "Classical Music as Popular Music," *Journal of Musicology* 3 (1984), 1–18. A
myth-debunking, category-demolishing, realistic discussion of the uses and perceptions of our
"art music" heritage.

PARELES, Jon. "Records: *Another Green World*," *Crawdaddy* (June 1976), 78.

———. "I Am a Child: *More Songs About Buildings and Food*, Talking Heads," *Crawdaddy* 88
(Sept. 1978), 75.

———. "Records: Does this Global Village Have Two-Way Traffic? *My Life in the Bush of Ghosts*,
David Byrne and Brian Eno," *Rolling Stone* 340 (2 April 1981), 60.

———. "Riffs: Eno Uncaged," *Village Voice* 27 (4 May 1982), 77–8.

PARELES, Jon, and Patricia Romanowski, eds. *The Rolling Stone Encyclopedia of Rock & Roll*.
New York: Rolling Stone/Summit Books, 1983. 615 pp.

PAYES, Robert. "Review: *On Land*," *Trouser Press* 9 (Aug. 1982), 41.

PEEL, Mark. "Disc and Tape Reviews: *Ambient #4—On Land*," *Stereo Review* 47 (Nov. 1982),
105.

PETHEL, Blair W. "Keith Emerson, the Emergence and Growth of Style: A Study of Selected
Works." Ph.D. dissertation (Performance). Peabody Conservatory.

PEYSER, Joan. "The Music of Sound; Or, the Beatles and the Beatless," *Columbia University
Forum* 10 (1967), 16–22. Positive appraisal of progressive movements in rock. Peyser writes:
"The best of rock is moving with unprecedented speed into unexpected, more artistically
interesting areas."

PICCARELLA, John. "Riffs: Possible Arabias," *Village Voice* 26 (20 May 1981), 80.

PICHASKE, David R. *The Poetry of Rock: The Golden Years*. Peoria, Ill.: The Ellis Press, 1981.
173 pp. The "Booklist" in *Popular Music 3* comments: "Literary discussions of 1960s rock lyrics,
based on the author's college teachings."

PISTON, Walter. *Harmony*, 3rd ed. New York: W. W. Norton, 1962. 374 pp.

?. "*My Life in the Bush of Ghosts* by Byrne and Eno," *Playboy Guide to Electronic Entertainment*
1 (Fall/Winter 1981), 17.

POIRIER, Richard. "Learning from the Beatles," *Partisan Review* 34 (1967), 526–46. Through a thorough analysis of the lyrics of *Sergeant Pepper's Lonely Hearts Club Band*, Poirier argues that the music of the Beatles can indeed be appreciated through conventional aesthetic categories.

POLLOCK, Bruce. *In Their Own Words: Lyrics and Lyricists 1955–1974*. New York and London: Macmillan, 1975. 231 pp. Paul Taylor writes: "The work of the leading songwriters from the whole spectrum of popular music is discussed and analyzed with profuse, well-selected examples. There are quotations from interviews with most of the writers with some fascinating insights into their methods of working and inspirations, as well as outlines of their careers."

RAMBALI, Paul. "Brain Waves from Eno: Too Smart for Rock'n'Roll, Too Weird for Anything Else," *Trouser Press* 4 (June/July 1977), 15–19.

RANDEL, Don, ed. *The New Harvard Dictionary of Music*. Cambridge, Mass. and London: Belknap/Harvard University Press, 1986. "Electro-acoustic music" (John Appleton), "Improvisation, extemporization" (Bruno Nettl), "Synthesizer" (Dimitri Conomos).

?. "Review: *Another Green World*," *Records and Recording* (Feb. 1976), 67.

REES, Dafydd, and Barry Lazell. *Bryan Ferry and Roxy Music*. London & New York: Proteus, 1982. 96 pp.

ROBBINS, Ira. *The Trouser Press Guide to New Wave Records*. New York: Scribner's, 1983. 389 pp.

ROBINS, Wayne. "Records: Taking Rock's Future by Artifice: Roxy Music, *Country Life*; Eno, *Taking Tiger Mountain (By Strategy)*," *Creem* 6 (Mar. 1975), 66–7.

ROBINSON, Lisa. "Eno's Last Interview," *New Musical Express* (10 Aug. 1974), 5–6.

ROCK, Sheila. "Brian Eno," *Rock* (Nov. 1976), 92–3.

ROCKWELL, John. *All American Music: Composition in the Late 20th Century*. New York: Knopf, 1983. 287 pp. Rockwell's unusually broad view and perceptive insights are refreshing. There aren't many books where one can find Milton Babbitt and Neil Young treated equally.

———. "Art Rock," in Jim Miller, ed., *The Rolling Stone Illustrated History of Rock & Roll*. New York: Rolling Stone/Random House, 1976, pp. 322–6. Rockwell's aim is to trace manifestations of "self-conscious experimentation in rock." Discusses and critically evaluates all the major figures of progressive rock in probably the best existing general treatment of the subject.

———. "The Odyssey of Two British Rockers," *New York Times* (23 July 1978), II:16. On Eno and Robert Fripp.

ROGAN, Johnny. *Roxy Music: Style with Substance—Roxy's first ten years*. London: Star, 1982. 219 pp. Paul Taylor has written: "A very good study of the group's career not forgetting the solo efforts of all the members. There are lengthy quotes from the music press with an unusual section of notes on sources. . . . The author's knowledge of Roxy Music's development in terms of artistic presentation as well as musical style is evident, making this stand above the usual group history."

?. "The Heavy Hundred 1980: *Rolling Stone* Picks the Movers and the Shakers of the Music Industry," *Rolling Stone* 312 (6 March 1980), 9–17.

ROSE, Frank. "Eno: Scaramouche of the Synthesizer," *Creem* 7 (July 1975), 30 ff.

———. "Four Conversations with Brian Eno," *Village Voice* 22 (28 Mar. 1977), 69 ff.

ROSS, David. "Brian Eno," *Matrix/Berkeley* 44 (June/July 1981), n. p.

RUSH, George. "Brian Eno: Rock's Svengali Pursues Silence," *Esquire* 98 (Dec. 1982), 130–2.

RUSSEL, Tony, ed. *Encyclopedia of Rock*. London: Crescent Books, 1983. 192 pp.

SAGAN, Carl. *The Dragons of Eden: Speculations on the Rise of Human Intelligence*. New York: Random House, 1977. 263 pp.

SALEWICZ, Chris. "Texans Like Steak, Oil-Wells, Large Hats and Eno," *New Musical Express* (7 Dec. 1974), 42–3.

SALZMAN, Eric. *Twentieth-Century Music: An Introduction*. Prentice-Hall History of Music Series, H. Wiley Hitchcock, ed. Englewood Cliffs, N.J.: Prentice-Hall, 1974. 242 pp. One of the standard texts.

SANDNER, Wolfgang. "Frankfurt am Main: John McLaughlin und 'Roxy Music' erstmals in Deutschland," *Neue Zeitschrift für Musik* 134:8 (1973), 523.

SCHAFER, William. *Rock Music: Where It's Been, What It Means, Where It's Going*. Minneapolis: Augsburg, 1972. 128 pp. Hails new movements in rock as manifesting a clear "artistic intent." Cf. especially the chapter on "Concepts and 'Concept Albums,'" which refers to Cage, Ives, Riley, et. al.

SCHAEFFER, Pierre. *Traité des objets musicaux*. Paris: Editions du Seuil, 1968. 671 pp.

SCHNEIDER, Mitchell. "Brave New Eno: *Before and After Science*," *Crawdaddy* 84 (May 1978), 64.

SCHUMACHER, Ernst. *Small is Beautiful: Economics as if People Mattered*. New York: Harper & Row, 1975. 290 pp.

SHAW, Russell. "Record Reviews: *Before and After Science*," *Down Beat* 45 (13 July 1978), 36.

SHEPHERD, John. "A Theoretical Model for the Sociomusicological Analysis of Popular Music," *Popular Music* 2 (1982), 145–77. Extremely thought-provoking plea for analytical methods appropriate to the specific musical object. Shepherd's controversial approach sees an analogy between the dominating force of tonality in traditional art music and the vertical power-structures of industrial capitalism, whereas many forms of popular music are said to be more "horizontal" in structure and function.

SHEPHERD, John, Phil Virden, Graham Vulliamy, and Trevor Wishart. *Whose Music? A Sociology of Musical Languages*. New Brunswick, New Jersey: Transaction Books, 1980. 300 pp. Consists of individual chapters by one or more of the above authors, a fine bibliography heavy on theoretical aspects of the arts in society, and a twenty-nine-page Appendix of Musical Terminology (for the naive sociologist). All in all, an imposing effort whose rather fierce Marxist polemical aim is "to provide a re-evaluation of deep-seated assumptions underlying attitudes to music," leading to (among other things) "a *serious* reconsideration by university music departments of the value of all kinds of music (*including* present-day 'popular' forms), instead of their acting merely as a forum for so-called 'art' musics."

SHORE, Michael. "The Arts: Music," *Omni* 3 (June 1980), 26–7. *Omni*'s characteristic techno-yuppie breathlessness is in full swing in this sweeping historical account of the creative use of synthesizers and studio effects in rock and related genres. Includes a brief mention of Eno's contributions, concluding: "Eno showed us how to live with and love electronics and how to use them expressively, with felicity and taste."

SIMELS, Steve. "The Sixties Revisited: *My Life in the Bush of Ghosts* by Byrne & Eno; *The Flowers of Romance* by Public Image Ltd.," *Stereo Review* 46 (Aug. 1981), 86.

SLAWSON, Wayne. *Sound Color*. Berkeley, Los Angeles, and London: University of California Press, 1985. 266 pp. Slawson, "motivated by the assumption that composition with sound color requires a theory," examines and criticizes the major existing studies of timbre: Pierre Schaeffer's *Traité des objets musicaux*, Robert Erickson's *Sound Structure in Music*, and Robert Cogan and Pozzi Escot's *Sonic Design: The Nature of Sound and Music* (see the entries in this bibliography for more information). Slawson includes an 18-page bibliography on his subject. Slawson's own concept of "sound color," which is exceedingly well thought-out and formally precise, is not really concerned with "timbre" as such, which is a more general term encompassing such sound-characteristics as attack and decay, vibrato, and periodic and aperiodic fluctuations in pitch and amplitude, as well as the harmonic or overtone structure of sounds. Although tempted to broaden Slawson's evocative term "sound color" for the purposes of this book, I have usually stuck with the traditional terms "timbre" and "tone color," which I have used more or less interchangeably, relying on their accustomed if inexact connotations to carry the argument.

SMITH, Rod. "What is Spacemusic!," *FM 91 Public Radio* (California State University, Sacramento, Feb. 1987), 5 ff.

?. "Review: *Here Come the Warm Jets*," *Stereo Review* (Dec. 1974), 102–3.

STONE, Ruth. "From the Editors: Hijacking Music," *SEM Newsletter* 21 (Jan. 1987), 2.

STRIEBEN, Joachim. "Brian Eno—ein Avantgardist der Rockmusik," *Musik und Bildung* 11 (Mar. 1979), 190–1.

SUTHERLAND, Sam. "Reviews: *The Catherine Wheel*, David Byrne," *High Fidelity* 32 (Feb. 1982), 75. Review of Byrne's score for Twyla Tharp's Broadway dance production; Eno is credited with instrumental support on three tracks, but "exerted a wider influence than those listings might suggest."

TAGG, Philip. "Analysing Popular Music: Theory, Method and Practice," 2 *Popular Music* (1982), 37–67. Excellent discussion of the problems confronting the would-be analyst. Stresses the importance of locating significant non-musical association-producing elements in the analytical object. Several well-thought-out charts, including a comparison of folk, art, and popular music, a chart of the analytical process, and a checklist of parameters of musical expression.

TAMM, Eric. "Materials for Rock Music Research," *Cum Notis Variorum* 90–93 (March–June 1985). Categorized bibliography of available sources.

TANNENBAUM, Rob. "A Meeting of Sound Minds: John Cage and Brian Eno," *Musician* 83 (Sept. 1985), 64–70, 72, 106.

TAYLOR, Paul. *Popular Music Since 1955: A Critical Guide to the Literature.* Boston: G. K. Hall, 1985. 533 pp.

TAZZI, Pier Luigi. "Milan: Brian Eno, Chiesa di S. Carpoforo," *Artforum* 23 (Feb. 1985), 97–8.

TRUNGPA, Chogyam. *Cutting Through Spiritual Materialism.* Edited by John Baker and Marvin Casper. Berkeley: Shambhala, 1973. 250 pp.

TUDOR, Dean. *Popular Music: An Annotated Guide to Recordings.* Littleton, Colorado: Libraries Unlimited, 1983. 647 pp.

TURNER, Anna and Stephen Hill, eds. *Spacemusic: Music by Mail, 1986.* San Francisco: Hearts of Space, 1986. 97 pp.

WADDINGTON, Conrad. *Towards a Theoretical Biology.* An International Union of Biological Sciences Symposium. Chicago: Aldine, 1968. 4 vv.

WAHLSTROM, Billie and Caren Deming. "Chasing the Popular Arts through the Critical Forest," *Journal of Popular Culture* 13 (1980), 412–26. Concentrates on myth and archetype as carriers of cultural values.

WALSH, Michael. "The Heart Is Back in the Game: Hypnotic and Infectious, Minimalism Is Emotional in Its Appeal," *Time* 120 (20 Sept. 1982), 60–2. Survey of the impact of the music of Reich, Riley, Glass, et. al. on the contemporary audience. Eno is mentioned as an Art-Rocker "whose own music has been influenced by the minimalist aesthetic."

WALTERS, Charley. "Records: Eno's Electronic Sonic Exotica: *Another Green World*," *Rolling Stone* 212 (6 May 1976), 67–8.

WARD, Ed. "Riffs: Meetings with Remarkable Men," *Village Voice* 24 (17 Sept. 1979), 65. Unabstractable piece in which Ward professes to be in touch with an all-seeing guru (Stravinsky's ghost) whose wisdom he hopes will give him the straight dope on Eno's music. "He loves sound and he will play with it forever, and if he composes directly onto tape then yes, he is a musician," is the Russian's final word.

WARD, Ed, Geoffrey Stokes, and Ken Tucker, *Rock of Ages: The Rolling Stone History of Rock & Roll.* New York: Rolling Stone/Summit, 1986.

WENNER, Jann. *Lennon Remembers: The Rolling Stone Interviews.* San Francisco: Straight Arrow Books, 1971. 189 pp.

WHITMONT, Edward. *Return of the Goddess.* New York: Crossroad, 1984. 272 pp.

WICKE, Peter. "Rock Music: A Musical-Aesthetic Study," *Popular Music* 2 (1982), 219–43. An extremely involved study from a socialist point of view that finds the "aesthetics" of rock primarily in the audience's experience of sensory-motor response. Includes an extraordinary bibliography of predominantly German sources.

WICKE, Peter, and Gunter Mayer. "Rock Music as a Phenomenon of Progressive Mass Culture," *Popular Music Perspectives: Papers from the First International Conference on Popular Music*

Research, Amsterdam, June 1981. Goeteborg and Exeter: International Association for the Study of Popular Music, 1982, pp. 223–42.

WILLIAMS, Richard. "Roxy Music," *Melody Maker* 47 (29 July, 1972), 14–5.

———. "Crimso Meets Eno!," *Melody Maker* 47 (4 Nov. 1972), 9 ff.

———. "Roxy Split," *Melody Maker* 48 (28 July 1973), 3 ff.

WILLIS, Paul. *Profane Culture*. London and Boston: Routledge and Kegan Paul, 1978. 212 pp. The annotation in the "Booklist" in *Popular Music 1* reads: "Excellent, thoughtful account of the homologies between the music and the lifestyle of different youth cultures."

WILSON, Olly. "Black Music as an Art Form." *Black Music Research Journal* (1983), 1–22. Wilson tackles the topic elegantly and systematically, defining black music concisely in musical as well as racial terms, summarizing formalist and expressionist definitions of art, and outlining a distinction between art and entertainment. He then analyzes in detail two examples of Afro-American music as art, the work song "Katie Left Memphis," and Miles Davis's recording of "On Green Dolphin Street." The former represents "basic" or "folk" art, the latter a tradition in which "the music exists clearly as an object of 'intrinsic perceptual interest' and thus is compatible with western concepts of art."

WIMSATT, W. K., and M. C. Beardsley, "The Intentional Fallacy," *Sewanee Review* 54 (1946), 468–88.

WINKLER, Peter. "The Harmonic Language of Rock," unpublished paper first delivered to the Keele University/Sonneck Society conference on American and British music, Keele, England, July 5, 1983. In an lucid presentation including many examples and voice-leading graphs, Winkler argued that "though its roots are in simple diatonic relationships, the harmonic language of rock has the potential to transcend the limits of triadic structure and tonality that governed earlier popular music."

———. "Toward a Theory of Popular Harmony," *In Theory Only: Journal of the Michigan Music Theory Society* 4 (1978), 3–26. Deals, through voice-leading principles, with the harmonic syntax of popular music, particularly jazz.

WOLCOTT, James. "Records: Nearer My Eno to Thee: *Another Green World, Discreet Music*," *Creem* 7 (Apr. 1976), 60.

ZALKIND, Ronald. *Contemporary Music Almanac, 1980/81*. New York: Schirmer; London: Collier Macmillan, 1980. 944 pp.

ZELINKA, Tom. "Eno interview," Australian Broadcasting Commission, Radio Station JJJ, 1977. Quoted extensively in Eno and Mills, *More Dark Than Shark*.

?. "Review: *Here Come the Warm Jets*," *Zoo World* (23 May 1974), 37.

ZWERIN, Michael. "Brian Eno: Music Existing in Space," *International Herald Tribune* (14 Sept. 1983), 7.

BIBLIOGRAPHY UPDATE 1995

This selective list represents items that have come to my attention since this book was originally published in 1989. A sampling of literature on Eno can be found in the Eno World Wide Web project's "Bibliography of Books and Magazines." For the period before 1989, the main Bibliography in this book remains definitive.

BERTONCELLI, R. *Brian Eno*. Milano, Italy: Arcana Editrice, 1982.

COE, Jonathan. "Music Without Knobs," *The Wire* (Oct. 1990). "Everyone sees synthesizers as the great breakthrough but what they are, in fact, is the aphex of Renaissance music making, in the second part of our occasional series in music in the 90's. Brian Eno unzips a warm jet at democracies. In art and new technology. Jonathan Coe takes a tiger by the tail by strategy."

DEROGATIS, Jim. "Don't Look Back," *Request* (Feb. 1991). "Rock instigators Brian Eno and John Cale move ahead and apart with *Wrong Way Up*."

DESTEFANI, F., and MASSONI, F. *Brian Eno: Strategie oblique*. Milano, Italy: Gammalibri, 1983.

DILIBERTO, John. "Music for Listeners," *Audio* (Mar. 1993). "Purist producer/artists, sick of gloss, discover distortion."

DOERSHUCK, Robert L. "One Vision Beyond Music: On Simplicity, Context & the Neccesity of Urgency," *Keyboard* (June 1989). Long interview.

ENO, Brian, and KELLY, Kevin. "Unthinkable Futures" and "Unthinkable Stories," *Whole Earth Review* 79 (Summer 1993). Some hypothetical futures from a conference on the WELL, an online system.

————. "Brian Eno talking at Irvine, Orange County, USA, November 1987," *Stride* 33-1/3 [UK poetry/music magazine] (1992).

————. "Eno on Miles Davis," *The Wire* (Dec.-Jan. 1993-1994).

FROST, Mark. "Summit Meeting," *Option* 37 (Mar.-Apr. 1991). Transcription of public talk/interview.

GREENWALD, Ted. "Pop Goes the Eno," *Creem* (Feb.-Mar. 1991). "A wayward art-rocker rediscovers songs, discusses *Wrong Way Up*, and other issues."

KOPF, Biba. "Sombre Reptile," *city limits* (Oct. 11-18, 1990). Biba Kopf meets Brian Eno, the lizard king of contemporary electronics, discusses *Wrong Way Up*, and other issues.

MCLELLAN, Jim. "The Life of Brian," *i-D* [UK style magazine] (1993, issue/date unknown).

MORLEY, Paul. "Thoughts of a Coriander King," *The Guardian* (1993, precise date unknown). Discusses Eno's "Perfumes Defence and David Bowie's Wedding" talk.

OLDFIELD, Paul. "Eno: A Patter of Life and Death," *Melody Maker* (October 13, 1990). Interview.

ORLANDO, Antonio. Feature on Eno and *The Shutov Assemby*, *MAX* 114 (Feb. 1993). In Italian.

PRENDEGRAST, Mark. "Brian Eno: After the Heat," *Variant* 13 (Winter/Spring 1993). "Brian Eno's recent re-emergence into the British limelight (via a mainstream record deal with Warner Brothers) led to much press coverage and little or no insight. Most writers trawled through the back catalogue, glutted themselves on post-modernist babble, and threw the word Ambient around like a cliché."

————. "Brian Eno: Thoughts Words Music and Art, Part One," *Sound on Sound* [UK music technology magazine] (Jan. 1989); "Part Two" (February 1989). Extensive article on Eno, Opal, and Eno's collaborators.

REBOIRAS, Ramon. "Eno es el mensaje (Eno is the message)," *Cambio* 16 (June 7 1993). Discusses new video installations, *Neroli*, etc.

SAVAGE, Jon. "Interview with Eno," *The Guardian* (Nov. 26, 1993).

SINKER, Mark. "Discourse Fever," *Spin* (Dec. 1990). "Brian Eno, pop's most uncompromising egghead, is back with two new albums. And he's still talking all that jazz."

————. "Taking Modern Culture by Strategy," *The Wire* 104 (Oct. 1992). Interview.

TAMM, Eric. *Robert Fripp: from King Crimson to Guitar Craft*. Boston and London: Faber and Faber, 1990. Includes discussions of Fripp's collaborations with Eno.

————. "Soul Robots: Eno and Fripp with Bowie," in Elizabeth Thomson and David Gutman, *The Bowie Companion*. London: Macmillan, 1993.

Z, Pamela. "Brian Eno: Ambiguity, Yams and Ju-Ju Spacejazz," *Mondo 2000* 4 (date unknown, probably 1991 or 1992). Interview. Also has D'Cuckoo feature where they describe working with Eno.

ENO DISCOGRAPHY

This discography is based on Eno's own list of his works to 1986. (See Brian Eno and Russell Mills, "Biographical Notes," *More Dark Than Shark* [London: Faber and Faber, 1986], 138–9.) I have reorganized and amplified it, added identifying record, cassette, or CD numbers, and omitted the sections of "selected commissions to score music," "selected uses of *Music For Films*," "video works," and "audio-visual installations." Recordings within each section are listed chronologically. The information under each listing is taken from the recordings themselves, and occasionally from other sources.

Solo Progressive Rock Albums

ENO, Brian. *Here Come the Warm Jets*. Editions EG ENO 1, 1973.
   Produced by Brian Eno.
   Keyboards: Nick Kool and the Koolaids, Nick Judd, Andy Mackay
   Guitars: Robert Fripp, Phil Manzanera, Paul Rudolph, Chris "Ace" Spedding
   Bass Guitars: Busta Cherry Jones, Bill MacCormick, Paul Rudolph, John Wetton, Chris Thomas
   Percussion: Simon King, Marty Simon, Paul Thompson
   Saxophone septet: Andy Mackay
   Slide Guitars: Lloyd Watson
   Backing vocals: Sweetfeed
   "Eno sings all other vocals and (occasionally) plays simplistic keyboards, snake guitar, electric larynx and synthesizer, and treats the other instruments."
   Authors: Eno, Eno/Manzanera, Eno/Fripp, and Eno (arr. Thompson/Jones/Judd/Eno).
ENO, Brian. *Taking Tiger Mountain (By Strategy)*. Editions EG ENO 2, 1974.
   Produced by Brian Eno.
   Eno: vocals, electronics, snake guitar, keyboards
   Phil Manzanera: guitars
   Brian Turrington: bass guitar
   Freddie Smith: drums
   Robert Wyatt: percussion and backing vocals
   "Special Guests":
   The Portsmouth Sinfonia: strings
   The Simplistics: chorus
   Andy Mackay: brass
   Phil Collins: drums
   Polly Eltes: vocals
   Authors: Eno, Eno (arr. Turrington), Eno/Manzanera.
ENO, Brian. *Another Green World*. Editions EG ENO 3, 1975.
   Produced by Brian Eno and Rhett Davies.
   Phil Collins: drums, percussion
   Percy Jones: fretless bass
   Paul Rudolph: bass, snare drums, "assistant castanet guitars," guitar
   Rod Melvin: Rhodes piano, piano
   John Cale: viola
   Brian Eno: synthesizer, guitar, tape, organ, piano, Yamaha bass pedals, synthetic percussion, guitars, digital guitar, treated rhythm generator, farfisa organ, Hammond organ, Peruvian percussion, "electric elements and unnatural sounds," prepared piano, Leslie piano
   Robert Fripp: "Wimshurst guitar," "restrained lead guitar," "Wimborne guitar"
   Brian Turrington: bass guitar, pianos
   All compositions by Brian Eno.
ENO, Brian. *Before and After Science: Fourteen Pictures*. Editions EG ENO 4, 1977.
   Produced by Brian Eno and Rhett Davies.

Paul Rudolph: bass and rhythm guitar
Phil Collins: drums
Percy Jones: fretless bass, analog delay bass
Rhett Davies: agaong-gong and stick
Brian Eno: voices, synthesizer, guitar, synthesizer percussion, piano, chorus, metallics, bell, mini-moog, CS80, AKS, piano
Jaki Liebezeit: drums
Dave Mattacks: drums
Shirley Williams: brush timbales
Kurt Schwitters: voice
Fred Frith: guitar
Andy Fraser: drums
Phil Manzanera: guitar
Robert Fripp: guitar
Achim Roedelius: grand and electric pianos
Möbi Moebius: Bass Fender piano
Brian Turrington: bass
Authors: Eno, Eno (arr. Jones/Eno), Eno/Roedelius/Moebius, Eno (arr. Frith/Eno).

ENO, Brian. *Rarities*. Editions EG ENOX 1, 1983. (EP released only in ten-album boxed set *Working Backwards 1983–1973*, Editions EG EGBS 2, 1983.)
Produced by Brian Eno and Rhett Davies.
Authors: Brian Eno, Linda/Campbell-Peretti/Creatore/Weiss/Stanton, Brian Eno/Daniel Lanois/Roger Eno.

ENO, Brian. *More Blank Than Frank: Songs from the Period 1973–1977*. EG EGLP 65, 1986.
Not exactly a "greatest hits" collection, this is a selection of Eno's progressive rock songs he chose to include in a record that tied in with the release of the book *More Dark Than Shark* (see full listing under Eno in "Materials by and About Eno" below).

Solo Ambient Albums

ENO, Brian. *Discreet Music*. Editions EG/Obscure EGS 303, 1975.
Produced by Brian Eno.
Side One: "Discreet Music," "recorded [and performed, by Eno himself] at Brian Eno's studio 9.5.75."
Side Two: Three Variations of the Canon in D Major by Johann Pachelbel, "performed by the Cockpit Ensemble conducted by Gavin Bryars (who also helped arranged the pieces)."

ENO, Brian. *Music for Films*. Editions EG EGS 105, 1978.
Produced by Brian Eno.
Percy Jones: bass guitar
Phil Collins: percussion
Paul Rudolph: guitar
Bill MacCormick: bass guitar
Dave Mattacks: percussion
Fred Frith: electric guitar
Robert Fripp: electric guitar
John Cale: viola
Rod Melvin: electric piano
Rhett Davies: trumpet
All other instruments by Eno
All compositions by Brian Eno.

ENO, Brian. *Ambient 1: Music for Airports*. Editions EG EGS 201, 1979.
Produced by Brian Eno.

Voices: Christa Fast, Christine Gomez and Inge Zeininger
Eno: synthesizer and other instruments
"All compositions by Brian Eno except 1/1 which was co-composed with Robert Wyatt (who also played acoustic piano on this track) and Rhett Davies."

ENO, Brian. *Ambient 4: On Land.* Editions EG EGED 20, 1982.
Produced by Brian Eno.
Michael Beinhorn: synthesizer
Axel Gros: guitar
Bill Laswell: bass
Jon Hassell: trumpet
Michael Brook: guitar
Dan Lanois: live equalization
"All compositions by Brian Eno except 'Lizard Point' by Eno, Beinhorn, Gros and Laswell."

ENO, Brian. *Apollo: Atmospheres & Soundtracks.* Editions EG, ENO 5, 1983.
Produced by Brian Eno and Dan Lanois.
Composed and played by Brian Eno, Daniel Lanois, and Roger Eno.

ENO, Brian. *Music for Films, Vol. II.* Editions EG EGSP-2, 1983.
Produced by Brian Eno and Daniel Lanois.
Composers: Eno, Eno/Lanois, Lanois (arr. Eno), Eno/Roger Eno, Eno/Roger Eno/Lanois.

ENO, Brian. *Thursday Afternoon.* EG EGCD 64, 1985. (Compact disc only.)
Origination team: Brian Eno, Daniel Lanois, Roger Eno
Mix team: Brian Eno, Michael Brook, Daniel Lanois
Assembly team: Brian Eno, Michael Brook

ENO, Brian. *Glint (East of Woodbridge.)* Artforum International Magazine, Inc. Evatone Soundsheets 861222XS, 1986. Tear-out disc included as part of *Artforum* 24 (Summer 1986).

Rock Collaborations
WITH ROXY MUSIC

ROXY MUSIC. *The First Roxy Music Album.* Atco SD 36-133, 1972. Eno: synthesizer and tapes.
ROXY MUSIC. *For Your Pleasure.* Atco SD 36-134, 1973. Eno: synthesizer and tapes.

WITH DAVID BOWIE

BOWIE, David. *Low.* RCA AYL1-3856, 1977. Eno: coauthorship of one piece; general studio collaboration.
BOWIE, David. *"Heroes."* RCA AYL1-3857, 1977. Eno: synthesizers, keyboards, guitar treatments, coauthorship of four pieces.
BOWIE, David. *Lodger.* RCA AYL1-4234, 1979. Eno: ambient drone, prepared piano and cricket menace, synthesizers, guitar treatments, horse trumpets, Eroica horn, piano, coauthorship of six pieces.

GERMAN SYNTHESIZER ROCK

CLUSTER and Eno. *Cluster and Eno.* Sky 010, 1977. Eno: instruments, coauthorship.
ENO, Moebius and Rodelius. *After the Heat.* Sky 021, 1978. Eno: instruments, lyrics, coauthorship of music, coproduction.

WITH TALKING HEADS AND DAVID BYRNE

TALKING HEADS. *More Songs about Buildings and Food.* Sire SIR M5 6058 (cassette), 1978. Eno: coproduction with Talking Heads.

TALKING HEADS. *Fear of Music.* Sire SIR M5S 6076 (cassette), 1979. Eno: coproduction with Talking Heads.

TALKING HEADS. *Remain in Light.* Sire SIR M5S 6095, 1980. Eno: bass, keyboards, percussion, voices, vocal arrangements, coauthorship of all music and some words, production.

ENO, Brian, and David Byrne. *My Life in the Bush of Ghosts.* Sire M5S 6093 (cassette), 1981. Eno: guitars, basses, synthesizers, drums, percussion, and found objects, coproduction with Byrne, coauthorship with Byrne.

BYRNE, David. *"The Catherine Wheel."* Songs from the Broadway production choreographed and directed by Twyla Tharp. Sire SRK 3645, 1981. Eno: bass, "prophet scream," vibes.

OTHER ROCK COLLABORATIONS

MATCHING MOLE. *Matching Mole's Little Red Record.* CBS S 65260, 1972. Eno: synthesizer.

AYERS, Kevin, John Cale, Brian Eno, Nico. *June 1, 1974.* Island, 1974. Eno: synthesizer, vocal.

CALVERT, Robert. *Captain Lockheed and the Starfighters.* United Artists, 1974.

GENESIS. *The Lamb Lies Down on Broadway.* Atco SD 2-401, 1974. Eno: "Enossification."

LADY JUNE. *Lady June's Linguistic Leprosy.* Caroline, 1974.

NICO. *The End . . .* Island ILPS 9311, 1974. Eno: synthesizer.

CALE, John. *Slow Dazzle.* Island ILPS 9317, 1975. Eno: synthesizer.

————. *Helen of Troy.* Island, 1975.

CALVERT, Robert. *Lucky Lief and the Longships.* United Artists, 1975.

MANZANERA, Phil. *Diamond Head.* EG, 1975.

QUIET SUN. *Mainstream.* Editions EG, 1975.

WYATT, Robert. *Ruth Is Stranger than Richard.* Virgin, 1975.

801. *801 Live.* Polydor/EG PD-1-6148, 1976. Eno: vocals, synthesizer, guitar, tapes, authorship of three pieces, coauthorship of one piece.

CAMEL. *Rain Dances.* Passport PB 9858, 1977. Eno: Mini Moog, electric and acoustic piano, random notes, bells.

MANZANERA, Phil. *801.* Polydor/EG PD-1-6147, 1977. Eno: "musician."

FRIPP, Robert. *Exposure.* EG EGLP 41, 1979. Eno: synthesizer, advice.

MATERIAL. *One Down.* Elektra 60206, 1982. Eno: coauthorship of one piece.

CALE, John. *Caribbean Sunset.* Island/Ze IT 8401, 1984. Eno: A.M.S. pitch changer.

Ambient Collaborations
WITH ROBERT FRIPP

FRIPP, Robert, and Brian Eno. *(No Pussyfooting).* Editions EG EGS 102, 1973. Eno: tapes and synthesizer, coproduction, coauthorship.

FRIPP, Robert, and Brian Eno. *Evening Star.* Editions EG EGS 103, 1975. Eno: loops and synthesizer, coproduction, coauthorship.

OTHER AMBIENT COLLABORATIONS

LARAAJI. *Ambient #3: Day of Radiance.* Editions EG EGS 203, 1980. Eno: production.

BUDD, Harold, and Brian Eno. *Ambient #2: The Plateaux of Mirror.* Editions EG EGS 202, 1980. Eno: instruments and treatments, coauthorship, production.

HASSELL, Jon, and Brian Eno. *Fourth World Vol. 1: Possible Musics.* Editions EG EGS 107, 1980. Eno: Prophet 5 (synthesizer) " 'starlight' background," "high altitude Prophet," "rare Minimoog" (synthesizer), treatments, coauthorship, coproduction with Jon Hassell.

HASSELL, John. *Dream Theory in Malaya: Fourth World Vol. 2.* Editions EG EGM 114, 1981. Eno: drums, bowl gongs, bells, mixing.

BUDD, Harold, and Brian Eno, with Daniel Lanois. *The Pearl.* Editions EG EGED 37, 1984. Eno: coauthorship with Budd, co-production with Lanois.

BROOK, Michael, with Brian Eno and Daniel Lanois. *Hybrid*. Editions EG, 1985.
ENO, Roger, with Brian Eno and Daniel Lanois. *Voices*. Editions EG EGED 42, 1985. Eno: treatments.

Rock Productions

CALE, John. *Fear*. Island ILPS 9301, 1974. Eno: Eno [*sic*], executive coproduction.
ULTRAVOX. *Ultravox!* Island ILPS 9449, 1977. Eno: production.
DEVO. *Q: Are We Not Men? A: We Are Devo!* Warner Brothers BSK 3239, 1978. Eno: production.
CONTORTIONS, Teenage Jesus and the Jerks, Mars, and DNA. *No New York*. Antilles, 1978.
EDIKANFO. *The Pace Setters*. Editions EG, 1981.
U2. *The Unforgettable Fire*. Island 90231-4 (cassette), 1984. Eno: background vocals, instruments, treatments, coproduction and coengineering.
————. *The Joshua Tree*. Island 7 90581-1, 1987. Eno: coproduction.

The Obscure Label

Note: Simon Emmerson, "Seven Obscure Releases," *Music and Musicians* 25 (Jan. 1977), 20–2, documents, discusses, and critiques Obscure's contribution to the development of British experimental music.

BRYARS, Gavin. *The Sinking of the Titanic*. Obscure/EG OBS 1, 1975. Eno: production.
HOBBS, Christopher, John Adams, and Gavin Bryars. *Ensemble Pieces*. Obscure/Editions EG OBS 2, 1975. Eno: vocals, production.
ENO, Brian. *Discreet Music*. Editions EG EGS 303, 1975. (See above under "Solo Progressive Rock Albums.")
TOOP, David, and Max Eastley. *New and Rediscovered Musical Instruments*. Obscure/Editions EG OBS 4, 1975. Eno: production.
STEELE, Jan, and John Cage. *Voices and Instruments*. Obscure/Editions EG OBS 5, 1976. Eno: production.
NYMAN, Michael. *Decay Music*. Obscure/Editions EG OBS 6, 1976. Eno: production.
PENGUIN CAFE ORCHESTRA. *Music from the Penguin Cafe*. Obscure/Editions EG Obscure 7, 1976. Eno: executive production.
WHITE, John, and Gavin Bryars. *Machine Music*. Obscure/Editions EG OBS 8, 1978. Eno: bottle, electric guitars, production.
PHILLIPS, Tom, Gavin Bryars, and Fred Orton. *Irma—An Opera*. Obscure/Editions EG OBS 9, 1978. Eno: production.
BUDD, Harold. *The Pavillion of Dreams*. Obscure/Editions EG EGS 301, 1978. Eno: voices, production.

Other

CARDEW, Cornelius. *The Great Learning*. The Scratch Orchestra. Eno: voice. Deutsche Grammophon DGG 2538216, 1971.
PORTSMOUTH SINFONIA. *Portsmouth Sinfonia Plays the Popular Classics*. Transatlantic, 1973. Eno: production.
PORTSMOUTH SINFONIA. *Hallelujah*. Transatlantic, 1974. Eno: production.
Peter and the Wolf (various artists). RSO, 1975.
Jubilee film soundtrack (various artists). EG, 1978.
SHECKLEY, Robert. *In a Land of Clear Colors*. Limited edition of 1000 copies with book. Galeria el Mensajero, Ibiza, 1979.
Dune film soundtrack (various artists). Polydor 823 770-1 Y-1, 1984. Eno: production, "Prophecy Theme."
DE SIO, Theresa. *Africana*. Polydor, 1985.

Discography Update 1995

This selective list represents items that have come to my attention since this book was originally published in 1989. Further Eno discographies can be found in the Eno World Wide Web project on the Internet.

Key:

1 - Solo Album
2 - Solo Single
3 - Album production or coproduction
4 - Remix production
5 - Primary collaboration
6 - Guest appearance / secondary collaboration
7 - Selected commissions to score music

1986

3   THE FALLING: Carmel (2 tracks) (London)
     (compilation for CD) (EG)
3   POWER SPOT: Jon Hassell (ECM)

1987

3   THE SURGEON OF THE NIGHTSKY
     RESTORED DEAD THINGS BY THE
     POWER OF SOUND: Jon Hassell
     (Intuition)

1988

6   THE WHITE ARCADES: Harold Budd
     (Opal/Warner Bros.)
5   MUSIC FOR FILMS VOL. 3: Eno/Lanois/
     Budd/Brook/Jones/Laaraji/Mahlin/Theresin
     (Opal/Warner Bros.)
5   YOU DON'T MISS YOUR WATER: *Married
     to the Mob* Soundtrack: Jonathan Demme
     (Warner Bros.) (USA Film)
3   FLASH OF THE SPIRIT: Jon Hassell
     (Intuition)

1989

3   ZVUKI MU: Zvuki Mu (Opal/Warner Bros.)
6   YELLOW MOON: The Neville Brothers
     (A&M)
3   WORDS FOR THE DYING: John Cale
     (Opal/Warner Bros.)
6   RATTLE & HUM: U2 (Island)

2   ANOTHER GREEN DAY/DOVER BEACH/
    DEEP BLUE DAY: Eno (Editions UK)
6   ACADIE: Daniel Lanois (Opa/Warner Bros.)

1990

3   EXILE: Geoffrey Oryema (Real World)
5   WRONG WAY UP: Eno/Cale (All Saints)

1991
3   ACHTUNG BABY: U2 (Island)

1992

1   NERVE NET: Eno (WEA)
1   THE SHUTOV ASSEMBLY: Eno (WEA)
2   ALI CLICK: Eno (WEA)
2   FRACTAL ZOOM: Eno (WEA)
3   JANE SIBERRY: Tracks (WEA)
6   COBALT BLUE: Michael Brook (4AD)
3   COMPLETE SERVICE: YMO (Alfa)
4   UNBELIEVABLE: EMF - remix, *Red Hot &*
       Dance (Epic)

1993

4   I FEEL YOU - Depeche Mode (Sire)
7   MR. WROE'S VIRGINS, with Roger Eno - Feb.
1   NEROLI: Brian Eno (Caroline)
3   T.B.A.: James (Polydor)
3   ZOOROPA: U2 (Island)

OTHER MUSIC CITED

Listed here are LPs, singles, and compositions referred to in the text, alphabetically by composer, performer, or title, whichever is most pertinent. Neither the records nor the scores listed here are necessarily the first editions, but the date of first publication, or in some cases the date of composition, is given where appropriate.

Actual Voices of Ex-Slaves.

ANTHONY, Ray. "Peter Gunn." Capitol 4041, 1959.

BEACH BOYS. *Pet Sounds.* Reprise 2MS 2083, 1966.

———. "Surf's Up."

BEATLES. *Abbey Road.* Apple PCS 7088, 1969.

———. *The Beatles.* Apple PCS 7067/8, 1968.

———. "Dr. Robert," from *Revolver.*

———. "Eleanor Rigby," from *Revolver.*

———. *Help!* Parlophone PCS 3071, 1965.

———. "Let It Be," from *Let It Be.* Apple PXS 1, 1970.

———. *Magical Mystery Tour.* Capitol SMAL 2835, 1967.

———. "Nowhere Man," from *Rubber Soul.*

———. *Revolver.* Parlophone PCS 7009, 1966.

———. *Rubber Soul.* Parlophone PCS 3075, 1965.

———. *Sergeant Pepper's Lonely Hearts Club Band.* Parlophone PCS 7027, 1967.

———. "Within You Without You," from *Sergeant Pepper's Lonely Hearts Club Band.*

BEETHOVEN, Ludwig van. Symphony No. 5 in C minor, Op. 67. *Ludwig van Beethoven: Fourth and Fifth Symphonies in Full Orchestral Score.* New York: Dover, 1976. (Completed 1808.)

BEETHOVEN, Ludwig van. Symphony No. 9 in D minor. *Ludwig van Beethoven: Eighth and Ninth Symphonies in Full Orchestral Score.* New York: Dover, 1976. (Completed 1824.)

BERG, Alban. *George Büchners Wozzeck: Oper in 3 Akten,* Op. 7. Klavierauszug von Fritz Heinrich Klein. Wien: Universal Edition, 1926. (Composed 1917–21.)

BROWN, Arthur. "Fire." Atlantic 2556, 1968.

CAGE, John. *45' for a Speaker,* in his *Silence* (Middletown, Connecticut: Wesleyan University Press, 1976), 146–93. (Composed 1954.)

———. *4'33".* 1954.

CARLOS, Walter. *Switched-on Bach.* Columbia Masterworks MS 7194, 1968.

COLEMAN, Ornette. *Skies of America.*

DAVIS, Miles. "In a Silent Way."

DEBUSSY, Claude. "Pagodes," from *Estampes,* in *Claude Debussy: Piano Music 1888–1905.* 2nd ed., corrected by Beveridge Webster. New York: Dover, 1973. (Composed 1903.)

DEUTER. *Nirvana Road.* Kuckkuck 068, 1984.

DIDDLEY, Bo. "Who Do You Love."

DON AND JUAN. "Chicken Necks."

DYLAN, Bob. *Blonde on Blonde.* 1966.

———. *Bringing It All Back Home.* 1965.

———. *Highway 61 Revisited.* Columbia 9189, 1965.

———. *Infidels.* Columbia AL 38819, 1983.

———. "Rainy Day Women #12 & 35." Columbia 43592, 1966.

———. "The Wicked Messenger," from *John Wesley Harding.* Columbia 9604, 1968.

FAST, Larry. *Synergy: Computer Experiments, Vol. 1.* Audion SYN 104, 1980.

FRIPP, Robert. *God Save the Queen.* Polydor MPF 1298, 1980.

———. *Let The Power Fall: An Album of Frippertronics.* Editions EG EGS 110, 1981.

———. *Exposure.* EG EGLP 41, 1978.

GENTLE GIANT. *Octopus.* CBS KC 32022, 1973.

GLASS, Philip. *Songs from Liquid Days.* CBS FM 39564, 1986.

HANDEL, Fr. "Hallelujah Chorus" from *The Messiah*. Ed. by T. Teritus Noble. Rev. according to Handel's original score by Max Spicker. Vocal score. New York: G. Schirmer, 1912. (1741.)

HAYDN, Franz. String Quartets. *Collection de quatours pour 2 violons, viola et violoncelle*. Ed. nouv., revue et corrige critiquement. Leipzig: C.F. Peters, 191?.

HENDRIX, Jimi. "Hey Joe," from *Are You Experienced*. Warner/Reprise RS 6261, 1967.

———. "Little Wing," from *Axis: Bold As Love*. Warner/Reprise 6281, 1968.

———. "The Star-Spangled Banner," from *Woodstock* (various artists). Cotillion SD 3-500, 1970.

HORN, Paul. *Inside* [the Taj Mahal]. Epic 26466, 1968.

The Human Voice in the World of Islam. Tangent TGS 131.

HYKES, David. *Hearing Solar Winds*. Harmonia Mundi HM 558 607, 1980.

KING CRIMSON. *Discipline*. 1981. Warner/EG BSK 3629, 1981.

———. *Larks' Tongues in Aspic*. Editions EG EGKC 6, 1973.

———. *Red*. Editions EG EGKC 8, 1974.

KINKS. "Well Respected Man." Reprise 0420, 1966.

KITARO. *Silk Road I & II*. Gramavision 18-7019-1, 1986.

LISZT, Franz. *Totentanz (Danse macabre), Paraphrase über Dies Irae für Piano und Orchester*. Leipzig: C.F.W. Siegel, 1865. (Composed 1950.)

"Little Puppy."

Les Liturgies de l'Orient.

"Living with a Hernia."

MURPHY, Walter, and the Big Apple Band. "A Fifth of Beethoven." Private Stock 45073, 1976.

Music of Bulgaria. Nonesuch H 72011, 1966.

OLDFIELD, Mike. *Tubular Bells*. Virgin V2001, 1973.

OLIVEROS, Pauline. *Sonic Meditations*. Baltimore, Md.: Smith Publications, 1974.

PACHELBEL, Johann. *Kanon für 3 Violinen und Bass*. Continuo-aussetzung von Caspar Diethelm. Winterthur: Amadeus, B. Päulen, 1980.

PARLIAMENT. *The Clones of Dr. Funkenstein*.

PICKETT, Bobby "Boris" and the Crypt-Kickers. "Monster Mash." Garpax 44167, 1962.

PINK FLOYD, *Dark Side of the Moon*. Capitol SMAS 11163, 1973.

Les Plus Grandes Artistes du Monde Arabe. EMI.

POUSSEUR, Henri. *Exercises pour Piano: Impromptu et Variations, 2*. Milano: Edizioni Suivi Zerboni, 1959.

PRESLEY, Elvis. "Heartbreak Hotel." RCA 6420, 1956.

PROCOL HARUM. "Whiter Shade of Pale." Deram 7507, 1967.

REED, Lou. "Walk on the Wild Side," from *Transformer*. RCA LSP 4807, 1972.

REICH, Steve. *Four Organs*. Capitol/Angel S-36059, 1973. (Composed 1970.)

———. *It's Gonna Rain*.

———. *Music for a Large Ensemble*. Warner Brothers ECM-1-1168, 1980. (Composed 1978.)

———. *Tehillim*. Warner Brothers ECM-1-1215, 1982.

———. *Violin Phase*. Warner Brothers ECM-1-1168, 1980. (Composed 1967.)

RIFKIN, Joshua. *The Baroque Beatles Book*.

RILEY, Terry. *In C*. Columbia MS 7178, 1968.

———. *A Rainbow in Curved Air; Poppy Nogood and the Phantom Band*. Columbia MS 7315, 1969.

RIOS, Miguel. "A Song of Joy." A&M 1193, 1970.

RIVERS, Johnny. "Secret Agent Man." Imperial 66159, 1966.

ROACH, Steve. *Structures from Silence*. Fortuna FOR-LP024, 1984.

ROCHES. *The Roches*. Warner Brothers BSK 3298, 1979.

ROLLING STONES. *Beggar's Banquet*. London 75391/PS 539, 1968.

———. "Mother's Little Helper." London 902, 1966.

———. "(I Can't Get No) Satisfaction." London 9766, 1965.

———. *Their Satanic Majesties Request*. London 80021/NPS-2, 1967.

SATIE, Erik. *En Habit de Cheval.* Paris: Rouart, Lerolle, 1911.

———. *Le Fils des Etoiles.* Paris: Rouart, Lerolle, 1951.

———. *Morceaux en Forme de Poire.* Paris: Rouart, Lerolle, 1911.

———. *Vexations.*

SCHOENBERG, Arnold. *15 Gedichte aus Das Buch der hängende Gärten von Stephan George,* Op. 15. Wien: Universal Edition, 1952. (Composed 1908.)

———. *Fünf Orchesterstücke,* Op. 16. Leipzig: C.F. Peters, 1912. (Composed 1909.)

———. *Dreimal sieben Gedichte aus Albert Girauds Pierrot lunaire,* Op. 21. Wien: Universal Edition, 1941. (Composed 1912.)

SILHOUETTES. "Get A Job." Ember 1029, 1958.

SIMON AND GARFUNKEL. "Bridge Over Troubled Water." Columbia 45079, 1970.

SLY AND THE FAMILY STONE. "Everyday People." Epic 10407, 1969.

———. "Thank You (Falettinme Be Mice Elf Again)." Epic 10555, 1970.

SMITH, Patti. "Gloria," from *Horses.* Arista AL5-8158, 1975.

STOCKHAUSEN, Karlheinz. *Aus den Siben Tagen: Kompositionen Mai 1968.* Wien: Universal Edition, 1968.

———. *Gesang der Junglinge.* Deutsche Grammophon Gesellschaft, SLPM 13881, 1963. (Composed 1956.)

———. *Klavierstück XI.* London: Universal Edition, 1957.

STRAVINSKY. *Ebony Concerto.* New York: Boosey & Hawkes, 1973. (Composed 1945.)

———. *The Rite of Spring.* New York: E. F. Kalmus, 1933. (Composed 1911–13.)

SUPREMES. "Reflections." Motown 1111, 1967.

Virtuoso Harp Music.

VANGELIS. *Chariots of Fire: Music from the Original Soundtrack.* Polydor 825 B84-1.

VARÈSE, Edgar. *Poème electronique,* from *Music of Edgar Varèse, Vol. I.* Columbia ML 5478, 1960. (Composed 1958.)

VIVALDI, Antonio. *The Four Seasons.* Electronic realization by Patrick Gleeson. Varese/Sarabande VCD 47212. (Composed ca. 1725.)

WEBERN, Anton von. Symphony, Op. 21. Wien: Universal Edition, 1956. (Composed 1928.)

WHO. "Baba O'Reilly," from *Who's Next.* MCA-1691, 1971.

———. *Tommy.* MCA2-10005, 1969.

XENAKIS, Iannis. *Bohor I,* from *Electro-Acoustic Music.* Nonesuch H-71246, n. d.

YES. *Close to the Edge.* Atlantic SP 19133, 1972.

YOUNG, La Monte. *Composition 1960 #3.*

———. *Composition 1960 #6.*

———. *X for Henry Flynt.* 1960.

About the Author

Eric Tamm was born in New York City in 1955 and spent his early years listening to Mozart, Swedish folk-pop tunes, Chet Atkins, Louis Armstrong, Ella Fitzgerald, and Episcopal hymns. A little later—around 1964—he heard the music of the Beatles and something inside him changed forever. His first band was called the Humbugs and did covers of songs by the Beatles, the Monkees, the Rolling Stones, Bob Dylan, and the rest of the usual late-60s groups.

In college Tamm studied the history of Western theology and comparative religions, travelled in Israel and Europe, and spent a year in Tamil Nadu, India. Reading Kierkegaard, Jung, and Nietzsche brought him back to his senses, and when he returned to the U.S., he threw away the philosophy books and began concentrating on music.

Ten years of study ensued: Tamm received the B.Mus. from Immaculate Heart College in Los Angeles (1978), the Master of Arts in music from Cal State Northridge (1982), and the Ph.D. in musicology from the University of California, Berkeley (1987). He taught music—history, theory, rock and roll, contemporary music, and piano—at San Francisco Bay Area colleges and universities from 1983 to 1990. He is the author of *Robert Fripp: From King Crimson to Guitar Craft; Right-Brain Musical Improvisation;* and numerous critical articles on popular and classical music.

Dr. Tamm developed an abiding passion for high technology, musical and otherwise, and currently works as a senior writer at PeopleSoft, Inc., a leading vendor of client/server business software applications. He plays lead guitar and sings in a rock band, the Raving Daves, composes music for films and corporate videos, and manages Yak Productions, which records and publishes rock and roll, ambient, neo-classical, progressive rock, electro-acoustic, new age, and MIDI music.

This book is available in hypertext format (Microsoft Windows). For more information, please contact:

Yak Productions
1532 Francisco Street
Berkeley, CA 94703

CPSIA information can be obtained at www.ICGtesting.com

226111LV00007B/37/A